Russia's VIRTUAL Economy

Russia's VIRTUAL Economy

Clifford G. Gaddy

Barry W. Ickes

BROOKINGS INSTITUTION PRESS
Washington, D.C.

Copyright © 2002
BROOKINGS INSTITUTION PRESS
1775 Massachusetts Avenue, N.W., Washington, D.C. 20036
www.brookings.edu

Library of Congress Cataloging-in-Publication data
Gaddy, Clifford G.
  Russia's virtual economy / Clifford G. Gaddy and Barry W. Ickes.
     p.   cm.
  Includes bibliographical references and index.
   ISBN 0-8157-3112-4 (cloth : alk. paper)
   ISBN 0-8157-3111-6 (pbk. : alk. paper)
    1. Russia (Federation)—Economic policy—1991– 2. Russia
  (Federation)—Economic conditions—1991– 3. Structural adjustment
  (Economic policy)—Russia (Federation) I. Ickes, Barry William. II.
  Title.
   HC340.12 .G33 2002
   330.947—dc21   2002008413

                9 8 7 6 5 4 3 2 1

  The paper used in this publication meets minimum requirements of the
American National Standard for Information Sciences—Permanence of Paper
      for Printed Library Materials: ANSI Z39.48-1992.

                   Typeset in Sabon

          Composition by Oakland Street Publishing
                  Arlington, Virginia

          Printed by R. R. Donnelley and Sons
                 Harrisonburg, Virginia

Foreword

Has Russian economic reform been a success or a failure? Indeed, what standard should be used to make such a judgment? Today, a full decade after Russia officially embarked on what were described as "radical market reforms," there is no consensus answer to those basic questions. Rather, the answers differ so fundamentally as to remind us of the wide divergence of views about the old Soviet economy. Then, the divide between opinions followed the ideological fault lines of the cold war. While ideology (although of a different kind) sometimes plays a role in today's debates, the current disagreements arise mainly because the Russian economy is just plain hard to comprehend.

One response to the perplexing course of Russian transition has been to abandon the attempt at rational explanation and simply concede, "it is Russia." The authors of this book have a different attitude. Clifford Gaddy and Barry W. Ickes believe that it is possible to describe the course of Russian economic reform in terms of rational behavior, provided one understands the constraints that economic actors actually face. The key to that understanding, they argue, is to recognize that the Russian economy has evolved into a hybrid form that combines elements of the market with institutions and behaviors that have a distinct, non-market character. In this book they take this hybrid system—the one they have termed the "virtual economy"—head on. Their purpose is to develop the tools to analyze how it operates and to show how these tools can both solve some of the major riddles of the Russian economy and provide a framework for thinking about its future.

The virtual economy idea gained much of its notoriety around the time of Russia's financial crisis of August 1998. The explosion of barter and nonmonetary payment presented a puzzle. For many, the virtual economy model proved useful in trying to understand that puzzle. In recent years, as the share of nonmonetary payments has decreased, some might question the model's continuing relevance. The goal of the virtual economy analysis, however, was not to explain barter but to explain the lack of restructuring in the economy. Viewed in this light, the complexities of Russia's economy have not decreased. Hence, Gaddy and Ickes argue, the virtual economy model is still the best way to understand the Russian economy.

The authors owe a debt of gratitude to a very large number of people who have, in various ways, assisted them in this project. They would like to offer special thanks to three individuals whose intellectual contributions and advice have helped shape the authors' understanding of the Soviet economic system and today's Russian economy. Gregory Grossman forced them to pay attention to the tension between the formal and informal nature of the Soviet-type economic system. Gur Ofer stressed the importance of the structural features of the Soviet economy and their continuing relevance for the Russian transition. They owe a special debt to Richard Ericson for advice and encouragement at all stages of this project. Above all others in the field, Ericson has established a standard of rigor, depth, and balance in his analyses of first the Soviet and now the Russian economy. The authors believe that, in a real sense, this book is their best effort to flesh out his insights about the implications for transition of an economic structure created without regard for opportunity cost.

Edward Dolan, Sergei Guriev, Sergei Izmalkov, Vijay Krishna, Thomas Richardson, John Steinbruner, and Andrei Volgin made special contributions to the research and the ideas. Michael Alexeev, John Anderson, Anders Aslund, Robert Axtell, Bruce Blair, Victoria Bonnell, George Breslauer, David Brown, Ronald Childress, Steven Durlauf, Joshua Epstein, Yegor Gaidar, Fiona Hill, Andrei Illarionov, Juliet Johnson, Andrei Kozlov, Jim Leitzel, Robert Litan, John Litwack, Vladimir Mau, John Odling Smee, John Roemer, Peter Rutland, Ben Slay, Pekka Sutela, Janine Wedel, Victor Winston, Thomas Wolfe, and Yevgeny Yasin provided helpful comments and criticism. Three anonymous reviewers read a preliminary version of the manuscript and offered valuable suggestions.

Participants at seminars given at the Bank of Finland Institute for Economies in Transition (BOFIT), Columbia University, Harvard University, Indiana University, James Madison University, the U.S. National Intelligence Council, the Stockholm School of Economics, the U.S. Treasury Department, the University of California (Berkeley), the University of California (Davis), the University of Illinois, the University of Michigan, and the World Bank made insightful comments and suggestions.

The Hebrew University (Jerusalem), the William Davidson Institute of the University of Michigan, and the International Monetary Fund provided a stimulating research environment for Barry Ickes as he worked on portions of the manuscript.

At Brookings, Richard Haass, former director of foreign policy studies, provided the initial encouragement to undertake the book project and made helpful comments on a preliminary draft. Carol Graham and Peyton Young, co-directors of the Center on Social and Economic Dynamics, supported the project at all stages. Julian Hendley, Bridget Butkevich, Frederick Hodder, and Marjory Winn provided research assistance. Deborah Styles edited the manuscript. Marjory Winn and Tanjam Jacobson edited and proofread the two indexes. Carlotta Ribar proofread the text pages.

Brookings is grateful to the John D. and Catherine T. MacArthur Foundation for generous financial support of this project.

The views expressed in this volume are those of the authors and should not be ascribed to any person or institution acknowledged above or to the trustees, officers, or other staff members of the Brookings Institution.

MICHAEL H. ARMACOST
President

Washington, D.C.
June 2002

Contents

Figures

Tables

Boxes

CHAPTER ONE

Introduction

"We hoped for the best, but it turned out as usual."

—*Viktor Chernomyrdin*

Economic reform in Russia has been anything but the smooth process envisioned by many in 1991. The general problem of reform seemed straightforward. The essential task was to remove the distortions created by central planning. Once the restrictions on economic behavior were lifted, the market would develop. Of course, it was recognized that there would be bumps along the way, but these would not distract from the task at hand. The main requisite was the will. Transition would be like turning a great ship in a choppy sea: set a course designated "market economy" and hold on. There might be great tossing and turning, but if the captain and crew could hold the course, the ship would eventually reach its destination.

In practice, the Russian transition has turned out to be vastly more complicated—so much more so that a better image might be that of replacing the propeller engines of a passenger airplane with jet engines . . . during flight. Attempting this is not only complex and unprecedented; it is highly likely that the airframe may be completely unsuited to the new engines. As time passes, the passengers worry less and less about the unpredictable turns and sudden changes in elevation. They forget about how soon, or even whether, they will reach the planned destination. Rather, their overriding concern becomes the sheer struggle to stay aloft—survival.

Regardless of the metaphor one chooses, the difficulties that Russia has encountered in the transition have posed an interesting set of problems for analysts. Trying to understand the reasons for these difficulties has become a growth industry among observers of the Russian economy. Most analyses of what went wrong fall into one of two camps:

—*Technocratic:* The wrong policies were adopted, embodying either too much or too little therapy.

— *"Russia is different":* Russia's unique culture and history ensured that the policies promoted by market reformers would not work.

These arguments share the premise that the choice of policies made the reform path so arduous. Of course there is a great difference between camps over what the bad choices were. In the technocratic view the problem is that the wrong policy settings were chosen for transition to the market economy.[1] In the "Russia is different" view the problem is that the chosen path was inconsistent with Russian history and culture. It is, of course, tempting to focus on bad choices because it makes blame easier to assign and because it makes the difficulties of transition seem potentially avoidable. It is not clear, however, that succumbing to this temptation enhances understanding.

Our approach to the problem of Russian transition is different. We focus on the inherent difficulties of the process stemming from the economic structure bequeathed by central planning. We would not argue that no mistakes were made along the way. However, we do not believe that the principal causes of the rocky road were remediable policy errors. Instead, we emphasize the inherited problems, primarily a vast industrial structure that could not compete in a market setting. This heavy industry sector, where the bulk of industrial employment still is located, has been the most resistant to reform; and it is the continued presence of this sector that most negatively affects Russia's growth prospects. Had it been possible to quarantine this sector of the economy and let it decline slowly, the transition might have been different. In the absence of such insulation, however, what happens to this sector affects the whole economy and politics. In particular, when this industrial structure was shocked by the sudden collapse of central planning, economic agents adapted their behavior to survive in the new setting. Optimists had assumed that agents would adapt their behavior in a manner consistent with a market economy. In fact, they adapted

---

1. Notice that "technocrats" disagree over the nature of the mistake. Some argue that shock therapy would have worked if it had been fully implemented. See, for example, Aslund (1999). Others argue that the shock therapy approach (in the form of the so-called Washington Consensus) was inherently deficient; it ignored the role of institutions and locked Russia into an inferior path. See, for example, Roland (2000).

their behavior in a different manner, to a mode consistent with what we call the virtual economy. Explaining this process and what it means for economic development in Russia is the purpose of this book.

Our goal is to provide a method of analysis—a model that can be used to think about transition in Russia. We believe that without such a model it is not only difficult to understand developments in Russia, but is even harder to think about how Russia can escape the virtual economy trap.

Some readers may ask, Why is this relevant now? In the year 2000, Russia's gross domestic product (GDP) grew 9 percent. Although the growth rate slowed to 5 percent in 2001, it still represents a great improvement over the first seven years of transition. Barter is down, and Russia is repaying its debts to the International Monetary Fund at an accelerated pace. Perhaps, one might argue, the problems that we are concerned with are in the past now. Perhaps Russia has finally achieved the critical steps that make growth self-sustaining.[2]

Although there are some positive signs of change in Russia, as always it is best to think about Russia as an iceberg: it is what is below the surface that must be watched carefully. Consider then figure 1-1, which shows the percentage of loss-making industrial enterprises in Russia during transition. What is remarkable about this picture is that despite the real depreciation of the ruble and high oil prices, the share of loss makers continues to be exceptionally large, nearly 40 percent.[3] There was a one-time improvement after the August 1998 crisis, but subsequently the share remained stable.[4]

What this suggests is that there continues to be a large core of enterprises that survive *despite* their performance rather than because of it. The future for this core cannot be ignored in thinking about how Russia will develop. When the dinosaurs became extinct, niches were opened for mammals to

2. We are tempted to note that we have heard this all before. In 1996 and 1997 we read about the coming Russian boom. Of course, things are different now: GDP is growing and tax revenues are up. However, the reason why things are different is precisely the real depreciation of the ruble that occurred after August 17, 1998. This has changed the economy significantly. Combined with high oil prices, the devaluation has put Russia in a far better situation than before August 1998. However, as is evident from figure 1-1, this improved environment has not changed some of the key fundamentals of the economy.

3. In absolute numbers, the loss makers total around 60,000 large and medium-sized industrial enterprises. See sources for figure 1-1.

4. The share of loss makers is higher now than in the early years of transition. The relatively higher profitability in 1992–95 is surely due to the high inflation of those years, which covered up losses. Similarly, the real appreciation of the ruble up to 1998 accelerated the number of loss makers.

FIGURE 1-1. Percentage of Loss-Making Industrial Enterprises, 1992–2001

Percentage

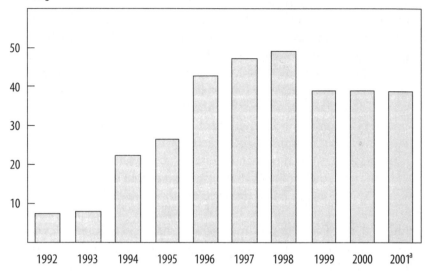

Source: For 1992–99, *Rossiyskiy statisticheskiy yezhegodnik* (2000, table 21.31); for 2000, *Interfax* (2001, no. 22); for 2001, *Interfax* (2002, no. 47).
a. January–September 2001.

develop and thrive; bit players in the previous era evolved into the dominant forms of life. In Russia, however, the dinosaurs—this large industrial core—survive, and as long as they do, they inhibit economic progress. Because of their sheer size and their importance for employment, these enterprises have a political and social significance far in excess of their economic importance.[5] The virtual economy thus remains relevant.

What Is the Virtual Economy?

Many understand the virtual economy to be synonymous with the phenomenon of widespread barter, other nonmonetary transactions, and taxes

5. This was recognized by President Vladimir Putin in his recent address to the Asia-Pacific Economic Cooperation (APEC) summit: "We are . . . worried about [the gap] between the real economy and the 'virtual' economy, a gap that is fraught with new shocks. . . . We are for the liberalization of economic regimes, but we are categorically against a situation in which the dying off of entire branches of the national economy in developing countries or in so-called 'developing markets' would upset the social balance, a situation that would exacerbate social-economic and political tensions not only in individual states but in entire regions of the world" Putin (2001b).

paid in kind.[6] This is *not* how we have used the term, however, for this confuses a symptom with the disease. The lack of restructuring in the Russian economy is the fundamental problem that the virtual economy model addresses. It is rather easy to understand why there may be forces that do not want to change. We do not need a complex argument to understand why economic transition may threaten the position of certain elements in society. The difficult part is to understand how these agents can succeed at blocking changes that have large economic advantages. The most threatened agents, after all, are those who work in or direct enterprises that are value destroying: the loss-making dinosaurs, the most prominent legacy of the Soviet period. The point of introducing markets is precisely to create the pressure on these enterprises to reform or die. During the first decade of economic reform in Russia, privatization was carried out on a massive scale, and overt subsidies to enterprises were reduced practically to the point of elimination. How enterprises could survive in this environment without restructuring thus presents a serious puzzle.

The virtual economy is the outcome of agents' adapting their behavior to an environment that threatens their survival. It is characterized by a set of informal institutions that permits the production and exchange of goods that are value subtracting, that is, worth less than the value of the inputs used to produce them. Enterprises can continue such production because they have recipients who are willing to accept fictitious ("virtual") pricing of the goods at levels that mask their unprofitability. Buyers and sellers collude to hide the fictitious nature of the pricing (that is, the discrepancy between the virtual prices and the true, market, prices). In the classic form of the virtual economy, they do so by avoiding money: they use barter and other forms of nonmonetary exchange, as well as even more intricate subterfuges. Since value is being destroyed as the system operates, there also has to be a source of value infusion. The ultimate "value pump" in Russia today is the fuel and energy sector, above all one single company, Gazprom—Russia's natural gas monopoly.[7] In exchange for the rights to keep what it earns from exports, Gazprom pumps value into the system by supplying gas without being paid for it (or, more generally, at a cost that is

6. When we began working on this book, nonmonetary transactions were the primary mechanism for redistributing value to enable loss makers to survive. Shocks to the economy since August 1998 have reduced the amount of barter, but clearly they have not eliminated the redistribution of value; otherwise, how would these loss makers survive?

7. For simplicity, we continue to use Gazprom as the stand-in for the value-producing part of the economy. This is a great convenience, and it also reflects the overwhelming importance of that company in the Russian economy.

low enough to keep enterprises operating). Gazprom subsidies—which then lead to arrears to the government—are the primary way in which unprofitable activity is supported today in Russia.

The system survives because it meets the needs of so many actors in the economy. Workers and managers at industrial dinosaurs benefit because the virtual economy postpones the ultimate reckoning for loss-making firms. Government, especially at the subnational level, where much of the important action takes place, benefits because it maintains employment and continues providing social services. Gazprom also benefits, however; the value transfers it makes to the virtual economy are the price it pays to be able to appropriate the massive rents from exports. One side of the transaction for Gazprom is the value that must be pumped into the economy; the other side is the value that leaks out.

This is not to argue that people would not be better off if the virtual economy were replaced by a functioning market economy. There are great inefficiencies in the virtual economy. It is a clear impediment to growth and development. The key point is that the equilibrium is stable; it does not pay for any actors to depart from the behaviors that characterize it.[8] This is surely the most pernicious effect of the virtual economy—those who try to play by the normal market rules are penalized relative to those who play by the virtual economy's rules.

This brief description identifies several of the key themes that recur throughout this book and that distinguish our view of Russia's economy from most others. These interconnected and interdependent themes include (1) an emphasis on the *initial conditions* that Russia faced as it began its transition; (2) the *impermissible* nature of the consequences of serious reform policies; (3) behavioral *adaptation* by agents in the economy; and (4) the extent to which so many agents in the economy participate in what we refer to as "the *loot chain*."

Initial Conditions

Acknowledging the importance of Russia's initial conditions goes farther than the simple realization that Russia's starting point for market reform was bad. It also requires knowing what those initial conditions were and how they helped shape the subsequent behavior of agents. The first basic fact is that restructuring was not a realistic prospect for a great many Russ-

8. This is especially so for policymakers, since changing this system requires radically restructuring the source of incomes for households. We return to this subject when we discuss the "loot chain," below.

ian enterprises: they began the transition too far away from viability.[9] Of course, a sufficient infusion of outside resources can guarantee successful restructuring for any enterprise, because this makes it possible to reconstruct the entire enterprise from scratch. Therefore, any meaningful notion of restructuring has to consider the opportunity cost of making a given enterprise viable. For most Russian enterprises, the cost of reaching viability was prohibitive. This pandemic condition was hidden from view by the nature of Soviet pricing. Indeed, the transfer of value from the raw materials sector to manufacturing was a critical feature of the Soviet economy. This transfer of value through Soviet pricing hid the true features of the Soviet economy.[10] In effect, Soviet pricing was like a distorting mirror at the carnival. The reflection distorted the relative importance of sectors in arbitrary but systematic ways. The illusion that these enterprises were value producing, when in fact they were value destroying, was one key initial condition of the transition.

A second basic fact was the social importance of the nonviable enterprises. This is also a legacy of the Soviet system. Enterprises were more than just productive units; they were also the major providers of social services. The industrial "dinosaurs" established under the dictates of communist central planning still employ millions of people and support entire cities and regions across the country. Because of the social importance of these enterprises, their viability cannot be assessed solely in terms of their physical capital. Enterprises and their directors accumulate *relational capital* (see chapter 3) to influence the behavior of officials whose actions can affect their survival. Our analysis of enterprise behavior focuses on the interaction of physical, human, *and* relational capital.

The third basic fact is the degree to which value-adding activity in Russia is concentrated in the resource sectors. The Russian economy, like the Soviet economy from which it is descended, is and has been primarily an economy driven by resource industries. Although the Soviet economy produced missiles, cars, planes, and space stations, the bulk of value added was produced in the energy and other raw materials and basic commodities sectors.[11] Little has changed today.

---

9. We formalize the notion of "too far away" in chapters 3 and 4, using the concept of market distance. The analysis was first developed in Gaddy and Ickes (1998).

10. This is explained most carefully in Ericson (1999).

11. This is a statement about valuation. Soviet prices reflected the preferences of the political leadership, which placed greater value on defense output than does the market economy of Russia. Transition has resulted in a dramatic change in relative prices owing to this change in the system of valuation. See Gaddy and Ickes (2001b).

These initial conditions may seem self-evident to any student of the Russian economy. It is thus all the more remarkable that these conditions are ignored in most of the technical debates about Russian reform. Most debates on reform focus on the speed and comprehensiveness of measures or on the sequence in which reforms must be carried out.[12] Those debates may differ over diagnosis of where reform has gone wrong, but they share a common methodology. The focus is on the intended goal of market reform, not the initial conditions in which this transition is to take place.[13] The debates thus produce a laundry list of needed reforms, all of which are sensible, but no framework within which to understand their interaction and, more important, no way to understand why the economic system rejects these interventions.[14]

Impermissibility

A second key notion underlying our approach comes from the observation that while policymakers—the reformers—in Russia adopted one conventional measure after another in their attempt to transform Russia into a market economy, very few of those measures were ever fully implemented, and the intended effects were rarely achieved. Incomplete implementation and policy reversal have been the norms in the Russian transition. To understand why, we focus on the role of initial conditions and behavioral adaptation, rather than on exogenous political forces alone. This is facilitated by the notion of an "impermissibility constraint," which refers to restrictions on the set of feasible policies that arise from the prevailing values and norms of society.

When policy measures violate the impermissibility constraint, modifications in the implementation prevent them from having their full and intended consequences. These modifications arise precisely because the consequences of complete and proper implementation are politically

12. See, for example, Aslund (1999) and Roland (2000) for examples from opposite ends of the shock therapy–gradualism divide.

13. Ironically, informed discussion of transition policy resembles nothing more than the arguments of the followers of Stanislav G. Strumilin—the "teleologists"—in the great debates about Soviet planning in the 1920s. The teleologists argued that planning must be based on the goal, not on the initial conditions.

14. Kontorovich (1988) provided a classic analysis of how the Soviet economy rejected reforms that were alien to the fundamental mechanisms of the system. Much like antibodies defending the host, the economy reacted to reforms that threatened the primary means of allocation. No similar analysis has, to our knowledge, been conducted with respect to the Russian economy. In chapter 5 we present an analysis of this phenomenon in an evolutionary framework.

intolerable. Russia did not formally reject the policies themselves; instead, it continued with a pretense of market reform. The nation's leadership proclaimed reform policies, while enterprises and other agents continued to behave in ways that rendered the policies ineffective.

Our mode of analysis is to incorporate political factors as constraints and then analyze how economic behavior and equilibria are affected. Considering the impact of political constraints on the reform process does not, by itself, represent a significant departure from previous analyses. But unlike previous studies we do not treat political constraints as exogenous.[15] We root them in the inherited legacy of the Soviet economy. They arise precisely from the specific problems of transforming the Soviet economy. And we study how agents can act to affect these constraints by investing in relational capital.

By treating political factors as impermissibility constraints, we are trying to study the interaction of economic policies with political constraints and to analyze how the economic outcomes arise from this interaction.[16] The course of transition in Russia has followed its particular path precisely because impermissibility constraints have often been binding. Of course, the fact that these constraints have been binding does *not* mean that policymakers have always been cognizant of them. In fact, the failure to consider these constraints has often led to perverse, or unintended, outcomes of economic reforms.

Adaptation

The third fundamental point in our conception flows from the preceding two. Given Russia's peculiar combination of special initial conditions, along with its simultaneous commitment to reform policies and unwillingness to accept the consequences of those policies, agents had a uniquely propitious environment in which to adapt their behavior to survive. They had to adapt

15. Shleifer and Treisman (2000) use political constraints to explain the paradox of selective success of reforms. For example, they study the impact of a decentralized federal structure in inhibiting certain types of economic reforms. For the most part, however, they assume these constraints to be exogenous to the transition process.

16. Our approach to political considerations via the concept of impermissibility follows the approach that has become the convention in information economics. This convention treats incentive constraints as fundamental primitives of economic models; indeed incentive constraints play a role symmetrical with resource constraints in determining equilibria. Our approach is to consider impermissibility constraints in a similar fashion. Thus, as with incentive constraints, one can consider outcomes that would be feasible in a first-best (perfect information) environment. However, actual equilibria depart from the first best because the impermissibility constraints do, in fact, bind.

to an environment that threatened their very existence. At the same time, the incompleteness with which policies were implemented failed to wipe out behaviors that were antithetical to reform. The attempt to reform the Russian economy has thus had significant effects—the key problem is that they are not always the *intended* ones. The idea of adaptation is especially relevant for the robustness of the virtual economy. It means that the virtual economy is not some half-reformed economic system or a flawed version of the ideal. It is a mutant system, with laws of behavior and evolution all its own.

The "Loot Chain"

Finally, we stress the way in which income from control of assets is passed down as payoffs through what we call the loot chain, a notion that was introduced by Gregory Grossman in reference to the Soviet economy. In the USSR, wealth diverted from the official state economy into private hands was shared among networks of individuals in the form of payoffs, bribes, and other schemes. Over time an ever greater proportion of people's incomes depended on the chain of corruption and side payments. In post-Soviet Russia, the loot chain has reappeared thanks to the virtual economy. The living standards of a huge number of people depend on the chain of production and distribution of goods and services in the virtual economy system. In the virtual economy, value redistribution, in contrast to looting pure and simple, occurs in a form that parallels and is intertwined with actual productive economic activity. This makes it especially difficult for agents to discern what their own value and the value of their assets would be in a well-developed and transparent economy. Basic ideas of a market economy, such as the relationship between individual effort and reward, become almost impossibly obscure. One's static position in the production process—for instance, membership in the work force of a particular enterprise—is more important for success than individual skills and abilities. This aspect of the loot chain phenomenon significantly affected privatization of enterprises in Russia.

The loot chain is also a constraint on the future evolution of the economy. Individuals are dependent on the current system at the same time that they cannot know what an alternative system will offer. The uncertainty causes them to resist abandoning the prevailing system. This ingrained bias in favor of the status quo means that while Russians may or may not vote for "reform" politicians, they are unlikely to permit reform politicians to dismantle the virtual economy.

Plan of the Study

Chapter 2, "Illusion versus Reality," sets the stage for investigating the paradoxes of the Russian economy as they emerged especially in the years 1996–97. At that time the Russian economy looked as if it were on the way to recovery. However, the measures being cited to support that view were highly selective. A different reality lay beneath the surface. Enterprises were defying the logic of economic reform, but they were by no means acting contrary to economic self-interest. The enterprises did not restructure because they had found mechanisms that allowed them to survive. These included barter, so-called offsets, and fictitious or "virtual" pricing. These phenomena were most striking in the run-up to the August 1998 crisis. Since then the manifestation has changed, but not the underlying virtual economy structure.

As we explain in chapter 3, the roots of these virtual economy mechanisms lay in the Soviet system, especially the production relationships that had developed under the Soviet command economy. We introduce the idea that these relationships represent a peculiar type of asset, which we call "relational capital," that supplements the enterprise's conventional physical and human capital. Thanks to relational capital, market reform policies did not necessarily compel the enterprise to restructure in a market sense in order to survive. To analyze enterprise behavior in this setting, we also use the notion of market distance, which measures how costly it is to restructure the enterprise so it can compete in the market environment. We use the concepts of relational capital and market distance to reevaluate how to think about reform. In the conventional account, enterprises differ only in their degree of inefficiency. We supplement this picture with the degree of relational capital the enterprise possesses. The resulting two-dimensional picture we term r-d space. This structure allows not only for market-oriented activity, but also for behavior characteristic of the virtual economy.

Chapter 4 analyzes enterprise behavior in the Russian context using the two-dimensional space of market distance and relational capital. It focuses on explaining how enterprises choose between becoming more competitive *in* the market or more protected *from* the market.

The virtual economy was in large part a reaction to incomplete shock therapy—an adaptation that we compare in chapter 5 with a biological mutation. An evolutionary analysis of the development of the virtual economy allows us to study the process by which policies are rejected and altered. The analogy with mutation allows us to talk about rejection of policies.[17] This is important because the transition in Russia has not been characterized by failures to reform, but rather by failures of reform to stick. Chapter 5 also introduces the notion of leakage of value from the virtual economy system.

In chapter 6 we briefly digress from the analysis of the individual enterprise to show how the enterprise interacts with other parts of the economy. A stylized four-sector "virtual economy" serves to illustrate how fictitious pricing allows value to be transferred across sectors of the economy.

The next three chapters examine the implications of the continued operation of the virtual economy. Chapter 7 considers what happens as the system "runs out of value." We introduce the notion of "shrinkage" and contrast it to true restructuring. We show the effects of shrinkage on the manufacturing sector and on households. Chapter 8 describes the effect of the virtual economy on government and the public sector. The state itself begins to shrink; it is fragmented and weakened. The public sector cannot perform its functions. In chapter 9 we use the framework we have developed to analyze the Russian economy in the aftermath of the August 1998 financial crisis. Has the crisis provided a way out of the virtual economy, or is the recovery that followed more virtual than real?

The final chapter focuses on the eternal Russian question, "What is to be done?" Because the virtual economy is a complex system, where behavior has responded to policies and constraints, no simple solutions for exiting from it exist. Any policies that might lead to real reform of the system must account for the complex of factors that generate this equilibrium. To make progress on formulating such a set of policies, we use the metaphor of a corporate restructuring exercise. We treat Russia as if it were "Russia, Inc." and examine how a group of corporate receivers would structure a plan for this company. We then examine how the political realities of Russia would affect the corporate restructuring plan and develop a "real world" version of the plan. This sets the stage for discussing the potential for its implementation—is there a sufficient reason for Russia to reform?

17. We first explored the evolution analogy in Gaddy and Ickes (2001c). See also Aoki (2001, pp. 271–74).

CHAPTER TWO

Illusion
versus
Reality

"Russia is in the process of becoming one of the great markets and economies in the world.... Established institutions can't afford to be away."

—David Mulford, Chairman,
Credit Suisse First Boston Europe, February 1997

Studying the Russian economy is like examining an iceberg. Only a part of the object is visible above the surface, and failing to recognize that it is not the whole is misleading and dangerous. This has long been a truism for those analysts of the Soviet economy who emphasized the role of the shadow or second economy and those who stressed the differences between the formal and the informal economic systems.[1] In the post-Soviet Russian economy it has been especially important to separate illusion from reality. Yet time and again, evaluators of Russia's economic reform have failed to peer below the surface of the economy, and as a result, they missed its essence.

Perhaps the most striking case of confusing illusion and reality arose in the period leading up to Russia's financial crisis of August 1998. In the months from 1996 through the spring of 1998, the Russian economy seemed to be booming. Yet, at the same time, there was a proliferation of some of the most curious nonmonetary payment schemes recently seen in the modern world. For a long while, these schemes were treated as a bizarre counterpoint to an otherwise positive development. Later, their seriousness was revealed. Analysis of these elaborate schemes, however, actually illu-

1. Gregory Grossman pioneered the study of the Soviet second economy. Ed Hewett's (1988) classic study of the late Soviet economy devoted special attention to the differences between the Soviet economic system as it was designed to work and the way it actually worked.

FIGURE 2-1. Monthly Inflation in Russia,[a] February 1992–September 1997

Percentage change in consumer price index

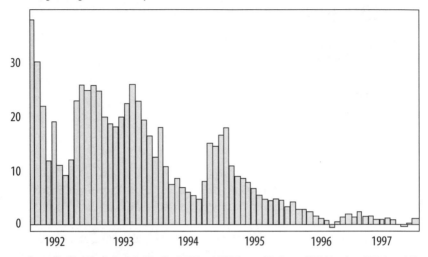

Source: The World Bank, *Statistical Handbook 1994 and 1996: States of the Former USSR* (data from 1992 through May 1996); IMF, *International Financial Statistics,* May 1997 and November 1997 volumes (data from June 1996 through September 1997).

a. Based on weekly observations of prices of 120 goods and services in 130 cities.

minates the value transfers that sustain loss-making enterprises. That is why we focus here on this case; it most clearly illustrates how the value transfers that underlie the virtual economy operate. Since the heyday of these nonmonetary schemes in 1996–98, the form of the value transfers to loss-making enterprises has changed; the substance has not.

By the summer of 1996, Russia clearly could pride itself on some major formal achievements: it had managed to stabilize the ruble, privatize enterprises on a vast scale, develop bankruptcy procedures, even create a modern stock market. Boris Yeltsin, who had initiated these reforms after assuming the presidency of Russia in 1991, won a second term in the summer of 1996. His reelection was taken as a guarantee that economic reform would continue in a stable political environment. By some appearances, it did. Inflation, for instance, still exceeded 15 percent a month in early 1995. After that it dropped steadily. For the month of August 1996, the recorded level of inflation was negative, and it stayed low through 1997 (see figure 2-1).

A related success story was the stability of the ruble. Stabilizing the external value of the ruble was an essential instrument in the fight against inflation and also a measure of its effectiveness. In the early years of the transition, the ruble had so consistently and rapidly lost value against the

U.S. dollar that dollarization of the economy had become widespread.[2] The apparently successful fight against inflation was centered on a policy of maintaining the value of the ruble against the dollar.[3] This policy—the so-called ruble corridor—allowed the ruble to maintain its value against a very strong U.S. dollar better than almost any other currency in the world in 1996–97.[4] By the late summer of 1997, Russian policymakers were so confident of the ruble's future stability that they declared that as of January 1998, old rubles would be replaced with new bills, removing three zeroes from all prices.[5]

The fledgling Russian stock market reflected this general sense of optimism and became its symbol, especially in 1997. The main stock market index, the RTS Index, began 1997 at a value below 200.[6] Within six months, it had broken the 500 barrier and was continuing upward (see figure 2-2), earning Russia the honor of having "the best-performing stock market in the world."[7]

The optimism about Russia's economic performance and future prospects was not new. Throughout the course of transition in Russia there had been a heavy dose of wishful thinking, mainly because of a genuine desire to see the country succeed. As time passed, however, many interests vested in giving a rosy picture also developed. Private investment companies were trying to attract clients. Western economists and others had given advice to Russian policymakers. Western governments had given money and other assistance. Members of these groups interacted with each other and

2. The ruble value of Russian holdings of dollars in 1994 was approximately equal to ruble M2, the broad measure of the money stock (OECD 1995, pp. 37–38).

3. The use of the exchange rate as a nominal anchor in the fight against inflation is not atypical. Indeed, as noted by Stanley Fischer (2001, p. 18), "There are few instances in which a successful disinflation from triple-digit inflation has taken place without the use of an exchange rate anchor, particularly in countries that have suffered from chronic monetary instability."

4. The ruble corridor allowed for the depreciation of the ruble against the dollar, but at a rate lower than the inflation differential, so that the ruble strengthened in value in real terms.

5. The ruble's perceived strength in the year leading up to the monetary reform decision in August 1997 is illustrated rather dramatically by the following exercise. Imagine that on August 1, 1996, someone had given you $1,000 on condition that you had to convert that $1,000 into a foreign currency and keep it there for one year before converting it back into dollars. You were offered the choice of keeping your prize in German marks, French francs, Japanese yen, Swedish kronor, or . . . Russian rubles. The best choice would have been the ruble.

6. The Russian Trading System was founded in July 1995. Its official indicator, the RTS Index, has been calculated since September 1, 1995.

7. For instance, Betsy McKay, "Record-Setting Russian Bourse's Allure Grows along with Country's Economic, Political Strides," *Wall Street Journal*, July 7, 1997, p. C13.

FIGURE 2-2. Russian Stock Market (RTS-1), September 1, 1995–August 8, 1997

Index, September 1995 = 100

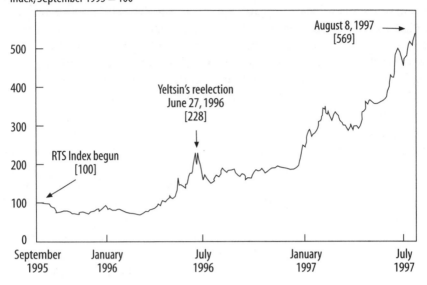

Source: Russian Trading System (RTS) website, rtsnet.ru.

strengthened their shared perception of an improving Russian economy. This produced a veritable chorus of optimistic voices about Russia.

The excessive optimism reached the point of downright giddiness in some cases. In the fall of 1996, U.S. ambassador to Russia Thomas Pickering publicly made the following predictions about Russia's economic future:

> [Let] me predict that within three years . . . doing business in Russia will become more structured, predictable, and less risky. . . . Russian tax laws and accounting standards will approach Western norms and standards. . . . The Russian Far East will become as economically vibrant an area as other parts of the Pacific Rim—including Singapore, Japan, Taiwan, Korea, and California's Silicon Valley. . . . Americans will . . . travel to Sochi and Samara as easily and as regularly as they now travel to Chicago or Cleveland; and . . . when they travel there, they will be able to stay in four-star hotels, eat at McDonald's, and rent American cars. . . . Russia will be one of America's major trading partners—and we will consider our trade relations with Russia to be as important as our relationships with Europe or Japan.[8]

8. Pickering (1996).

The Missing Pieces

These optimistic scenarios were based on selective perception. While there clearly were some bright spots in Russia's economic performance, there seemed to be a general tendency to downplay, or even ignore, two critical elements. The first was what was happening (or rather, what was *not* happening) in the core sector of the economy—manufacturing industry. The second was the unprecedented and growing scope of demonetization of the economy. Russian manufacturing enterprises seemed not to be adapting at all to the new market economy. They were not modernizing or changing their behavior. Meanwhile, more than two-thirds of transactions among the largest of these enterprises were conducted without the use of money. Lack of restructuring, on the one hand, and demonetization of the economy, on the other, were the most important facts about the economy that simply did not fit the picture of the apparent boom. Analyzing the link between the lack of restructuring and demonetization will help to show how the virtual economy operates.

Manufacturing Industry

The primary role of industrial manufacturing was an important Russian legacy of the Soviet economy. Employment in that sector accounted for 30.3 percent of total employment in 1991 (compared with 19 percent in the United States).[9] Because so much of Soviet urbanization had been based on industrial development, every major Russian city depended on manufacturing. Unless the manufacturing sector could be transformed, it would be hard to justify claims that Russia was on the road to the market. Nevertheless, many signs suggested that Russian manufacturing industry was not changing in a way that would make it more viable in the market economy. Ironically, one of the clearest was the stock market.

The same RTS index that had soared in 1996 and 1997 showed how far behind Russian manufacturing was. As of January 1, 1998, the market capitalization of the RTS list—that is, the market price of all the outstanding shares of stocks in the index—was $63 billion.[10] Only three companies—the oil companies Lukoil and Yukos and the national electrical power producer, United Energy Systems (UES)—accounted for nearly half of the

9. Construction accounted for another 12 percent of employment in 1991. See OECD (1995, p. 6). U.S. figure is for 1988, from *Statistical Abstract of the United States* (1990, table 650). Construction accounted for another 7 percent.
10. RTS website, rtsnet.ru.

TABLE 2-1. Russian Industry: Market Value versus Employment Shares
Percentage

Sector	Sector's market capitalization as a percentage of total RTS market capitalization, January 1, 1998	Employment in the sector as a percentage of total employment in the economy, 1995
Oil and gas	50.0	0.9
Electric power	29.9	1.1
Telecommunications	14.0	1.3
Manufacturing	1.0	20.6

Source: Market capitalization shares calculated from data from Russian Trading System (RTS) website, www.rtsnet.ru; employment shares calculated from data in *Rossiyskiy statisticheskiy yezhegodnik* (1997, p. 111) and *Promyshlennost' Rossii* (1996, pp. 78–79).

market capitalization. Altogether, the oil, gas, and electricity sectors accounted for 80 percent. One of the largest companies in Russia, the natural gas monopoly, Gazprom, was not on the RTS list. An alternative stock market index that did include Gazprom—the Moscow Times Index— showed an even greater degree of concentration of market capitalization. The top three companies on that index (Gazprom, UES, and Lukoil) accounted for 60 percent of its market capitalization.

Meanwhile, where was traditional manufacturing? It represented only 1.0 percent of the stock market's value. This was as good a summary as any of the lack of success in transforming the Russian economy (see table 2-1). Despite all the talk about stabilization and privatization, the core of the Russian economy remained almost completely outside the new market economy.

The striking differences in the market capitalization of various sectors of the Russian economy are illuminating.[11] One reason frequently given for low levels of market capitalization of Russian enterprises is poor corporate governance and weak protection of shareholder rights. While this is important, it cannot explain the differential, as all the sectors are part of the same underdeveloped environment. Moreover, almost all of the most notorious examples of minority shareholder abuse have taken place in oil and gas, not manufacturing. The huge discount, relative to the employment share, of Russian manufacturing must be due to something else.

---

11. Two factors account for the low market capitalization of Russian manufacturing. First is the low valuation of the enterprises that are listed on the RTS. Second is the fact that most manufacturing enterprises are not listed on the exchange. Of course, the second factor is related to the first: the fact that few enterprises are listed is due to the low expected return from listing, because investors do not place high values on their prospects.

The low valuation of Russian manufacturing relative to other sectors reflects the market's assessment of the relative competitiveness of this sector. While manufacturing appeared to be central to the economy, its actual value was much smaller than generally recognized. It is instructive to compare the data in table 2-1 with data from the Soviet period on the share of industrial value added that various sectors produced. For example, in 1989 electrical energy accounted for 3.8 percent of industrial value added, and fuels accounted for another 8.1 percent. Meanwhile, just *one part* of the manufacturing sector—machine building and metalworking—accounted for 39 percent.[12] Hence, in terms of its contribution to valued added in Soviet prices, the machine building and metalworking sector was *ten times* as large as electrical energy, whereas in 1998 the market assigned the entire manufacturing sector a value that was less than 6 percent that of electricity production.

What accounts for this drastic change in the valuation of the two sectors? Many transition processes have affected this, especially external liberalization of the economy and the decline in military spending. External liberalization enhanced the value of the natural resource sectors and increased the competitive pressure on domestic manufacturing. The decline in military spending eroded the markets for a large part of the assets in manufacturing. As a result, manufacturing enterprises entered an environment where their relative fitness decreased dramatically. Yet the sheer size of this sector—as shown by employment—maintained its social and political importance and the illusion of its economic performance. In economic terms this misperception was a product of Soviet pricing, which generated a false notion of the sectoral sources of value added.[13] In a sense, then, the importance of the manufacturing sector in Russia was an economic illusion, but continued to be a political and social reality. This discrepancy is the single most important fact explaining the nature of the Russian transition.

The Legacy

Russian manufacturing's biggest problem is not the poor corporate governance environment or corruption. Rather it is the starting point: manufacturing was not competitive when reform began in 1992.[14] It was,

12. These shares were practically unchanged from 1980 (3.8 percent, 7.8 percent, and 39.1 percent, respectively). IMF and others (1991, vol. 1, table B.2, p. 89).

13. Chapter 3 amplifies this topic, considering the roots of the virtual economy. The best analysis of this subject is in Ericson (1999).

14. Subsequent chapters introduce the concept of market *distance,* an important element of our analysis of the lack of competitiveness of Russian enterprises.

of course, universally recognized that Russia had almost no private owner-ship, but this proved easier to remedy than the more fundamental problem: uncompetitive assets. Even by official Soviet standards, more than one-third of equipment in Russian industry was physically obsolete. It was quite lit-erally junk; it could not even produce *Soviet* goods.[15] Even this is a very conservative estimate, however. It does not consider how little of this equipment was technologically suited to produce anything that had more market value than the inputs used to produce it. Soviet planning practice, which emphasized output over costs, set physical rather than economic obsolescence as the criterion for removing a machine from the factory. As long as the machine could produce anything at all, it was kept in produc-tion. The result was very low replacement rates for capital equipment.[16]

Outdated equipment was not the only problem. The geographic location of industry in the Soviet economy was not guided by economic principles. Ignoring transportation costs, Soviet planners made decisions about the location of enterprises for reasons other than economic. This often led to enterprises' being compelled to work together even though they were at opposite ends of this huge landmass. Ed Hewett described one notorious example: "Minenergo (Energy and Electrification), for example, ships sawn timber produced by construction firms at the Bratsk and Krasnoiarsk hydro-electric stations in Siberia 3,000–5,000 kilometers away to its enterprises in the European USSR. Simultaneously Minlesbumprom (timber, pulp, paper, and wood) ships sawn timber to Siberia from its enterprises in the European USSR."[17]

Soviet location policy ignored not only transportation costs, but also the costs associated with Russian climate. Russia is obviously a cold country, but Soviet investment policies greatly exacerbated the problem. During the Soviet period, population grew most rapidly in regions that are far colder than the population centers were during the years of the tsarist empire. In 1897, of the ten largest cities within the confines of the current Russian Fed-eration, only one—Kazan—had a mean January temperature below minus 13 degrees Celsius. By 1997, six of the top ten largest cities had such tem-peratures (Novosibirsk, Yekaterinburg, Omsk, Chelyabinsk, Ufa, and Kazan), and each of the six was home to more than one million residents. As a result of such policies Russia became a colder country during the Soviet

15. That is, in a closed economic environment without higher quality imports.
16. See, for example, Cohn (1979). One reason for the predominance of outdated equipment was the preference for plant over equipment in Soviet investment policy.
17. Hewett (1988, p. 173).

period.[18] Extreme cold increases the cost of economic activity—energy use, health maintenance, and many other factors—thus reducing the competitiveness of enterprises located in these regions and the attractiveness of these regions to foreign investors.

Because of location policies, much of Russian manufacturing inherited an extra liability. However, the most important legacy of the Soviet period was the inefficiency of the assets themselves, as capital, labor and technology were combined in a manner that ignored economic rationale. As Richard Ericson put it, the Soviet system created a "structure of production—location, capital, employment, materials and energy use, etc. . . . without any regard for economic opportunity costs, in an environment free of economic valuation and only subject to consistency in arbitrarily measured accounting units." It thus left Russia with a "structure of capital and economic activity that is fundamentally nonviable in an environment determined by market valuation, and hence requires massive transformation at its very roots."[19]

What happened in the postcommunist era hardly helped to improve the poor starting position. A key feature of economic reform was liberalization of the economic environment—domestic and external. Russian enterprises would be forced to compete with one another and with foreign companies. The seemingly unassailable logic was that in order to survive, enterprises would have to modernize and restructure.[20] In fact, liberalization did produce competition with foreign companies, but it did not cause modernization. Rather than devoting more attention to modernization, enterprises spent less and less each year to renew their woefully obsolescent plant and equipment.[21] In 1997 the overall level of capital investment in the economy's production sectors (industry, agriculture, transportation, and communications) was only 17 percent of what it had been in 1990. In the core manufacturing sector of metalworking and engineering products, real spending on plant and equipment in 1997 was no more than 5.3 percent of the 1990 level. While one could reasonably argue that in the Soviet period

18. By a measure of temperature per capita (TPC)—the average temperature across regions weighted by population—Russian TPC fell by about one degree centigrade between 1926 and 1998, while in the United States TPC rose by about three degrees. See Gaddy and Ickes (2001a).

19. Ericson (1999).

20. Chapter 4 explains how enterprises developed alternative survival strategies.

21. As restructuring involves doing things in a better way, some may argue that there is no necessary connection between restructuring and investment. Chapter 3 offers an argument that this intuition is typically not correct, explaining why investment is crucial to restructuring in transition.

enterprises had overinvested (as well as misinvested) and that therefore a decline in investment rates might be natural, this was clearly an overcorrection, as is evident in the aging of the capital stock. In 1990 the average age of industrial plant and equipment was 10.8 years; by 1996 it had risen to 14.9 years.[22] One Russian study claimed that as much as two-thirds of equipment was already obsolete in 1991.[23] With only negligible amounts of new equipment purchased and equipment scrapped in the years after that, the capital stock of Russia's manufacturing enterprises grew even more obsolete in every year that passed.

Given that such a huge segment of Russian industry was so poorly equipped to compete, it was not surprising that a large part of it was unprofitable. Perhaps more surprising is the trend. The share of industrial enterprises reporting net losses was 47.3 percent in October 1997, up from less than 27 percent in 1995.[24] According to one authoritative survey, the share of enterprises in "good or normal" financial condition even in the "boom" year of 1997 was less than one-quarter of the total.[25]

An important argument for markets is that those firms that lose money disappear. This did not happen in Russia. While enterprises that failed to modernize did lose money, they continued to operate. Bankruptcy in Russia was a rarity. There were more corporate bankruptcies in the United States in an average four-week period than in Russia in an entire year. It would thus appear that despite the obvious lack of success, nothing was changing in Russian industry, yet that was not true, either. Remarkably, rather than just withering away, or even remaining moribund, these companies expanded their loss-making output! In 1997, for example, Russia's industrial enterprises produced more output and employed more workers than they did in 1996. Industrial output in constant prices rose 1.9 percent in 1997. Overall unemployment fell, as did underemployment: short working days or weeks and involuntary leaves decreased by 32 percent in the first three quarters of 1997 compared with the previous year. Large and medium-sized industrial enterprises hired 6.6 million new workers in the first nine months of 1997; as a percentage of payroll this was a higher rate than for the same period in 1996. All the time, they were deeper in the red: real profits fell by 5 percent in 1997. To be sure, there were some exceptions, but they were few and far between. While a few enterprises were moving

22. *Rossiyskiy statisticheskiy yezhegodnik* (1997, p. 340).

23. Akoryan (1992).

24. All data are from Goskomstat as reported in *Interfax* (1997, nos. 14, 51/52) and (1998, no. 4, p. 88).

25. *Russian Economic Trends* (1998, no. 4, p. 88).

toward the market, most others were not. Taken as a whole, Russia's enterprise sector, especially the manufacturing core, was showing every sign of moving away from the marketplace rather than successfully adapting to it.

Bad Managers?

What could explain the failure of Russian enterprises to restructure? For many observers, it was easiest to blame the managers, notably those described as the "Red Directors"—the Soviet-era executives who held on to their positions in the new period. Some people considered them congenitally incapable of market thinking and behavior. Others more benignly attributed their nonmarket behavior to ignorance and thought that might be remedied by proper education. In 1997 Vice Premier Boris Nemtsov argued that Russia "is now short not only of money but also of well-trained executives. All positive macroeconomic gains achieved in Russia over the past few years will fall flat unless enterprises are managed properly."[26] Boris Yeltsin echoed that opinion when he called for 5,000 managers annually to be sent to the West for training.

Clearly, there *was* something different about the way Russian managers behaved. Research confirmed this. As sales plummeted, managers did not shed labor, but instead hoarded it. Why? Many studies suggested a "paternalistic" mentality on the part of the directors. In one survey in 1995–96, 60 percent of enterprises reported that they had significantly more workers than they needed. Fully 71 percent of those surplus-labor enterprises explained that the reason they kept the unneeded workers was a sense of social responsibility. The managers simply could not bring themselves to fire workers, even though they knew that keeping them on the payroll was wasteful.[27]

The profit motive, axiomatic for explaining the behavior of firm owners in western economies, would thus appear to have been weak. Again, however, what is most interesting is the trend that was apparent by 1996. Surveys seemed to indicate that the profit motive was declining in importance as market reform was said to be proceeding. One series of surveys tracking the attitudes of enterprise directors over a three-year period reported that the proportion of directors who mentioned profit as one of their top two goals declined from 31 percent in 1994 to 27 percent in 1995

26. Nemtsov went on to argue that "the catchword 'cadres decide everything' is today no less urgent than fifty years ago." Alexandra Akayeva, Moscow, December 22, 1997, RIA Novosti.

27. *Russian Economic Barometer* (1997, p. 305).

and to 21 percent in 1996. In fact, in the fourth quarter of 1996, the percentage had dropped to 12 percent! By comparison, in that quarter, 27 percent listed maintaining or increasing employment as a top priority, while 59 percent mentioned maintaining or increasing output.[28]

How could such antimarket attitudes and behavior persist? It was understandable that enterprise directors might act paternalistically and fail to recognize the importance of profits in the early period of transition. The question is how this could persist throughout this period, especially in the purported boom. A key part of the explanation lay with the other major phenomenon that was at odds with the picture of successful reform in 1996–97: the disappearance of money as a means of exchange in the economy.

Re-Demonetization

It is perhaps understandable that observers failed to pay adequate attention to the lack of restructuring in manufacturing industry. The overall facade of success in the economy obscured it. The demonetization of the economy—or, more accurately, the "re-demonetization"—was a phenomenon that was frequently noted.[29] Nevertheless, its implications were generally missed. Throughout the economy, transactions were occurring where either no payment of any kind was made or the payment was in the form of goods rather than money. Both phenomena—nonpayment (or arrears) and in-kind payment—infected the entire economy: transactions between enterprises (to suppliers and customers) and within the enterprises (wages to workers), enterprise obligations to the governments (taxes and other contributions), the government's obligations to enterprises (for government contracts), and the government's obligations to its population (pensions, child benefits, and so on). The entire economy seemed to be caught in a vicious circle of arrears and in-kind payment.

---

28. *Russian Economic Barometer* (1997, p. 305).

29. This point is argued in Ickes, Murrell, and Ryterman (1997). The Soviet economy was essentially demonetized (with the partial exception of the household sector) because plan decisions rather than purchasing power determined the quantity and assortment of goods and services produced. Money was primarily a record-keeping device. Command over goods and services derived not from possession of the means of payment, but from relations to power and personal identity. With the early 1992 price liberalization, the Russian economy began to be monetized, as command over purchasing power meant command over goods and services. The growth in barter thus represented re-demonetization, because once again "who you know" became critical to the ability to acquire goods and services, especially in the production sphere.

To some extent, both the scale and the interconnectedness of the barter and arrears phenomena were recognized at the highest policymaking levels. In his 1998 State of the Nation message, President Boris Yeltsin told his fellow citizens: "The Russian market is still crammed with barter deals and is suffocating on mutual arrears. Enterprises live on borrowed resources, yet are unwilling to pay debts. Reasons are many. One key reason is that the budget is unrealistic. This country is an economy of irresponsible debtors. This practice is wrong. Continuing it is unacceptable. It is senseless and pernicious to try and dupe the economy."[30]

Russia's barter economy actually comprises a wide range of nonmonetary means of payment.[31] These include direct exchanges of goods (true barter), either bilaterally or through "chains" with multiple participants; offsets (where debts accrued by one party were later paid off not in money but in goods); and promissory notes called *veksels*. *Veksels*—the name for which is derived from the German *Wechsel*, meaning "bill of exchange"— are a widespread form of nonmonetary payment that spanned the gamut of use from a substitute for money to essentially a form of barter. One particularly important phenomenon was tax offsets. An enterprise owing taxes to the government would conclude an agreement settling those tax obligations by delivering goods or performing services for the government.[32]

Many observers have noted the growth of barter in the Russian economy.[33] The monthly surveys of industrial enterprises conducted by the Russian Economic Barometer research institute constitute the most complete time series of barter. They show that the surveyed enterprises steadily, almost monotonically, increased their use of barter from about 5 percent of all transactions in 1992 to close to 50 percent in 1997 (see figure 2-3).[34] The

30. Yeltsin (1998).

31. Much of the literature, including some empirical studies, tends to combine the various types of noncash payments under the term barter. This can lead to some confusion. For example, some respondents consider a narrow definition of barter as strict bilateral exchange of goods and report low levels of barter despite the almost nonexistence of cash sales. Confusion of definition can cause difficulties in assessing the causes of barter. For example, tax evasion may not be a motive for the narrow definition of barter (direct goods exchange), but it may be a critical reason for the use of such a mechanism as tax offsets (the broad definition).

32. Tax offsets can resemble barter or *veksels*. They resemble *veksels* when the government agency issues a security that can be used to offset taxes. Examples of those securities, such as KOs and KNOs, appeared as early as 1993. Tax offsets can also resemble barter when goods delivered but not paid for result in cancellation of a tax obligation.

33. See OECD (2000, chapter 2) for an informative discussion. See also the papers in Seabright (2000).

34. The Russian Economic Barometer (REB) conducts monthly surveys of around two hundred enterprises selected from a fairly stable pool of about five hundred enterprises.

FIGURE 2-3. The Rising Role of Barter in Industrial Sales, 1992–97

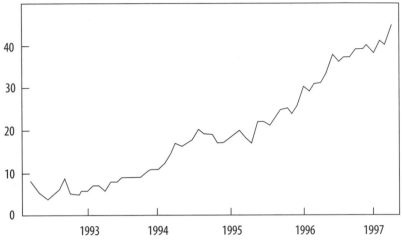

Source: *Russian Economic Barometer* (1997, no. 4, p. 71).

pattern displayed in figure 2-3 is corroborated by other work. In a 1994 survey of 150 Russian enterprises, Ickes and Ryterman found that the incidence of barter had increased from 5 percent of the value of transactions in 1992 to approximately 20 percent in 1994.[35] A follow-up survey of the same category of enterprises reported a further increase to approximately 40 percent in 1996.[36]

The phenomenon was nationwide; only the city of Moscow appeared to be a relative exception to the trend. Table 2-2 gives an idea of the growth of barter from 1992 to 1997 in six Russian regions.

The pool comprises almost exclusively enterprises that were state owned before 1992. It has none with fewer than fifty employees that were created de novo after 1992 and none with more than two thousand employees. The mean and the median sizes are fewer than five hundred employees. As a result of the REB's sampling method, its mean enterprise is smaller than the mean for all industry. This is important, since barter rates tend to be higher among the very largest enterprises. While the REB's barter index is probably consistent (that is, it reflects the trend over time), it underestimates the actual extent of barter in Russian industry.

35. Ickes and Ryterman (1994).
36. Hendley and others (1997).

TABLE 2-2. Estimated Percentage of Industrial Output Sold through Barter in Selected Russian Regions, 1992, 1997

Year	Barnaul	Yekaterinburg	Moscow	Novosibirsk	Saratov	Voronezh
1992	11	9	7	13	13	19
1997	64	46	15	47	49	35

Source: Hendley, Ickes, and Ryterman (1998, p. 102).

Causes of Barter

Although the widespread use of barter was generally recognized, its significance was downplayed.[37] Many observers at first regarded the increase in barter in Russia as a transitory phenomenon. Barter and arrears had been characteristic of the earliest phase of transition in many other former planned economies, but they disappeared quite rapidly once the financial system developed and the macroeconomy stabilized. In Russia, however, the importance of barter and nonpayments continued to grow over time.

Early in the Russian transition, some observers argued that barter was the natural response of many enterprises to the high inflation, or the high inflation tax, that prevailed in Russia after prices were liberalized at the beginning of 1992.[38] Prices rose at rates as high as 200 percent a month in the early months of 1992 and then at monthly rates of 25 percent in the second half of the year. To make matters worse, the rates fluctuated greatly (see figure 2-1). Prices varied not only in time, but also across the territory of Russia and across different branches of the economy. The rapidly declining, and highly uncertain, value of the ruble begged for an alternative medium of exchange. At the retail level, ordinary Russians circumvented the ruble

37. An important exception is David Woodruff (1999). He argues that demonetization represents a significant development in the transition. He emphasizes that many enterprises could not pay cash for needed inputs, such as energy, and that barter was a means of reducing the price of these key inputs. He places much of the blame for this on rules that prevented Gazprom from reducing prices to these enterprises. Hence he argues that barter was a means for natural monopolies to engage in price discrimination. See Ericson and Ickes (2001) for a model of the virtual economy with Gazprom as a price-discriminating monopolist.

38. This is a curious argument. Price liberalization raised the price of the inventories that enterprises held at the beginning of 1992, which should have led to a windfall gain. But the inadequate payments system that existed in Russia—payments often taking two months to travel from buyer to seller—meant that the real value of money balances held in the production sector was heavily taxed. A slow payments system results in inflation's placing a huge tax on its users: it is essentially a transfer from enterprises to the government.

by using the U.S. dollar for their buying and selling.[39] No matter what happened to the ruble's value, dollar prices remained steady. The dollar was also used as a store of value.

Curiously, though, even as inflation was tamed and the value of the ruble remained fairly steady against the dollar in late 1994 and early 1995, the use of barter did not diminish, but instead grew. An alternative explanation was needed. A very popular one, especially during the period of financial stabilization, was to attribute the growth of barter to a shortage of liquidity created by stabilization.[40] The argument is that the high real interest rates, by making it hard for enterprises to borrow, forced them to transact without the use of money.

In the course of financial stabilization, real interest rates went from negative to significantly positive. The combination of a tight monetary policy and a loose fiscal policy, financed by issuing government securities (GKOs and OFZs), led to high real interest rates. This certainly had the effect of raising the cost of borrowing. Nevertheless, a reduction of inflation ought to result in greater use of money, not less, as people expect that the currency will retain its purchasing power. In a well-functioning economy, a tight money policy would lead not to more barter, but to greater holdings of real money balances.

The liquidity explanation of barter does have the advantage of getting the timing right: barter began to increase as the economy experienced high real interest rates. Most of the empirical support for the theory, however, comes from survey responses of directors who state that they accept barter because their customers lack liquidity. A problem with this evidence, however, is that if it is advantageous to the buyer to pay with goods rather than with money, then buyers will act strategically. That is, they will pretend to be liquidity constrained when they may not be, in order to qualify for barter. If enterprises act strategically, then the seller's information may not be the most accurate indicator of the liquidity position of the buyer.

Some empirical evidence that casts doubt on the liquidity hypothesis comes from a study by Sergei Guriev and Barry Ickes that avoids the problem of uninformed sellers and strategic buyers. They matched data on the

39. In January 1993 a presidential decree required all payments to be made in Russian currency. This did not prevent people from holding their wealth in dollars (and German marks), and exchange windows (often inside shops) proliferated, allowing Russians conveniently to convert their dollars back into rubles only at the time of immediate purchase.

40. For arguments to this effect, see Commander and Mummsen (1998) and Morozov, Pinto, and Drebentsov (2000).

proportions of revenues in cash and noncash form taken from a survey of directors with the Goskomstat database of Russian enterprises, which contains the financial accounts of all large and medium-size industrial enterprises in Russia. This allowed them to compare the share of noncash payments with the enterprise's financial position. They concluded that there was no discernible relationship between the use of barter and the financial condition of the enterprise.[41]

The point of this discussion is not to argue that the liquidity squeeze that began with financial stabilization played no role in the growth of noncash payments. Rather, it is to point out that once noncash payments became a widespread phenomenon, the possibility of using them became part of the strategies of all agents. As barter proliferated, it became a "normal" way of doing business. Chapter 4 will explain the importance in the Russian economy of judicious management of the types of payments that are used and to whom they are made. Knowing when to use cash and when to use barter is often the key to economic survival in Russia's virtual economy.

Perhaps the most intriguing fact with respect to barter (and other forms of nonmonetary payment) was that the impetus to barter often came from the seller.[42] This suggests that the motivations for barter may not be limited to the ones suggested so far. One alternative explanation is that barter allowed enterprises to survive Russia's onerous tax system.[43] The first and most obvious use of barter in this regard is to allow enterprises to avoid taxes. A second—subtler and more peculiarly Russian—is not to evade taxes, but to pay them—only not in cash.

Barter and Tax Evasion

Barter in some cases allows enterprises to avoid declaring some income. But even more important than tax reporting is tax collection. Barter allows the enterprises to avoid the first line of tax collection in Russia today: the banking system. Any enterprise that is in arrears to the government for unpaid taxes is by law subject to having its bank accounts blocked. All transactions that flow through the banking system are available for collection by the

41. Guriev and Ickes (1999). The directors survey was conducted by the Center for Business Trends at the Institute of Economy in Transition in the autumn of 1996, 1997, and 1998. Similar results are reported in Hendley, Ickes, and Ryterman (1998).

42. Hendley and others (1997).

43. See, for example, Yakovlev (1999) and Yakovlev (2000). Yakovlev argues that tax evasion is the primary motive for barter and nonmonetary transactions in Russia, and he provides survey evidence about how this is accomplished.

State Tax Service for enterprises that are delinquent on their tax obligations. This provides a direct incentive for enterprises with tax arrears to avoid using the banking system, as the effective tax rate on revenue is 100 percent.

Enterprises have various approaches to avoiding the banks. They hold multiple accounts, opening new ones and closing old ones at a rapid rate, trying to stay one step ahead of the tax inspectors. Use of offshore accounts is another technique. Using cash—that is, banknotes—is a third. Clearly, however, another way to avoid using the banks is to avoid money altogether by making and receiving payments in the form of barter or *veksels*.

Legally, barter transactions are taxable. Many, though far from all, barter transactions actually are recorded for the tax authorities, the statistics agencies, and others to see. Enterprises thus incur a tax liability on sales for which they are paid in barter goods. However, the burden then falls on the tax collection end. Since no money is deposited in the enterprise's bank accounts, the convenient and automatic mechanism of direct deduction does not work. The enterprise never received cash from the sale and thus has no cash with which to pay taxes.

If barter constituted only a relatively small percentage of enterprise sales, with the rest in monetary form, then the tax authorities might realistically expect the enterprise to be able to pay enough in cash from its other sales to cover the taxes incurred on the barter transaction. However, when barter and other related nonmonetary payments constitute as much as 90 percent of all sales for some enterprises, enterprises simply do not have the cash and will not pay. The same goes for other obligations of the enterprise—to suppliers of material inputs, utilities, and so on.

Barter also plays a more direct role in tax evasion by allowing enterprises to record the value of transactions in ways that reduce overall tax incidence. There has been a change in the way barter prices have been used in this regard over the period of the transition. In 1993–94, barter was used as a means of settling accounts between traditional business partners. Through direct contacts between buyers and sellers, prices on goods exchanged by barter were often chosen in mutual agreement so as to minimize taxes. Barter prices could be higher or lower than the corresponding market prices, depending on the potential tax liabilities of the parties.

By allowing its suppliers to charge higher-than-market prices, a profitable enterprise could inflate its production costs, thereby reducing its apparent profits and lowering its tax obligation. Of course the other party to the transaction would have greater accounting revenues, but if this enterprise were a loss maker, the transaction would not result in increased tax liability. Appendix A presents two cases showing how loss-making enterprises can facilitate tax evasion through barter.

Tax Offsets

Evidence on the role of tax evasion as a motivation for barter is mixed. Some studies find survey evidence in favor of the tax-evasion hypothesis,[44] while others do not.[45] In most cases, however, these studies focus the question too narrowly, asking, typically, whether enterprises use barter to *evade* taxes. A more appropriate question would be whether enterprises use barter to reduce the *effective* tax burden. Enterprises often use barter not to *evade* taxes, but in order to *pay* taxes, only in a way advantageous to the enterprise. This is the practice of tax offsets.

Consider, for example, an enterprise that is able to supply the local government with services in lieu of taxes. The enterprise could pay its tax liability in money, but this would require selling its output for cash. Alternatively, the enterprise could negotiate with the government to supply some service as an offset for taxes. If the enterprise has resources that are not fully utilized, supplying a service to the government is likely to reduce the effective tax burden on the enterprise. This would not be the case if the enterprise faced a perfectly elastic effective demand for its output, that is, if it could always charge the same price for each additional unit sold. In that case it could use the resources to produce and sell the output to obtain the cash with which to pay taxes. However, most Russian enterprises operate at a point on their demand curve where it is highly inelastic. If they want to increase cash sales, they have to offer a steep discount on the price. In that case negotiating an offset with the government is often the preferred option.[46]

Once the government is willing to engage in tax offsets, the options open to enterprises expand. Now the enterprise can potentially pay its taxes not only with its own products, but also with products it receives in barter deals from other enterprises. This greatly reduces the cost to the seller of accepting goods rather than cash. This is especially true when the noncash

44. Hendley, Ickes, and Ryterman (1998).

45. Commander and Mummsen (1999) also point out that tax rates did not increase dramatically in 1995, which makes it hard to understand how tax evasion could be the primary explanation for the rapid growth of barter since then.

46. This is an example of "Igor's second rule of managerial behavior," described in chapter 3: an enterprise should have the capability to provide municipal services so that it can offset local taxes.

receipts take the form of *veksels* from the natural monopolies, such as Gazprom or UES. The essential point is that once the government is willing to engage in tax offsets, enterprises face two effective tax rates, depending on whether taxes are paid in money or goods. This, in turn, alters the return to barter sales among enterprises.

Chains of Barter

A major shift in Russia's barter economy occurred in 1995, when multilateral barter chains proliferated.[47] This was the basis for the temporary stabilization in the decline in output in 1995.[48] A report from a leading Russian economics research institute, the Institute for the Economy in Transition (IET), noted:

> The barter chain itself turned out to be a special kind of consumer of the output. But its needs differed from the needs of liquid demand. The barter chains frequently reminded one of the "production for production's sake" of the [Soviet] planned economy, when a quasi-cooperation gave rise to closed autonomous systems that served only themselves. In a number of enterprises which we surveyed, the share of output necessary simply to support the viability of the chain itself was as high as 30 percent.[49]

The IET concluded that the growth of barter, especially multilateral barter, had not only quantitative but also qualitative features. "In several of the enterprises we studied in the past two years [1995–96], we saw a growth in production not of liquid output [output that could be sold for cash] but of output that enjoyed demand in the barter schemes."[50] The task of finding products that would be acceptable to the power companies became paramount. It compelled many enterprises to shift the structure of their output not to meet true market demand, but to attempt to satisfy directly or indirectly the rather specific needs of the natural monopolies. This created the conditions for the exact opposite of market restructuring—an adjustment away from the market.

47. Multilateral barter chains were observed as early as 1992. However, barter was less frequent, especially after the rapid increase in Central Bank credit beginning in July 1992. Most of these chains recreated links inherited from the Soviet period, and trust based on this history was an important element supporting such complex transactions.

48. According to Goskomstat, industrial output growth was -18.5 percent in 1992, -13.3 percent in 1993, and -20.9 percent in 1994. In 1995, it fell by "only" 3.3 percent.

49. IET (1999).

50. IET (1999).

As barter spread outside of traditional multilateral chains and began to be used with nontraditional customers, the quality of the goods exchanged deteriorated. Enterprises faced two prices for their product: a barter price and a cash price. Given the bias in Russian law against cash discounts, enterprises chose instead to offer lower quality goods in exchange for barter, while reserving better quality products for cash sales.[51]

One result of the proliferation in barter was a curious investment "boom" among the least likely candidates. One economics weekly wrote: "One can observe a paradoxical pattern: the worse the enterprise's economic condition . . . the higher its level of investment 'activity.'" The solution to this apparent riddle, the writer explained, was that these weak enterprises, surviving through the system of barter and offsets, ended up receiving huge amounts of some of the most popular barterable goods—construction materials of various kinds—which they then had to put to use by building something or other. As a result, around 60 percent of capital investment was construction of new residential and production buildings. But these projects never get finished. "Under conditions of the traditional Russian practice of construction delays, [these investment projects] have a zero or even negative economic effect."[52] In terms of economic efficiency, the only consolation is that a substantial portion of the construction materials delivered to the construction sites does end up in socially useful projects, albeit through illegal channels, since workers pilfer them and use them to build garages or dachas for themselves or their friends and neighbors.

Veksels

Although barter allows enterprises to avoid the use of money, it is very costly in time and effort required to make deals work. In more technical terms, the transactions cost of barter is high and is evident in the number of middlemen who specialize in barter.[53] This is especially true of multilat-

51. Russian law is biased against cash discounts, a practice that developed because Russian enterprises evaded taxes by selling output at very low prices to "daughter" companies, which then resold the output at market prices. The tax obligations were shifted to the daughter companies, which managed to vanish before the taxman arrived. To avoid this, Russian tax law now bases taxes on costs of production, which makes discounting extremely costly. See, for example, Tompson (1998) and Woodruff (1999).

52. *Ekonomika i zhizn'*, no. 12, 1999, p. 1.

53. These costs may be the fixed costs of finding potential trading partners. Guriev and Ickes (1999) report that the likelihood that an enterprise will barter this year is positively related to previous use of barter, consistent with the notion of a fixed cost of barter. They also find that the cross-sectional distribution of barter across enterprises is

eral barter, which requires the creation of chains of exchanges. One means of reducing the transaction costs involved in barter is to use *veksels*. These promissory notes, issued by commercial banks, governments, and enterprises, serve as an alternative medium of exchange. The use of *veksels* became widespread in 1997: by one estimate, the outstanding stock of these instruments had grown by the spring of that year to roughly two-thirds of the value of all rubles in circulation (ruble M2).[54] Enterprise *veksels* are issued by large established firms, such as Gazprom and UES. These notes circulate among chains of enterprises that owe goods to the issuer. Eventually the note is redeemed by some customer of the issuer. They are particularly useful in relieving the problem of mutual nonpayments.

What makes *veksels* interesting in the current context is that they, like direct barter, are another way for a tax-delinquent enterprise to circumvent the tax authorities' claim on bank deposits. Because *veksels* circulate outside the banking system, an enterprise with a blocked account can make and accept payments and avoid seizure of funds by the tax collectors. Again, like barter, although receipts received in the form of *veksels* are legally taxable, the payments technology allows much greater opportunities for evasion.

The "Three Fat Boys"

Any discussion of barter in Russia is incomplete without taking into account the role of three key entities that support the system. These are the major natural monopolies known popularly as the "Three Fat Boys" (*tri tolstyaka*)—Gazprom (the natural gas monopoly), RAO UES (the electricity monopoly), and MPS (the state railways). All three frequently complained that they collected as little as 10 percent of their revenues in cash.[55] Needless to say, almost all enterprises in Russia are consumers of the output of these three companies: rail freight transport, gas, and electricity. The three also account for about 25 percent of revenues to the federal budget. Hence,

---

rather uniform, except at the tails. That is, very few enterprises barter for less than 10 percent of sales or for more than 80 percent of sales. The former result is again consistent with the notion of a fixed cost of barter, while the latter follows from what we call Igor's third rule (see chapter 3): *Set up some barter operations for the rest of your inputs, especially fuels, electricity and so on.* Because all enterprises need to purchase gas and electricity, the widespread use of barter is easy to understand. Moreover, because the share of material costs in production varies across enterprises, it is not surprising that the share of barter does likewise.

54. OECD (1997, p. 178).

55. This, of course, is a fact that they typically cited when explaining their tax arrears to the government.

TABLE 2-3. Gazprom Deliveries, Sales, and Cash Receipts, 1997

Market	Deliveries (bn cubic feet)	Share	Price ($/1,000 m³)	Sales ($ million)	Share of sales	Cash receipts as share of total sales	Share of cash sales
Europe	121	0.25	88.5	10,707	0.39	1.00	0.70
CIS	64	0.13	76.8	4,937	0.18	0.58	0.19
Domestic	301	0.62	47	11,536	0.42	0.15	0.11
Total	486	...	...	27,180	...	...	...

Source: Authors' calculations from Gazprom company data and data from Brunswick Warburg.

it is not surprising that they would be on one side of so many barter transactions. Moreover, the fact that everyone needs to purchase services from
the fat boys means that there is a ready demand for their IOUs. This special position put them at the core of the nonpayments system in Russia.
Having a product that is demanded by one of the fat boys is a key to survival in Russia.

Even among the three fat boys, the standout, as the pillar of the nonmonetary economy in Russia, is the gas giant, Gazprom. Gazprom is the
world's largest producer of natural gas, some 23 percent of world output,
while its proven reserves account for some 35 percent of world reserves.
Gazprom has essentially three distinct markets (see table 2-3). Exports to
the West are paid for entirely in cash. They account for approximately 25
percent of deliveries and 39 percent of total sales revenue, but 70 percent
of cash receipts. Domestic sales account for more than 60 percent of deliveries and 42 percent of sales, but only 11 percent of cash receipts.

Sales to the Commonwealth of Independent States (CIS) are a somewhat
mixed bag. For the most part Gazprom attempts to sell to the CIS only for
cash, but Belarus and Ukraine form two special cases. Lying along the route
of Gazprom's pipelines, Ukraine has been able to dramatically reduce the
proportion of its cash purchases by exercising its leverage over Gazprom's
main source of income. Gazprom cannot cut off supplies to Ukraine as a
penalty for nonpayment because Ukraine would retaliate by cutting off
exports to Europe. Consequently, Ukraine has been able to pay in large part
with goods, often swapped directly to the Russian government in lieu of
Gazprom's tax liabilities. It is somewhat less clear how Belarus is able to
obtain a similar deal, though geopolitics—the desire to form a union—and
the possibility of an alternative pipeline through its territory may be part of
the explanation. In any event, it is clear that by effectively subsidizing the

economies of Belarus and Ukraine, Gazprom is both an instrument and director of Russian policy toward these two countries.[56]

Noncash Production to Pay Taxes

In addition to the three fat boys, the other key player in the barter economy is the government—governments at all levels. Here again is an agent to whom nearly everyone has an obligation. The volume of accrued unpaid taxes, plus the huge fines and penalties levied for nonpayment, presents governments with an almost inexhaustible supply of debts. Governments themselves, in turn, owe many others. They are, like the natural monopolies, a key node for barter.[57]

Of all the forms of nonmonetary transactions observed in Russia, the mechanism of tax offsets is the most characteristic of the virtual economy. Russian governments at all levels grew increasingly willing to offset enterprises' tax obligations against goods or services delivered to the government. By the end of 1997, the accumulated tax debt was enormous. Industrial enterprises were particularly egregious delinquents. The sum owed by the enterprises at the end of 1997 (112 billion new rubles) was equal to 46 percent of the amount they actually remitted in taxes for all of 1997 (246 billion rubles).[58]

These enormous debts gave impetus to the practice of tax offsets. Tax offsets first arose as agencies of the federal government sought to evade restrictions on expenditures that had been imposed to meet IMF budget targets. They originated as promissory notes issued by government agencies and used to offset tax liabilities.[59] The notes took primarily two forms: KOs (negotiable notes) and KNOs (nonnegotiable notes). KOs (so-called Treasury *veksels*) were initially issued by the Ministry of Finance in 1994

56. The Russian government obtains Gazprom's willingness to supply customers for goods in exchange for the right to export for hard currency. The argument here is that exports to Belarus and Ukraine take on the appearance of domestic sales, offered at a discounted price for political reasons.

57. In many ways the natural monopolies may be thought of as an arm of government, as they were in the Soviet economy. The extent to which they are quasi government extends from governance (where their boards are still government-appointed in large measure) to policy (as in the case of Gazprom, where debts to the monopoly are paid directly to the Russian government).

58. *Interfax* (1998, no. 14).

59. According to a November 8, 1997, decree of Boris Yeltsin, the Russian government was prohibited from canceling debts to enterprises against tax arrears after January 1, 1998. Enforcement of this decree can be characterized as spotty at best.

and circulated as quasi money. They were replaced in 1995 with the non-negotiable KNOs, which in turn were eliminated in the summer of 1996. Tax offsets continue to be important, however, especially at the local level, but now they are in the form of direct barter or *veksels* issued by enterprises or banks.

Governments were motivated to join in the barter economy because they reasoned that if they could not get cash, it was better to reach some sort of settlement than to receive nothing at all. In some cases, especially at the local-government level, an enterprise could offer to deliver goods or services to the city or regional government in lieu of taxes. At the federal level, it was more common for the government to cancel tax arrears or taxes due by writing off the government's own debt (for state orders) to the enterprise in question. Once the practice was established with respect to past arrears, there was an anticipatory factor: enterprises began to feel confident that they could henceforth ship off products to the government, knowing that later they would be allowed to offset their taxes in an equivalent amount. Taxpayers also realized that there were many different ways to play this game. Often it was advantageous to bypass the financial agencies and deal directly with public-sector consumers, who in turn could seek retroactive approval of the fiscal authorities. This led to a highly decentralized system of bargaining between taxpayers and public-sector customers, with the fiscal authorities entering into the picture merely to rubber-stamp the deals already concluded. The story of how one hospital director in Kostroma province obtained bed linens illustrates the bottom-up nature of this process (box 2-1).

When the Kostroma official confessed he did not know the true proportion of nonmonetary budget receipts, he may have just been more honest than most of his peers. In fact, there are some statistics, but they are impossible to verify. Local and regional officials have good reason to understate the share of cash they receive: they fear it might be appropriated by higher levels of government. The federal government, at the same time, was under constant pressure by the International Monetary Fund to show higher figures for cash tax collections.

Table 2-4 shows the magnitude of the problem. Less than 60 percent of all federal taxes collected in 1997 were paid in cash; the rest were in the form of offsets. In twelve of Russia's eighty-nine regions, including some with the biggest and most paternalistic enterprises (Nizhny Novgorod, Sverdlovsk, Perm, and Kemerovo), cash accounted for less than 40 percent

BOX 2-1. The Kostroma Hospital Linens Story

The director and chief physician of a rural hospital in Kostroma, a region 300 kilometers northeast of Moscow, suffered from a shortage of bed linens. Woefully underfunded from the region's central budget and aware that she was unlikely to receive funding for such a relatively minor need, the director's response was to get on the telephone and contact the director of the region's largest textile mill. Inquiring almost rhetorically whether the mill had outstanding regional tax liabilities, she proposed that she and the director arrange to have a portion of the mill's taxes written off in exchange for the delivery of cotton fabric to the hospital. "I told him to go ahead and ship the fabric. I said I'd notify [the head of the oblast finance department] that we'd reached this agreement and would make sure he credited the mill's taxes."

The director recounted this incident to one of the authors in the presence of the regional finance department official in question. He confirmed that this was precisely the way it happened. He guessed that actions like this, from the bottom up, accounted for well over half of all his budget's revenues and outlays. Neither he, nor anyone else, he stated, knew the exact percentage: no statistics were kept on what percentage of payments were made in cash.

Source: Authors' interview in Sudislavl', Kostroma oblast, April 1997.

of federal tax payments.[60] Payments to local and regional budgets are even more dominated by barter and offsets.[61]

Virtual Accounting

The proliferation of nonmonetary payment creates confusion in the interpretation of statistics on economic performance. Payments in the Russian economy come in at least three forms: monetary, barter, and offsets. However, receipts are denominated in rubles in all cases, and they are typically

60. V. Butkevich, "Mezhdu proshlym i budushchim," *Ekonomika i zhizn'*, no. 5 (1998), p. 3.

61. For a sample of thirty-nine regions (of Russia's total eighty-nine), the average share of noncash tax revenues in 1996 was 60 percent for regional (oblast, kray, and republican) budgets and 43 percent for local (district and city) budgets. OECD (1997, p. 181).

TABLE 2-4. Federal Tax Collection, 1995–97

Trillions of 1997 rubles

Year	Total taxes due	Taxes collected in cash	Taxes collected in noncash form	Taxes not collected in any form
1995	366	190	60	116
1996	334	185	60	89
1997	334	135	95	104

Source: Authors' calculations from data in *Interfax Statistical Reports,* 1996–98.

recorded in rubles as if these three payment types were equivalent. This practice allows receipts to be recorded at values that may depart substantially from their true market values. In particular, enterprises that barter often record the value of the goods received in exchange at prices far above the true market value.

A concrete example is the best illustration of this phenomenon. The Karpov Commission reported the following data on one Siberian coal mine, *OAO Coal Mine Berezovskiy No. 1:*

> In the first half of 1997, the Berezovskiy Coal Mine . . . had sales totaling 551 billion rubles. Of those revenues, 335 billion were in *veksels,* 215 billion were in barter goods, and only 1 (one) billion was in cash.
>
> Those *veksels* [which were] issued by *Sibir'energo* [the regional electrical power producer]. . . can be sold for cash at an 80 percent discount, and sold for Siberian-produced goods at a discount of 54 percent.[62]

This information not only gives a conversion rate between *veksels* and cash (one *veksel* ruble equals 0.20 cash rubles), but also implies a rate of exchange between barter goods and cash: each barter ruble is worth 0.435 cash rubles.[63] These conversion rates in turn allow us to compute the actual cash value of the coal mine's nominal revenues (see table 2-5). The 335 billion rubles in *veksels* have a cash value of (335 x 0.20 =) 67 billion rubles. The 215 billion rubles in barter goods are really worth only (215 x 0.435 =) 93.5 billion rubles. Adding the one billion rubles actually received in

62. Karpov Commission Report (1997).

63. This can be computed as follows. A *veksel* with a face value of one ruble can be exchanged for barter goods nominally priced at 0.46 rubles (since the discount is 54 percent). Reversing the exchange, barter goods nominally priced at one ruble are equivalent to 1/0.46 = 2.17 rubles in *veksels.* But since each *veksel* ruble is worth 0.20 cash rubles, a barter ruble is worth (2.17) x (0.20) = 0.435 cash rubles.

TABLE 2-5. Recorded and Actual Revenues at the Berezovskiy Coal Mine

Form of payment	Recorded revenues (bn rubles)	Share of total revenues (percent)	Cash conversion rates	Implied cash revenues (bn rubles)	Share of market value of revenues (percent)
Barter	215	39.0	0.435	93.5	57.9
Veksels	335	60.8	0.20	67.0	41.5
Cash	1	0.2	1.0	1.0	0.6
Total	551	100.0	n.a.	161.5	100.0

Source: Karpov Commission Report (1997).

cash, the true value of the coal mine's sales was only (67 + 93.5 + 1 =) 161.5 billion rubles.

Thus the 551 billion in reported revenues represented a market (cash) value of 161.5 billion. The mine's output was being overvalued 3.4 times! Or, put another way, the users of coal were obtaining this resource for a much lower price than they ostensibly paid. The regional electricity producer, Sibir'energo, was obtaining coal for one-fifth the price it was nominally being charged. Users of electricity were no doubt similarly subsidized. Assuming that the domestic price of coal equals the world price, we can begin to imagine the extent to which value was lost from these domestic transactions.

The Berezovskiy coal mine illustrates a phenomenon that is widespread in the virtual economy: reports of economic performance that are seriously distorted. This makes it very difficult to assess quantitative performance data. For example, an increase in recorded industrial production may not indicate anything positive. First, the actual value of deliveries could be less than what is recorded. Second, the production could be used to offset taxes; that is, it could be production "for tax's sake."

Consider, for example, the effect on economic performance of a change in production at an enterprise that is producing a commodity, say steel, that has an actual cost of production of R1.5 per ton and a cash sales value of R1 per ton. Suppose, however, that when bartered for goods, the revenues are booked at R2 per ton. Performance data would indicate that an increase in production by this steel mill is good for society, leading to net profits of R0.5 per ton. In fact, however, expanding the output of steel from that mill actually represents a net cost.[64]

64. The proper interpretation of the social costs in this case depends on how the costs are distributed. Suppose that of the R1.5 it costs to make each ton of steel, only R0.3 goes to wages and capital, and the remaining R1.2 reflects purchased inputs from other enter-

Why would someone barter goods that are valued at R2 per ton for steel that has a cash value of only R1 per ton? This is a complex question, to which we will return later in this book, but a few points should be mentioned immediately. First, it is not clear from the example that the goods the mill received in payment for its steel are really worth R2 per ton; we only know that they are recorded that way. Presumably, for the steel purchaser (the seller of the barter goods), the potential net revenue from selling the barter goods must be less than R1 per ton. Otherwise, it would be more profitable to sell the goods and buy the steel for cash (at the "market," or cash, price of R1 per ton). But perhaps the market opportunities for the buyer are limited; hence, barter is a less costly route. Of course, the notion of *net* is important here as well. It may be that selling the goods for cash results in taxes and other costs that can be avoided by using barter.

One important reason why bartered goods may be recorded at a higher price than their cash value involves sales to the government. One of the advantages of tax offsets for enterprises is that the value at which the delivered goods will be recorded is an item of negotiation. Another is that paying taxes with unwanted production may be a key method for survival.

A Way to Survive

Payment of taxes in nonmonetary form has important implications for the governments themselves, an issue we examine later in this book. However, most critical for our immediate discussion is that tax offsets fundamentally changed the range of opportunities available to Russian enterprise directors. By allowing the enterprise to pay taxes by delivering goods for which there was no effective demand, tax offsets gave an incentive to avoid restructuring. For many enterprises it was easier to produce such goods than to restructure and earn additional monetary income to pay taxes in cash. Producing those goods allowed for use of idle capital and labor. The state of such enterprises can be seen in the example of one, the Tutayev Diesel Engine Plant in Yaroslavl oblast.[65]

Tutayev is typical of many enterprises in Russia's heavy industry. This plant, in a town of 45,000 in Yaroslavl oblast, employed 12,000 people in the 1980s. It is now a private company, although the state still holds a sub-

---

prises. Then this steel enterprise actually destroys value. Transformed into steel, the inputs are worth less than they were when they were unprocessed inputs. For more on value destruction, see appendix C.

65. Information on Tutayev from Malov and Mayn (1997).

FIGURE 2-4. Output and Employment at the Tutayev Engine Plant, 1990–96

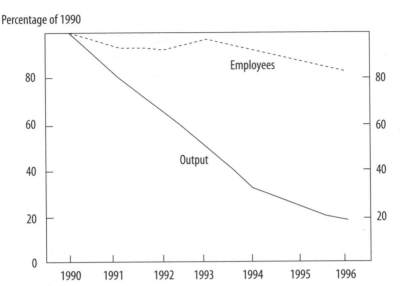

Source: Malov and Mayn (1997).

stantial minority stake. Tutayev was the major Soviet-era producer of diesel V-8 engines for tractor-trailer trucks, dump trucks, earth-moving equipment, and farm tractors. Reform has led to a near total collapse of production there. The plant has capacity to produce about 18,000 diesel engines annually. Its 1996 output was 401 engines—a capacity utilization rate of 2.2 percent. Since 1990 total sales of all products at the plant have plummeted by around 80 percent. Employment, however, was down by only 17 percent, reflecting the labor hoarding that is typical of Russian enterprises (see figure 2-4).

The company was not able to pay its suppliers, nor was it able to pay the government for taxes. Furthermore, naturally, Tutayev had problems making payments to workers as well. In 1996 it managed to pay only 61 percent of its wage bill. That included 36 percent that was paid in cash, with the rest paid in the form of foodstuffs, food coupons, and so forth. In January 1997 the situation was worse: only 34 percent of wages were paid at all.

TABLE 2-6. Sales by Product and Type of Payment for Tutayev Engine Plant, 1996

Percentage

Product	Sales	Paid by offsets	Paid in cash
Components for Yaroslavl Engine Plant	35	100	0
Spare parts for diesel engines	29	80	20
Diesel engines	7	70	30
Other products (heat, water, etc.)	29	100	0
Total	100	92	8

Source: Malov and Mayn (1997).

What is most interesting about Tutayev is the structure of payments for its products, that is, how much was paid in monetary form and how much in offsets (barter). Table 2-6 tells the story, showing that in 1996, 92 percent of total sales was paid for by offsets; for several categories of production, this figure was 100 percent. The plant relied on offsets to pay its taxes and to pay for inputs. Would Tutayev's director have preferred to sell more for cash? Given that only 8 percent of total sales was paid for in cash, one might suspect that the answer would be yes. In fact, however, the problem is more complex. The director explained that when he does sell for cash, to so-called commercial structures, "They pay only 50–60 percent of our official sales price." How should we interpret this? The answer is that the "official" price is a fictitious one from the point of view of market economics. The goods exchanged in offsets and barter sales are priced at twice the market price. Like most enterprises, Tutayev set its official price on a cost-plus-profit basis. Obviously Tutayev's costs were excessive compared with the price it actually received for output when sold in market conditions. Nonetheless, the enterprise continued to sell some output for cash. Tutayev's director observed: "This vicious practice in effect means that these various commercial structures are parasitizing our enterprise. *Nevertheless, it has been a vital necessity in current circumstances and has allowed the plant to obtain at least a minimum of cash.*" [Emphasis added.] This comment contains the key idea: an enterprise needs to obtain some cash to cover certain types of expenses, so it will sell some output even at a loss.

Illusion versus Reality

This chapter began with the images of apparent success of the Russian economic transformation in 1996 and 1997. It ends with a very different emphasis, that of rampant nonmonetary payments, enterprises that could not sell what they produced, and ingenious survival schemes. The fact is,

Tutayev and Berezovskiy Coal Mine No. 1 were more typical of Russia's reality in 1997, and more of its future, than the stock market. The apparent boom of 1997 was built on a facade. Much of industry was not restructuring. An illusion of growing prosperity was gaining acceptance, while enterprises found new ways to avoid the dictates of the market. These enterprises were able to survive thanks to their use of survival strategies such as nonmonetary payments and tax offsets.[66]

A multitude of causes contributed to the proliferation of nonmonetary payments in the period leading to August 1998. Without discounting the importance of the other causes, our analysis focuses on one particular aspect: the transfer of value to loss-making enterprises. This is where the role of the three fat boys and tax offsets is most crucial. This transfer of value is the essence of the virtual economy, and it enables enterprises to avoid restructuring.

The option of producing goods for barter and for tax offsets fundamentally changed the behavior of hundreds and thousands of "Tutayevs" in Russia during the transition process. This behavioral adaptation—something similar to a biological mutation—is what permitted enterprises to survive in the transition environment, where they ought to have gone extinct. The transition was supposed to be an example of a Darwinian process, whereby only those enterprises that could transform themselves into competitive operations would survive.[67] In the case of Russia, however, the dinosaurs have survived. They did so by adapting to the new environment, but not to the market.

66. Nonmonetary payments reached their peak just before the August 1998 crash. In the postcrisis period, nonmonetary payments have declined as a share of total sales, but they remain significant. Chapter 9 examines the causes of this decline—primarily ruble depreciation and high oil prices—and its implications for the virtual economy model.
67. We undertake an evolutionary analysis of the virtual economy in chapter 5.

CHAPTER THREE

Roots of the Virtual Economy

"We are stuck halfway between a planned, command economy and a normal, market one. And now we have an ugly model—a cross-breed of the two systems."
—Boris Yeltsin, State of the Union speech, 1999

At the heart of the virtual economy are enterprises, a legacy from the Soviet past, that struggle in a new economic environment. Unable or unwilling to restructure, these enterprises fight to survive in a system where competitive viability is supposed to be the determinant of success. Nonmonetary transactions, tax offsets, fictitious pricing—all of the characteristic elements of the virtual economy—are a response to this struggle to survive. This poses two fundamental questions for our analysis. First, why are there so many of these industrial dinosaurs that cannot be transformed? Second, how do they survive in a market system if they do not play by the market's rules? We will answer these questions in this chapter and the next.

Our first task is to understand the roots of this largely unreformed industrial sector. For the evolution of the virtual economy, this is the most important legacy that Russia's new economy inherited from the Soviet period. The Soviet Union bequeathed to Russia, to once again use Richard Ericson's formulation, a "structure of production—location, capital, employment, materials and energy use, etc. [that had been created] without any regard for economic opportunity costs, in an environment free of economic valuation." Russia thus ended up with a "structure of capital and economic activity that is fundamentally non-viable in an environment determined by market valuation, and hence requires massive transformation at its very roots."[1]

In the protected Soviet economy the market nonviability of individual enterprises and even entire sectors was largely hidden. Soviet statistics demonstrated that Russia produced a large share of value added in its industrial sector, and this picture survived western recalculations. It seemed consistent with a superpower. The inefficiency of this system was almost universally recognized, of course. That is why market reform was called for. What was missed was the distorted *image*. Like one of those mirrors at the circus that distorts the relative size of one's body parts, the image of the Soviet economy was distorted in terms of the relative contributions of various sectors in the economy. The importance of the industrial sector was magnified at the expense of the resource sector.

As the Soviet system was collapsing, and the inefficiency of the central planning system was almost universally accepted, the distorted image of the economy persisted. In the Soviet system the demand for military output was paramount, and protective tariffs, distorted pricing, and hidden taxes masked the noncompetitive nature of most nondefense production.[2] The distorted image concealed the transfer of value from the resource sectors to the manufacturing sector. It kept hidden the extent to which the manufacturing sector was destroying value. Liberalizing the economy and opening it up to trade removed the mask. It showed that many enterprises that previously produced value became destroyers of value when judged by the market metric.[3]

The Concept of Value Destruction

Russia's legacy of a large number of value-destroying enterprises and the fact that the continued existence of those enterprises requires redistribution of value from elsewhere means that the concept of value destruction itself lies at the heart of the virtual economy thesis. But because it is a notion that is fraught with confusion, it may be useful to comment briefly on it here. Appendix C contains further discussion on this important topic. Value destruction, or what economists term the production of negative value

1. Ericson (1999).
2. See Gaddy (1996), for a discussion of the overwhelming extent to which the Soviet economy was oriented to military production.
3. The problem, of course, was that the undistorted image that liberalization made possible was blamed, by many, on the policies of liberalization, rather than on the legacy of the Soviet system.

added, occurs when the market value of the inputs purchased for use in production exceeds the market value of the output itself.[4] Although it might seem to be a trivial point, value destruction does not mean that the products are without value. An enterprise may produce a useful product and still destroy value. Value destruction simply means that the product's market price is less than the price of the inputs that were purchased to make the product.

Notice that the concept of negative value added involves a comparison of a present configuration of production with an alternative use for the inputs. Negative value added implies that the alternative use of the inputs is more highly valued than the current use. Hence one could cease current production, sell the inputs, and then purchase a larger quantity of the original output. Perhaps the most fundamental point about value destruction is that the assessment of whether an enterprise produces value depends on what the market alternatives are. For example, an enterprise may produce value at domestic prices, but destroy value at world prices. The question then is whether world prices are an option or not. If the enterprise operates in a closed economy—that is, if the economy has no external economic relations, so there is no other way to procure the product aside from domestic production—then production at this enterprise may contribute to national income. Even if it is costly to produce the product, the price will cover this cost since there is no substitute available. Once the economy is open, however, continued production at that enterprise destroys value, because the inputs used there could more profitably be used elsewhere and the product imported from abroad. Many post-Soviet enterprises are in this position: the change in relative prices caused by external liberalization turned many enterprises that were value producing in the Soviet period into value destroyers.[5]

Soviet Pricing

To understand how Russia could end up with a significant part of its economy in such a predicament, it is useful to start by examining Soviet pricing. The central point, as emphasized by Ericson in the passage quoted above,

4. As we explain in appendix C, the strong version of negative value added means that the market value of output is less than the market value of the purchased inputs. A weaker form would compare the market value of output to the value of all inputs, including primary inputs such as labor and capital services. The latter is often referred to as loss making.

5. See also McKinnon (1993) for a discussion of negative value added at world prices.

is that resource allocation decisions in the Soviet Union were made without consideration of economic valuation, opportunity costs, or scarcity rents. This produced a price system that was not related to opportunity cost or to value. Prices were simply an accounting instrument to measure plan fulfillment.

Although Soviet prices were set arbitrarily, they were not set randomly. They were set according to specific rules of the system, and this produced some systematic biases. First of all, the planners underpriced raw material inputs, especially energy. They based raw materials prices only on the operating costs of extraction, while ignoring rent. In so doing, they disregarded the opportunity cost of using the resources now rather than in the future. The planners' overriding goal was to increase today's output. Scarcity pricing might have induced more conservation, but it would have militated against maximizing current production. This bias in raw materials prices fed into the system of industrial prices. Heavy consumers of energy were, in effect, subsidized. So, too, were heavy users of capital, thanks to the absence of interest charges. In short, costs of production were calculated on the basis of an incomplete enumeration of costs. This led to lower prices for inputs, especially resource inputs, than for final uses and thus an understatement of the share of gross output used in production and, hence, an overstatement of net output.

The Soviet system was not only characterized by incomplete cost-based pricing; it was also explicitly biased toward certain users. The Soviet leadership assigned priority in the economy to heavy industry, especially defense industry, and it was important that it appear that these sectors were producing value.[6] Accordingly, the price system was adjusted so that the same commodity might very well carry different prices if it were used by heavy industry or by light industry. Again, this initial pricing of inputs fed into the calculation of overall costs of production of these goods so that high-priority sectors would *appear* to have lower costs of production than low-priority sectors.[7]

6. An alternative, and from one point of view perhaps more correct, interpretation is to say that the end users of economic output in the Soviet regime—the Communist Party—placed such a high value on the output of the defense sector that value *was* being produced. The problem is that with the end of the Soviet regime and the Communist Party's rule, the value of that production has shrunk dramatically. We refer to this particular aspect of Russia's transition as the "Camellia Effect" in Gaddy and Ickes (2001b).

7. Ericson (1988) was the first to formalize the dual nature of the Soviet economy in terms of priority (military) and nonpriority sectors. His 1999 study shows how the input-output tables of the Soviet economy—which provided a seemingly consistent picture of the underlying structure—could appear to describe an economy where sectors are able

This nonscarcity-based pricing behavior had critical results for the perceived structure of the economy. First, as pointed out above, the economy appeared to be bigger than it really was. Second, since waste and distortions could be consistently hidden from view, the economy overall appeared to be more productive than it actually was. Third, since the arbitrary pricing resulted in artificial returns to specific activities, it distorted the picture of relative productivities and relative sizes of various sectors. From the standpoint of the Soviet leaders, the returns to specific assets were irrelevant, since they (or "the State") owned all property anyway. With the onset of transition, the true picture of the economy began to emerge. The overall size of the economy shrank (gross domestic product appeared to decline), and overall productivity dropped. Price liberalization revealed the extent to which value added in the Soviet economy was really created in the energy and raw materials sector.[8] For many people, however, it had the effect of making reform appear to be the destroyer of the manufacturing sector.

Market Distance—"d"

The Soviet economy was highly protected from the world market. Liberalization and opening to the world economy made clear the relative backwardness of most enterprises. We can think of this in terms of inefficiency, and certainly Soviet enterprises were inefficient, but emphasizing efficiency misses an important point.[9] Efficiency measures how well an enterprise uses its inputs:[10] it is a measure of the output that is obtained

---

to cover average cost when in fact they do not. The fundamental factor, of course, is pricing that is not based on scarcity. Since prices were based on costs and costs were measured arbitrarily, there was a "circularity in definition" that could not be eliminated within the structure of the Soviet system.

8. An interesting exercise to illustrate this point is to look at the sectoral distribution of Russian economic output during the Soviet period as measured in official Soviet prices and then compare that with what it would have looked like in world prices. The true contribution from electrical energy, fuels, and forestry and timber products becomes apparent. In Soviet prices, these sectors contributed 17.1 percent of total output in 1991. At world prices, they accounted for 51.6 percent of total output! See OECD (1995, chapter 1).

9. Peter Murrell (1991) suggested that too much emphasis on *static* efficiency in postsocialist economies deflected attention from *dynamic* efficiency, which refers to innovation and technical change. Our point is different.

10. Notice that if an enterprise is value destroying, eliminating all inefficiency will not rectify this problem. Improvements in efficiency involve movements from inside the production frontier to the boundary of the frontier. However, the gain implied by this may not be sufficient to overcome the fact that the enterprise produces the wrong thing in the wrong place.

from inputs.[11] But for suddenly emergent Russian enterprises the key notion is *competitiveness*. What is crucial is how well an enterprise can survive in this new, open, environment.[12]

One way to view the impact of liberalization on the Soviet economy is to invoke a spatial metaphor: liberalization revealed the distance that Russia would have to travel to compete in the world economy. Let d designate an enterprise's "distance to the market" at the start of transition. Our interest is in exploring the determinants of d across enterprises and economies. Clearly, d depends on the enterprise's initial endowments of the things that matter for market viability: physical and human capital, as well as the enterprise's marketing structure and organizational behavior, but also the characteristics of the good that the enterprise produces (its quality and cost of production). Our earlier discussion in this chapter clarifies another point: market distance also depends on market conditions. In a closed economy an enterprise may be perfectly viable and thus have zero distance. Yet, when faced with competition from the rest of the world, the same enterprise will find itself far from the point of market viability.

Formally, we will define an enterprise's d as *the amount of capital expenditure needed to enable the enterprise to produce a product that is competitive in the market*. Why do we define d in terms of investment? One might object that this exaggerates capital's role in competitiveness. For instance, might not Russian enterprises become competitive simply by reducing excess employment or by cutting costs in other ways? Moreover, why the emphasis on investment in new capital, given that Russian enterprises inherited what would seem to be more than enough capital from the Soviet period, when investment as a share of GDP approached 40 percent?

11. Economists distinguish between technical efficiency—which refers to obtaining more output from given inputs—and allocative efficiency—which refers to achieving optimal outcomes given available resources and compares how resources are allocated across activities. Hence, an enterprise can be technically efficient—that is, it produces according to the best recipes available for those particular inputs—but allocatively inefficient because the inputs could produce more valuable output if they were used to make a different product.

12. Former Soviet enterprises are often termed dinosaurs. This is an interesting terminology. Dinosaurs were not inefficient relative to their original environment. The problem was that the environment changed and then they became extinct. In the Russian context the fact that enterprises were inefficiently organized deflected attention from the fact that the environment changed in dramatic fashion. Efficiency gains are not sufficient to prevent extinction. A 10 percent increase in the caloric efficiency of dinosaurs would almost surely have been insufficient to improve their odds of surviving the end of the Cretaceous period. The same could be said for Soviet enterprises. Efficiency gains are not sufficient to overcome a mass extinction process.

One reason why we measure distance in terms of capital expenditure is to make clear the opportunity cost of reducing it. Even if the particular measure to reduce d at a specific enterprise requires reducing the work force, this still is costly;[13] otherwise, the enterprise would have already taken these actions. There is always some cost to reducing distance. But a second and more fundamental reason for measuring d in terms of the investment cost is one that illuminates an important subtlety of transition, namely that transition causes a divergence between the value of existing (inherited) capital and that of newly installed capital.

One may begin to grasp this point by recalling what happened to traditional models of investment in market economies during the energy crisis of the 1970s.[14] Those models predicted that investment would decline, given the tremendous increase in the price of energy. In fact, however, spending on new equipment and buildings soared. The reason for this discrepancy between model and reality was the divergence between the value of installed capital that was energy intensive and new capital that was energy saving. The conventional model ignored the sharp decline in the economic value of the existing capital stock as a result of the 1973 energy crisis. Installed capital was the result of investment decisions based on low energy prices; hence, its value fell dramatically once energy prices quadrupled. This in turn only increased the demand for new investment in energy-saving equipment. The result was a divergence between the value of installed capital (which lost value) and that of new capital (which had full economic value).

In today's transition economies, this problem is multiplied many times over. Not only energy prices, but the prices of virtually every input and output, change. Hence in the transition case, the contrast between the value of inherited capital and newly installed capital is all that much greater than in the post-1973 market economies. Even this description fails to capture the magnitude of the problem. It is not just that prices have changed dramatically. Instead, it is that the inherited structure of production was one where enterprises produced the wrong goods in the wrong way, with the wrong structures of capital and labor. This is precisely the point of the

13. Russian enterprises, for example, had to make severance payments when they laid off workers in the early parts of transition.

14. Models of investment based on Tobin's q theory worked quite well before the energy crisis, but they performed very poorly after energy prices rose. The reason is that Tobin's q is the ratio of the market value of the aggregate capital stock (equity) to its replacement cost. When energy prices rose, existing capital fell in value. Tobin's q would be less than unity and thus predict a decline in investment, but in fact investment increased because firms needed to replace existing equipment with energy-saving equipment. See Abel (1990, p. 706).

remark (quoted earlier in this chapter) by Richard Ericson that the Soviet economic system created a structure of production that was devoid of the concept of economic opportunity cost. Transition toward a market economy introduces opportunity cost to an inherited structure of production where this was not previously applicable. The extent to which the old allocation of resources diverged from one based on the new notion of cost is what determines the gap between the value of inherited capital and newly installed capital.[15] In sum, measuring market distance d by the need for new capital investment is a way of capturing the cost of filling the gap.

Distribution of d

If we were to compare enterprises in the economy by their level of d, what would we observe? Obviously we would see a great deal of variation. An enterprise that already produces a product it can sell in world markets at a price above cost will have a value of d equal to 0. A completely noncompetitive enterprise will have an enormously large d. Everyone else will be somewhere between. For example, an oil-producing enterprise will have a very low d. Its product is already right for the market. It may need only relatively small investments in marketing, and so on. A Soviet-style machine tool producer, at the same time, is likely to have a longer distance to travel. Of course, the distance that an enterprise must travel depends on the good that it produces. A TV-producing enterprise may have high d when it comes to its completely noncompetitive television sets, but if it converts its production to a different and much simpler product, it may have much lower d. In chapter 7, we examine such a case, that of a manufacturing enterprise that switches to a more primitive product (in this case, vegetables!).[16]

Transition starts with some initial distribution of d across the enterprises in the economy.[17] The greater the d_i, the less viable the enterprise. Market

15. This answers the question of why simply reducing the size of the labor force will not reduce d. That is not a measure that affects the gap between the lost value of installed capital and the demand for new capital. Reducing the labor force to meet cash flow constraints is a natural reaction of enterprises whenever budget constraints are hardened. But it is at best a defensive action, designed toward survival, not restructuring.

16. Notice that for the TV producer to become a vegetable producer, it had to write down the value of its capital stock, since much of the capital stock of the enterprise was useless in the production of vegetables.

17. Let μ_i be enterprise i's share of GDP (or employment). Then $\Omega \equiv \int_i (d_i \mu_i) di$ is a measure of the average distance of the economy. It thus represents the initial level of the gap that must be overcome in transition. An important point about Russian initial conditions is that Ω was larger than in other transition economies.

distance depends not only on current conditions but also on the ease or difficulty of changing them. An enterprise may currently be a loss maker, or even a value destroyer, but its d could still be low if the changes required to become viable were not particularly great. The question for the enterprise is the *cost* of shifting from value destruction to value-adding activity. How much investment will it take to make the shift, and what is the opportunity cost of that investment? Market distance captures the amount of effort that will be required to produce a commodity that can be sold profitably. It is thus a function of history and of the costs of restructuring (and of the external market environment).

If we were to compare the distributions of d in transition economies with those in market economies, we would make two important observations. First, the range of ds is greater in transition economies than in market economies. Second, the distribution of d is more skewed in the transition economy. These two observations follow from differences in the process of entry and exit in market and planned economies, since transition economies inherit the enterprises of the latter system. The enterprises in transition economies were created in a closed economy and without regard to opportunity cost. Once the economy is liberalized, both internally and externally, it is then not surprising that some enterprises have very high levels of d. This is a legacy inherited from the Soviet period. In a market economy, whether a new firm attempts to enter an industry depends on the founders' expectations about the new firm's competitiveness. They will enter if they expect the firm's potential costs to be lower (its productivity to be higher) than those of existing firms. No firm enters an industry in which it *expects* it will be noncompetitive. Of course, mistakes are made. Because of uncertainty, some firms enter with the expectation that they will be low-cost producers, only to learn that they are in fact high-cost producers. However, if the expected costs are sufficiently high before the decision to start the business is made, then entry will not occur. Over time the competitiveness of some firms declines, so d increases. However, if a firm in a market economy has too high a level of d, it will be forced to close. Competition and hard budget constraints cause high-d enterprises to shut down. Hence, the range of ds observed is much smaller in market economies.

The distribution of d across enterprises is more skewed in transition economies for similar reasons. In a developed market economy the distribution of d is always centered near zero. Most firms will have very low d because they enter only if they expect low d. If they do not have that expectation, they do not enter. If, after entering, they learn that d is not low, they will close up shop or exit from the market. In sum, at any given time in such a mature market economy, everyone's distance, d, to the market is low. In statistical terms, the distribution of d is right-truncated[18] for two reasons: firms with high ex ante costs do not enter, and firms with high ex post costs exit.[19]

In an economy emerging from socialism, the initial distribution is quite different. Enterprises have ds that would not be observed in a market economy. As mentioned in chapter 2, there are many reasons why this is so. Most fundamentally, in socialist economies entry was determined not by expectations of profitability or competitiveness, but rather by the need to fulfill plan targets. Second, insulation from the world economy meant that enterprises were created that produced goods for which the country might not have had a comparative advantage. Third, especially in the case of Russia, the priority given to defense production led to a proliferation of enterprises that produced goods whose market collapsed with the end of the Soviet Union. Fourth, since the geographic location of industry in the Soviet period was based on ignoring transportation costs (as well as the costs associated with extraordinarily cold temperatures), the location of enterprises in Russia is also a factor in increasing the d for many enterprises. For all of these reasons, the distribution of d in Russia at the onset of the transition had a much higher mean and was more skewed to the right than in a mature market economy. This extra mass of high-d enterprises is the burden of the Soviet legacy. This burden is the essence of the restructuring problem: so many enterprises must all radically reduce their distance to the market at the same time.[20]

Another way to think about the distribution of d at the onset of transition is as a representation of the *past mistakes* that must be overcome by economic reform. The greater is the average distance in the economy, the more onerous is the legacy. All postsocialist economies entered transition with a distribution of d that was skewed compared with that of a market

---

18. Of course, in all economies d is bounded below by zero.

19. See Ickes and Ryterman (1997) for an analysis of the implications of the absence of exit with regard to industrial dynamics in planned economies.

20. A full empirical picture of the initial distribution of Russian enterprises' d remains to be elaborated. The general picture is suggested in the work of Joseph Blasi. He divided Russian enterprises into four groups. Using our terminology, one could say that only one of Blasi's groups had low d; the rest had progressively higher amounts of d, up to the point of total nonviability. From the survey work conducted by his research team, Blasi concluded that "no more than a quarter of Russian enterprises" were in what we would term the low-d group, and that the remaining three quarters were in desperate need of restructuring. Blasi, Kroumova, and Kruse (1997, pp. 176–78).

economy. However, for reasons we have outlined, this degree of skewness is greater in Russia than elsewhere in the postsocialist world.[21]

One characterization of economic reform is to reduce the average distance in the economy. This occurs through three means: (1) exit of high-d enterprises; (2) entry of new (low-d) enterprises; (3) and reduction of the d of surviving enterprises. The essence of economic reform is to create institutions that support these three processes. For example, the imposition of hard-budget constraints may force the first process and induce the third one. If there are hard-budget constraints, the only firms that will enter a market are those that expect to be competitive.

Relational Capital

Market distance is an effective way of capturing an important condition of the enterprise. In an ideal market world, this would be the only condition that characterized the state of an enterprise. If the only important difference in enterprises were their initial level of d, then policies that put pressure on high-d enterprises would have the effect of pushing the distribution in the direction of the market. The problem of economic reform would be straightforward: put pressure on high-d enterprises, even if implementation remained a problem. This might, in fact, be characterized as the conventional wisdom concerning economic reform. While not without value, this view fails to explain the persistence of unrestructured, noncompetitive enterprises such as the Tutayevs and the Berezovskiy Coal Mines.

To explain the persistent survival of high-d enterprises we must consider a second dimension on which enterprises differ: that is the level of what we call *relational* capital. The conventional view of restructuring, that reform means reducing d, assumes that the enterprise has one set of resources—its physical and human capital—that it must use ever more efficiently in order to survive. Suppose, however, that the enterprise has another resource, *rela-*

---

21. The difference in one important economic legacy—degree of militarization—between Russia and a relatively successful postsocialist economy such as Hungary is telling. In the Soviet era, Hungary had no more than twenty defense enterprises, the largest of which had about six thousand employees. See Kiss (1999, pp. 31–33). Soviet Russia had nearly two thousand defense enterprises; over one hundred of those had more than ten thousand employees each. See Gaddy (1996, pp. 24–26). Relative to the population, the Russian economy was at least ten times more militarized than Hungary's. Of all the fully industrialized postsocialist economies, only Ukraine and Belarus come even close to having an endowment as unfavorable as Russia's. Russia, however, suffers from having enterprises located north of the Arctic Circle and in other inhospitable climes that distinguish it from all other cases.

tional capital, which it can draw on to enhance its chances for survival. An enterprise that has high relational capital can undertake transactions (bartering, using tax offsets, delaying payment) that other enterprises cannot get away with. Relational capital is support for informal activity that can aid the operation of an enterprise.

Let us designate relational capital as "r." At the onset of transition, enterprises differed in their inherited r, just as they differed in their d. Some enterprises (or their directors) had very good relations with local and/or federal officials. Relations with other enterprises also varied. What kind of relations, with whom, how solid they were, and so on, can be thought of as the enterprise's "stock" of relational capital. It is this stock that determines the types of transactions that can be supported (barter instead of cash payment, prepayment or not). To put it another way, relational capital is good will that can be translated into the ability to continue to engage in production and exchange without reducing the distance to the market. Relations, in other words, aid in production. The service flow from relational capital is an input to the production process; it increases the marginal product of other inputs. This is one important distinction between investment in relational capital and rent seeking.

While we may, in general, think of relational capital as support for informal activity, in the Russian case it takes on a particular aspect that we emphasize: high-r enterprises can escape the strictures of the budget constraint. Such enterprises can delay payments or barter at inflated prices when other enterprises, with low amounts of relational capital, cannot. Relations thus serve as a substitute for financial responsibility. There are many economies where relational capital is developed but enterprises are nonetheless financially responsible. In Russia, the use of relational capital to evade responsibility is an important element.[22]

Like any asset, relational capital yields a return to its possessor. In the case of r the benefit is the ability to undertake informal transactions. Relational capital enables transactions to occur where contract enforcement is difficult to obtain. In this sense, r bears resemblance to trust, or social cap-

---

22. Since the rest of the discussion will strongly emphasize the negative aspects of relational capital, it is important to recognize that relational capital can also be a positive asset for society. It supports informal contracting and other arrangements without which certain beneficial economic activities would not take place. In our discussion we emphasize how relational capital can be used to evade responsibility and the budget constraint. This process is crucial to our story, but it should not obscure the role of relational capital in a well-functioning economy.

ital.[23] Social capital, however, is usually thought of as a feature of the aggregate environment, or at least a feature of a network of agents.[24] Relational capital, in contrast, is a consequence of past investments at that enterprise, and the level of relational capital can vary across enterprises within the same economy or even the same community.[25]

Origins of Relational Capital

The relational capital of Russian enterprises was initially accumulated in the Soviet system and was embodied above all in the large industrial enterprises and their directors. Enterprise directors relied heavily on the accumulation and use of personal connections or "pull," known colloquially as *blat*.[26] *Blat* was critical to performance, especially fulfillment of the economic plan, in the highly distorted regime of central planning, where supply failures were a chronic aspect of economic life. Relations with local party officials were often crucial to obtaining scarce inputs. As Gregory Grossman has emphasized, informal economic activities were an essential feature of the Soviet economy. Ed Hewett described how this worked when he spoke of the Soviet enterprise director as a "master of triage." Because of inconsistent demands from the center, "enterprise management is forced to choose which parts of the plan to fulfill and which to violate. . . . Informal communication with all levels of the party and government bureaucracy is essential." The result, concluded Hewett, was a "world of special deals."

> The central planners, faced with the de facto inconsistency of their assigned objectives and the efforts of managers to serve many motives, begin to make special deals with each enterprise, through the ministries. The resulting relationship between the state and enterprises is

23. The importance of trust in economic development was emphasized in Fukuyama (1995). The notion of social capital was introduced by Coleman (1988), and Putnam (1993). Guiso, Sapienza, and Zingales (2000) provide an interesting empirical examination of the role of social capital. In their analysis trust allows financial development because it facilitates transactions that take place over time.

24. Fukuyama, for example, defines social capital as "an instantiated informal norm that promotes cooperation between two or more individuals." See Fukuyama (2000).

25. This perhaps reflects the fact that most analyses of trust use differences in this across countries to explain differential performance, whereas we are interested in explaining differential performance within an economy. Moreover, our concern is not only with the consequences of varying levels of r, but, more important, with decisions to invest in r.

26. Ledeneva (1998) provides the most comprehensive study of *blat* both in the Soviet period and in post-Soviet Russia. Fitzpatrick (1999) summarizes the importance of *blat* in the Stalinist era (pp. 62–65) and cites other important works on the topic.

far more complex and individualized than the regulations would suggest, as both sides are forced by circumstances to reach a tacit agreement that they will ignore regulations and norms in the service of higher goals. The enterprise must therefore pay constant attention to bureaucratic politics; the assiduous enterprise manager is rewarded with considerable benefits that may not even be achievable under the regulations. . . . *The successful "entrepreneur" in this system is not a person who develops new products and technologies, but one who successfully develops a workable relationship with the government and party authorities supervising his enterprises* [emphasis added].[27]

Privatization of Relational Capital

Relational capital was a vital asset in the Soviet system. The critical question for our purposes is how relational capital was passed forward to the post-Soviet system. The simple answer is that it was *spontaneously* privatized. This is an important aspect of economic transition in Russia. As Hewett described, plan fulfillment in the Soviet economy required enterprise directors to use informal skills. Their ability to accomplish this, and their position in the economic hierarchy, was critical to their incomes. While directors earned income from these positions, they did not legally own the source of these incomes. The demise of the planning system, which had already begun with Mikhail Gorbachev's reforms in the late *perestroika* period, had the effect of increasing the autonomy of enterprise directors. With the start of economic reform and privatization, the role of the enterprise director increased; other mediating actors (planners, party officials) played less and less of a formal role in economic allocation. Directors used this opportunity to appropriate the returns to the relationships they had developed and cultivated under the previous system. However, in order for directors to appropriate these returns, the enterprises had to continue to operate.[28] Much of the relational capital was both enterprise specific and person specific. To the extent that it was enterprise specific, the director could not cash out the relational capital. The primary form of these connections was relationships with directors of other enterprises, often in related lines of activity, and with ministerial officials and local government

27. Hewett (1988, pp. 198–99).
28. Survival is thus a key motive for enterprises in the early stages of transition. It is the only way for directors to preserve the assets they have accumulated in the enterprise. See Ickes and Ryterman (1994) for a discussion of the survival-oriented enterprise.

officials. The relational capital was worthless to the incumbent director unless he remained in that particular enterprise. He could not leave the enterprise and take the relational capital with him. Furthermore, because it was person specific, he could not sell it to someone else. Instead, in order to appropriate the rents accruing to his relational capital, he had to remain in the enterprise and keep it operating. The privatization of relational capital is thus an important part of the explanation of why directors fought to keep open enterprises that had few prospects in the market economy.

The privatization of relational capital in Russia thus predates that of physical capital. Although some enterprises were spontaneously privatized before the demise of the Soviet Union, the bulk of industry was not privatized until mid-1994, as part of the formal privatization process. Relational capital, however, could be privatized without a formal process. Hence, its privatization began as the authority of the Communist Party receded. Precisely because the Communist Party was the primary mediating authority with regard to relational capital, once its authority began to wane, enterprise directors could expropriate this asset for themselves. Because relational capital was an informal institution, it survived changes in the formal economic system.

One could argue, in fact, that during the interregnum between the demise of planning and the formal privatization program, relational capital was pivotal to the operation of the economic system. Its use allowed supplies to be delivered and goods to be shipped in the chaotic environment. Had not relational capital supported those transactions, the situation would surely have been even more out of control. The problem, however, is that the privatization of relational capital distorted the formal privatization process.

Relational Capital and Reform

In the Soviet system as it actually operated, informal relations were central because they increased the flexibility of the system. Nevertheless, a system of mediation was needed to impose some notion of social efficiency when prices could not provide that information. Officials—especially the local Communist Party leaders known as obkom and raikom officials—played the key mediating role. Of course even during Soviet rule these officials and enterprise directors were interested in personal well-being. However, their ability to exploit their position was limited by the Communist Party, directly in terms of monitoring and enforcement and, more important, indirectly through desire for advancement within the hierarchy. Career interests motivated officials and enterprise directors to fulfill the goals of the Party. This acted as a constraint on their ability to exploit relational capital.

Transition reduced the role of most officials in the economy, but the elimination of Communist Party authority meant that the restraints on behavior were reduced to an even greater extent. While officials still had loyalties to others in the bureaucracy, their actions were no longer constrained by the need to satisfy Party goals. Their own interests became paramount. Thus, while reform removed the formal rules of the old system (which had already eroded under Gorbachev), it left much of the informal system intact, but without its mediating links.

The paradox, then, is that under the Soviet system Communist Party officials had mediated and limited the use of relational capital. In transition the role of relational capital was enhanced by the formal changes in the system. The elimination of mediation made it easier (more economical) to invest in relational capital. The director had more power than before; there were now fewer people to please. The director could now directly appropriate the returns to investment in relational capital. Had relational capital not existed before privatization, the Russian-style privatization program would have had different effects. The initial conditions facing enterprises would have been such that the only survival strategy would have been to invest in reducing d. Privatization of relational capital altered the outcome.

r-d Space

Let us now use the concept of relational capital to revise our spatial representation of the Russian transition economy. There are now two state variables that describe the nature of an enterprise. Enterprises can be arrayed in terms of their level of relational capital as well as the dimension of market distance. The initial conditions of an enterprise can thus be described by a two-dimensional space, r-d space, in which each enterprise has its own location. Figure 3-1 shows the distribution of enterprises in terms of these initial conditions.

Enterprises with varying amounts of r and d will fall into different parts of r-d space. An enterprise for which both d and r are small, for example, would be like enterprise B, close to the southwest corner. This is a company that is already market viable, or close to being so, but does not have particularly good relationships. A small food-producing company might serve as an example; it is relatively competitive and market viable, but it must pay its bills and is worried about treatment by government officials. Conversely,

FIGURE 3-1. Enterprises in *r-d* Space

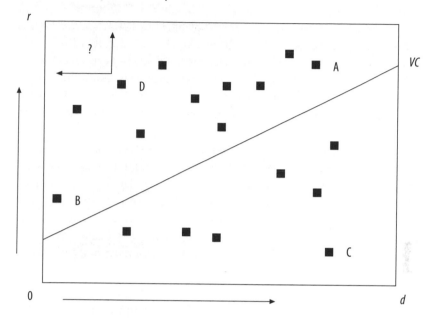

imagine an enterprise (A) whose market prospects are very poor (high *d*), but which has good relations. Russia's many giant defense enterprises typically fall into this category. Significant investment—perhaps prohibitive amounts—would be required to make these enterprises viable; yet good relations with officials may allow them to survive. A third class of enterprises lies to the southeast (enterprise C). Not only do they have poor market prospects (high *d*), but they also suffer from poor relations (low *r*). Finally, there are the enterprises in the northwest quadrant (D). They are the ones with relatively low *d* and high *r*. They can have good prospects for survival by virtue of either market viability or relational capital (and, of course, especially good chances if they can combine the advantages of both).

Viability Constraint

When enterprises are viewed solely in terms of market distance, it follows that the only means of survival is to reduce *d*. This produces a *unidimensional* view of reform in which progress can be viewed as moving enterprises toward lower levels of *d*. Adding relational capital, however, points to a trade-off that enterprises face as they try to survive. An enterprise can compensate for poor market prospects by exploiting its relational capital. Still, there may be some enterprises (like C in figure 3-1) with such poor initial combinations of both r and d that they are simply not viable. That is, not only are they situated far from the market, but the quality of their relations with officials and with other enterprises is so poor that their stock of r will not ensure their survival. This suggests that there will be some boundary within r-d space that separates enterprises that are viable—whether by competitiveness or relations—from those that are not. What will this viability boundary look like?

It is reasonable to assume that the minimum level of relationships needed to survive increases as the enterprise's market potential decreases: greater r is needed to overcome the disadvantage of large d. Thus we can imagine that the line that separates the region of viable enterprises from those that are not will have a positive slope. Such a "viability constraint" line is labeled VC on figure 3-1.

The shape and slope of the VC line, as well as its position, will depend on the institutional setting.[29] The general location of VC is influenced by the degree of openness of the economy. Enterprises that would be nonviable for a given d in an open economy may be viable if the economy is autarkic. Transparency and corporate governance are also important for the VC line. In a fully transparent economy, relations may compensate very little for distance. If officials are more corrupt, then relations become that much more important. It is also interesting to consider the minimum r necessary to maintain viability as d approaches 0. In a "pure" market economy (for instance, an Arrow-Debreu economy), relations are completely unimportant because all transactions are anonymous. Consequently, the viability boundary would be coincident with the d-axis—a ray straight up from the origin. In real world economies, however, relations may play a role even if the firm's d equals 0. Were relations not important in the U.S. economy, for instance, corporations would not likely spend millions of dollars on government relations offices in Washington, D.C., or in various state capitals. At a minimum, cultivation of the image of the "good corporate citizen" is motivated not purely by altruism. Furthermore, to the extent that relations are important, the viability boundary will not go through the origin, but rather intersect the r-axis at some point higher than 0. Indeed, one could think of certain characteristics of the VC

29. In figure 3-1 we have assumed the VC line to be linear, but this is just for simplicity. A plausible argument suggests that the slope of the VC line increases with levels of d. That is, at higher levels of d, proportionally greater r is needed to ensure viability.

line—its slope and its intercept—as a measure of the transparency and absence of corruption of an economy.[30]

Alternative View of Transition

Visualizing economies in terms of r-d space provides an alternative to the conventional approach in thinking about transition and reform. As we emphasized above, the conventional view of enterprises in transition was unidimensional: it included only the d-dimension. Accordingly, success in enterprise management was thought of in one dimension only: movement to the left on the d-axis in figure 3-1. Progress for the entire economy was viewed as a shift to the left of the entire distribution of enterprises (the average d gets smaller). In the r-d space view, however, success for an individual enterprise in the Russian economy can come from viability in either of *two* dimensions, not only the d (market) dimension, but also the r-dimension, the realm of relationships and nonmonetary transactions. Hence, a viable, even relatively flourishing enterprise is not necessarily one that has adapted to the market. It may have adapted to the informal regime of tax offsets and barter through the strategic use of relational capital.

Similarly, the real economic activity of these enterprises—their production of physical goods—must be viewed more critically. Increased output by enterprises that are surviving by exploiting r is not a sign of overall health in the economy, but quite the opposite. These enterprises are producing unprofitably, perhaps even destroying value. Hence, increases in recorded aggregate output for the economy may be due not only to increased output by successfully restructured enterprises, but also to increased production of noncompetitive goods by enterprises in the r-regime. This means that resumptions in GDP growth may not be the best indicators of restructuring.[31] Table 3-1 sums up the differences between the conventional and the r-d space views of economic reform.

Whether one views the enterprise sector in a single (d) dimension or in the two dimensions of r-d space is critical for how reform policy is under-

30. In this interpretation, the position of the VC line's intercept at $d = 0$ would be a corruption index, with different societies accepting different cutoff points as perfectly acceptable. In the case where VC is nonlinear, the level of d at the asymptote answers the question, "How inefficient can you be and still survive thanks to connections?" In the linear case the answer is given by the level of d where $r = r_{max}$ (that is, the level of d at the maximum level of relational capital).

31. This is not true, however, for properly measured GDP, which measures value added, not production.

TABLE 3-1. Comparing the Conventional View and the *r-d* Space View

Category	Conventional view	*r-d* space view
Distribution of enterprises	In only one dimension— market performance	In two dimensions: a market distance dimension and a relational capital dimension
Dynamics of enterprise development	All enterprises are moving in the same direction; only the speed of movement differs	Not all enterprises move in the same direction; there are (at least) two poles of attraction
"Success" for the individual enterprise	To move to the left of the "viability" line	To be viable in either dimension. A viable, even flourishing enterprise does not have to be one that has adapted to the market ("restructured"); it may have adapted to the informal regime of paternalism, tax offsets, etc., by means of relational capital
Progress in true restructuring of the economy	Shifting the distribution to the left (toward the "market")	Moving SW, lowering average r; reducing d is not enough if r is not also reduced
The meaning of GDP growth	Assumed to be unambiguously good	May be due in part to increased production of noncompetitive goods by enterprises in the r regime
	Monotonically increasing with a shift of the enterprise distribution to the left ("success in restructuring")	Therefore, not necessarily reflective of successful restructuring

stood. The conventional, unidimensional, view assumes that economic reform measures will have the greatest impact on those enterprises that have the highest level of d.[32] According to this assumption, for example, if budget constraints are tightened, enterprises that are farthest from the market will be under greatest competitive pressure. Similarly, it is assumed that if the economy is opened to international competition, the greatest impact will be on those enterprises that are most in need of restructuring. In the two-dimensional r-d space environment, the effects of market-type reforms need not have this property at all. Tightening the budget constraint will not necessarily put the most pressure on the enterprise that is most inefficient (has the highest d). If the enterprise has been endowed with high r, it may be insulated against the impact of this policy; it can use relations to evade the budget constraint. If tight budget constraints are enforced against enterprises that are lower in r, then the policy may, in fact, have greater impact on low-d enterprises than high-d enterprises.

32. We refer to this assumed property of economic reform as *monotonicity* (see chapter 5, pp. 106–08).

It is not just the initial levels of r that matter, of course. If the enterprise has *invested* in r, it will improve its resistance to policies of tight budget constraints. Investing in r is like taking a vaccine. It immunizes the enterprise against certain interventions that it may otherwise be vulnerable to. An enterprise that initially recognized the high costs of reducing d may have chosen to invest in r to achieve such immunity. Hence, the r-d space view leads us to consider not just where enterprises found themselves as transition began, but where they sought to go as it proceeded. The relevant issue for the enterprise is the relative returns to investing in reducing distance and in enhancing relational capital. The analysis of enterprise decisions to reduce distance and invest in relations is the key to understanding the process of restructuring and, through that, the further evolution of the virtual economy.

"Igor's Rules"

To analyze properly the enterprise director's decisionmaking process, we must ask, What is his goal? What is he trying to maximize? We conclude this chapter, and introduce the subject of the next chapter, by looking at a paradigmatic description of how the director does behave. From that we will attempt to deduce appropriate objectives that would motivate such behavior. Box 3-1 contains an excerpt from a conversation with a director who offers advice on successful management planning in post-Soviet Russia. Our analysis of what we call *Igor's Rules* is given below.

Rule 1: "Sell something to the federal government so you can offset your federal taxes."

The point of this rule is to use the federal government's debt to the enterprise that results from these sales as a way to offset the enterprise's federal tax bill. The smart enterprise manager does not even expect to be paid for his government contracts; he counts on the offset possibility. That means, however, that it makes little sense to deliver too much to the government. Enterprises following this rule are the explanation for the federal government's collecting only about 60–65 percent of its taxes in cash in 1996 and 1997 (recall chapter 2). The rest of the taxes were offsets.

Rule 2: "Be able to provide some services to the local government so you can offset your local taxes."

Igor's reasoning here is similar to rule 1, but applied to regional and local government levels. In fact, rule 2 is even more important than rule 1. Local governments are in general more inclined than the federal government to accept noncash tax payments. Moreover, since Russia's central govern-

BOX 3-1. "Igor" in His Own Words

"Igor" is the director of a large (approximately 10,000 employees) enterprise in the Urals. In a conversation with the authors about his own tax situation, he described in detail his use of barter deals and tax offsets. He summarized his strategy as follows.

"I have concluded that there are four things minimally you need to do to survive as an enterprise director in this environment.

"First of all, you need to have some percentage of your sales to the federal government. Ideally, you should get it right at about what you think you'll end up being assessed in federal taxes. You know you probably won't be paid for these federal government contracts, but you use them to offset your federal taxes.

"Second, you must have the capability to provide municipal services so as to be able to offset local taxes. The local government does not order the kind of products we produce, so we can only rarely use goods offsets. So we pay with services. We'll suggest repairing a school, for instance. The city government agrees. We have our large construction division, which works well for this. We do the work and then send over the receipts showing how much the paint cost, the lumber, etc. We don't really charge them for the labor.

"Third, you have to set up some barter operations for getting the rest of your inputs where possible, especially fuels, electricity, and so on. We are fortunate enough to have some products that are valuable for these utilities—they need high-tech communications systems—so they take our products and pay us in *veksels* that we can then redeem for oil, gas, electrical power, and so on, when we need them.

"Finally, you have to have some cash for your operations—mainly for urgently needed inputs for which you must pay in cash, in advance. What you really need is not necessarily dollars; just cash of any kind. Theoretically, there are paying customers inside Russia, who pay in rubles, but it's most reliable if you export. So I export steel. About 30 percent of what we make. [Although Igor is a producer of high-tech satellite and missile telemetry systems, he also had his own small steel mill.]

"I like to call these my 'four rules for successful management planning.' Oh, yes, there is a final rule: Whatever you do, don't make a profit! The governments take it all in taxes."

ment remains constantly behind in its transfers to the regions, the federal government itself can give the green light for an enterprise to deliver goods or services to the local government and be credited for payment of federal tax obligations.

Rule 3: "Produce some goods for barter with the gas and electricity companies."

Here, Igor is referring to the "Three Fat Boys"—Gazprom, UES, and the Railways Ministry.

Rule 4: "Export something to a hard currency market to get cash for essential needs."

Although one might infer from rules 1–3 that Igor is suggesting that enterprises can survive entirely without cash, this rule acknowledges that every enterprise needs some cash for its operations. Wage payments to workers are an obvious example. Another (not mentioned by Igor) is cash for bribes to government officials.[33]

Igor's Final Injunction: "Never make a profit!"

Of course what Igor really means is do not make a profit that can be observed.

What sort of enterprise can best follow Igor's Rules? The ideal would be a large, diversified, integrated, paternalistic enterprise with good relations with both federal and local authorities. Igor's own enterprise is precisely such an enterprise. As a high-tech defense plant, it not only enjoyed special political and social status, but also had integrated facilities that provided for flexibility in production. Its size alone ensured that it had a large stock of so-called social assets (day care centers, sports facilities, vacation housing, and so on), along with the infrastructure to support them—a construction division, heating plant, road crews, and so on. Following the prescribed formulas for market economic transition, the municipal government required Igor to divest himself of these assets. This provided Igor with a convenient way to handle local taxes. Just keep doing what he had done before: build and repair schools, clean the streets, and so on.

Not every enterprise is as ideally suited to follow all of Igor's Rules as Igor himself is. What is important, though, is that almost all of them follow *some* of the rules. Clearly, the extent to which the director concentrates on one or two and ignores the others will depend on his initial endowments.

---

33. One way to think of cash bribes, then, is to view them as investments in relational capital, r.

Enterprises that inherited a relationship with the federal government—as suppliers for a ministry, say—will tend to preserve that status. Other enterprises that lack a business relationship with the central government will instead nurture their relations with local governments. And so on.[34]

The most important implication—and perhaps most disturbing for Russia's future—is that Igor himself (or any other enterprise director who followed something like Igor's Rules) *could* produce more marketable output, but he does not. He could restructure, but he does not. Why? Because, as the next chapter will show, cash sales and the profits they bring can be costly to the enterprise and its manager.

---

34. It should be noted that Igor's first three rules also represent three separate and distinct causes of barter in the Russian economy. This suggests an empirical approach to measure the relative importance of various causes of barter.

CHAPTER FOUR

"Igor" in the Virtual Economy

"Whatever you do, never make a profit!"

—*Igor's Final Injunction*

Igor's explicit final injunction, "Don't make a profit!" sounds like complete confirmation of the argument in chapter 2: enterprise directors in Russia do not behave rationally. If that is true, then the lack of economic restructuring in Russia can be blamed on a shortage of qualified managers: too many of the people in charge of industrial enterprises simply do not have the proper goals for a market economy. We are convinced that this is not the case; enterprise managers are not the problem. In this chapter we will argue that managers like Igor are rational when they refrain from earning profits. They realize that under certain conditions profits can cost more than they are worth. The problem therefore is not the managers' rationality, nor is it their competence. It is that they are compelled to pursue their own self-interests in the context of an economic environment—the virtual economy—where rational adjustment does not necessarily lead to efficient results. The virtual economy channels the best efforts of honest and skilled managers into activity that ultimately is socially destructive. This chapter is thus concerned with the behavioral foundations of the virtual economy.

The Cost of Profits

Thé very idea that profits can be costly sounds strange, but it becomes less mysterious once we recognize the important distinction between formal profits and informal profits. Formal profits entail a number of risks that directors seek to avoid. First of all—and this, recall, was Igor's express concern—formal profits attract the attention of the tax authorities. This, we argued, was also one of the factors motivating the use of barter (see appendix A). Second, profits, even cash flow alone, attract the attention of criminal organizations (the so-called "mafiya," or protection rackets). Third, formal profits may make the enterprise a takeover target, either because it is already profitable or because its reported profits are so low relative to its assets—more precisely, relative to its "market distance," d—that it would attract those who see a chance to enhance the formal profits with a successful takeover. Fourth, natural monopolies with the power to price discriminate demand more money from customers whom they know are earning more cash.[1] Finally, an enterprise that reports high formal profits finds it harder to delay paying wages to workers or dividends to shareholders.

Informal profits, in contrast, do not entail any of these risks for the simple reason that they are hidden from view. Informal profits are best defined as economic surplus from commercial activity that is not transparent. In our analysis informal profits differ from formal ones only in their observability. Both types of profits are inputs to economic survival, but informal profits are more difficult to expropriate because they are hidden. They are thus more under the director's control than are formal profits. While other stakeholders may have claims against profits, be they formal or informal, their claims are much harder to enforce when the profits are informal.

Informal profits do have a cost, however. Because they render the enterprise's current performance and potential future success unobservable, they make it harder to attract investment. In an environment where external finance is potentially available, this may be a significant economic cost. In

1. This is the corollary to the argument, for example, of Woodruff (1999), who argues that barter in Russia is the means by which natural monopolies engage in price discrimination. Unable to charge lower cash prices to customers who cannot afford to pay the full price, the natural monopolies accept payment in kind at a lower effective price. Clearly, then, the enterprise has an incentive to appear to be unable to pay in cash. See Ericson and Ickes (2001) for a formal model of the virtual economy with Gazprom as a price-discriminating monopolist.

the virtual economy, where external finance is relatively unobtainable, informal profits may be preferable as a survival strategy.

Formal and Informal Activities

The types of activities that generate formal and informal profits differ. In the "iceberg" of today's Russian economy, the formal activities of enterprises compose the portion that lies above the surface. The product of the formal activities is what shows up in official statistics and what results in cash payment of taxes. Below the surface, Russian enterprises engage in informal activities aimed at earning informal profits. They are also the kinds of activities and transactions that characterize the virtual economy. Informal activities span a wide range in both form and motive. If these activities are for the personal gain of the owners, they may be driven by the desire to win unfair competitive advantage. Alternatively, they may represent looting on the part of an owner or manager. Informal economic activity is of course not unique to Russia. However, this chapter focuses on what is peculiarly Russian, or at least post-Soviet. It is the unprecedented scope and complexity of production and exchange of goods and services in a parallel, noncash economy. In many countries informal economic activities take the form of concealed monetary transactions, exemplified by the phrase "cash under the table." Again, while this form of informal activity is also widespread in Russia, the informal activities we are concerned with here are paid for by nonmonetary means.

Regardless of their form, the distinctive feature of all informal activities is a lack of transparency. Something is being concealed. It may be from the tax man, from shareholders, from the managers, from workers, from suppliers, from regulators, from politicians, or from the police. Clearly, from whom it is concealed depends on what it is that needs to be concealed. Someone's interests are suffering—people inside the company or outside. They may be employees, owners, competitors, or partners. If the informal activities exist on a large scale, there will also be parties from whom the activity is not concealed, parties who participate in the scheme. One of the things that is special about the current Russian virtual economy is that it has so many participants. These participants all have a stake in making the entire system work, whether they are consciously aware of that or not. The network of personal relationships among the participants holds the whole system together.

With whom does the enterprise have relationships? We have mentioned other enterprises with which it has transactions, those to whom the enterprise sells its output or from whom it purchases inputs. An equally critical relationship is with governments or, more correctly, with individuals at various levels of government and in different agencies within governments. Not only are these governments themselves purchasers of the output of the enterprise, but they are also protectors: they help the enterprise to remain within the world of nontransparency.

The dividing line between formal and informal activities is sometimes unclear. A good way to understand the distinction is to look at how the activities, and the transactions that flow from them, relate to the formal rules of the game (or system). Formal activities and transactions are consistent with the formal rules of the system and are in principle enforceable under those rules.[2] Moreover, even if the formal contract is not enforceable, the parties would be better off if it were, since it would enlarge the range of contracting opportunities. For instance, agents in a formal transaction may prefer not to use the courts in practice (courts being a classic third-party enforcement mechanism), but the fact that they can rely on courts in specified circumstances increases the probability of agreement.

In other words, even if participants in a formal transaction would prefer that the contract be self-enforced, they envision some circumstances where that transaction may be judged by the formal rules. Participants in an informal transaction, however, would *not* undertake the transaction if they anticipated its enforcement by formal rules of the game. Interpreted according to the formal rules, an informal transaction will be distorted; the obligations of the parties will be altered in ways that neither party is willing to accept. The parties to such a transaction desire that it be hidden from view precisely to avoid any possibility of adjudication by the formal system. Hence, the parties to an informal activity desire nontransparency as a mechanism to avoid enforceability by the formal system.

Why would agents prefer an informal transaction when this precludes any possibility of third-party enforcement? Clearly the costs of losing enforcement possibilities are outweighed in such cases by the benefits of

2. In practice many formal contracts are not enforceable because third parties cannot verify the actions. This is due to the nature of the transaction, not the desire of the parties to preclude enforcement. With informal activities, however, it is precisely the preferences of the agents that preclude verifiability. Thus agents in a formal transaction would benefit if third-party verifiability were feasible, as it would enlarge the range of contracting opportunities. However, parties to an informal transaction benefit from unobservability and desire to maintain it.

being able to circumvent the rules. Aside from outright illegal behavior, the prime factor governing such choices is the need for survival. Informal activities become important when playing by the formal rules threatens the agent's survival. This is most likely to occur subsequent to a significant change in the formal rules that jeopardizes many formerly viable operations. To survive, agents ignore the changes in the formal rules and continue to rely on strategies that were useful before the rule changes. Not all agents who engage in informal transactions are relying on them for survival. Informal activities induce pooling; that is, when enough agents do engage in such transactions, they shape the environment for others as well. However, some agents require informal activities to survive. This is why the authorities tolerate them.

Because informal transactions cannot rely on formal enforcement mechanisms, relational capital is necessary to support such activities. Of course, relational capital is always useful to inhibit opportunism—for both formal and informal activities. Even with formal activities, a cost-benefit calculation usually favors reliance on reputation and other relationship-based mechanisms over legal enforcement. For formal activities, however, there is a choice of enforcement mechanisms, since the formal rules could be appealed to. With informal activities, however, the reliance on relational capital is a necessity—there is no other choice.

There is another way in which the effect of relational capital is fundamentally different on informal and formal activities. The stocks of relational capital possessed by the parties to an informal transaction are the key determinant of the terms of trade, or the relative prices that the parties face in the exchange of their products. The terms of the informal transaction are incomprehensible without a sense of relational capital among the parties. This is not the case with formal activities. In formal transactions relational capital may support low-cost ways of enforcing contracts, but it does not determine the terms of trade; instead, opportunity cost and gains from trade are the primary determinants of the terms of trade.

Enterprises that engage in formal activity and those that engage in informal activity both strive to improve the terms on which they can trade in the future. However, their approaches are different. The formal enterprise's incentives are geared to developing opportunities (creating new and better products, marketing, reducing costs, and the like) to improve its objective position for competition. An enterprise may invest in physical and human capital, that is, in equipment and machines and in its employees' skills and abilities. An enterprise that operates in the informal regime based on personal relationships has different priorities; its main concern is to cultivate those relationships. That, too, is a form of investment. It requires effort, time, and possibly money, all things that are in scarce supply in any company. Thus it is consistent to say that both types of enterprises depend on investment in order to survive and succeed. In the terminology of *r-d* space, developed in the previous chapter, the formal enterprise invests in distance reduction; the informal enterprise invests in relational capital.

The Director's Decision Problem

In the previous section, for the sake of convenience, we spoke of enterprises as though they were exclusively formal (oriented toward the market) or informal (oriented toward relationships). In practice, the boundary between the two types is not so sharp. Even in market economies, firms will undertake both types of activities. In the context of Russia the same holds true. Igor is a good example. The problem for a director like Igor is not to choose which regime to operate in; instead it is to choose how much effort to devote to each type of activity.[3]

We can analyze the decision problem of a typical Russian enterprise by examining the decision of how to allocate effort (a scarce resource) to formal and informal activities. A convenient way to think about this problem is as a choice from a menu of actions that relate to the production of goods to be used in formal and informal transactions. We will call these goods "hard" and "soft" goods, respectively. Hard goods are market-viable goods that can be sold for money at a price that covers costs; goods that do not meet that description are soft goods.[4] The director must choose how to

---

3. Our approach thus contrasts with that of Johnson, Kaufmann, and Shleifer (1997), where the decision to engage in informal activities is a knife edge.

4. We will occasionally use the terms "cash" and "noncash" goods instead of hard and soft goods. However, a good's being sold for cash is not sufficient to qualify it as a hard good. A good can always be sold for cash if the price is discounted sufficiently: hence, the emphasis on the fact that hard goods can be sold for money *and* cover the costs of production. Both here and elsewhere when we use the term "cash," it is synonymous with "monetary," and we will also use the terms "monetary" and "nonmonetary." The terms should thus not be confused with the special Soviet (and now Russian) distinction between *beznalichnyye den'gi* (literally, noncash money, in other words, bank accounts, and the like) and *nalichnyye* (paper currency and coin). The distinction between cash and noncash production describes whether receipts are monetary or not, regardless of the type of money received.

allocate his own total effort $\bar{e}$ between producing hard goods (e_h) and soft goods (e_s) so as to maximize profits.[5]

We suppose that effort is the only variable input that the director chooses. Production of hard and soft goods thus depends on the allocation of effort and on the levels of r and d of the enterprise. Hence, we can write the production functions for the two goods as:

$$y_h = f(e_h, d, r) \tag{1}$$

for hard goods, and:

$$y_s = g(e_s, r) \tag{2}$$

for soft goods. We assume that the impact of increased effort is positive in both expressions. We also assume that increased distance reduces the level of hard-goods production at any level of effort.

Notice the asymmetry in these two production functions. The production of hard goods depends on relational capital, but the production of soft goods does not depend on distance. The former follows because greater relational capital makes it easier to procure inputs, and that helps any type of production, including hard goods (hence, the marginal product of increased relational capital is positive). However, the production of soft goods does not depend on how competitive the product is in the market-place. Instead, the production of soft goods utilizes inherited facilities—it depends on the supply of effort and the ability to obtain variable inputs, such as energy, that are critical to keep old production structures operating.

The amount of effort required to produce hard and soft goods is likely to differ. Hard goods tend to be high-effort products, especially when directed to export markets. They require marketing: since traditional customers are more likely to be illiquid, the hard-goods producer will need to attract new customers. Doing so may require a better product. Hard goods may also require new suppliers. For soft goods, however, less effort is needed for production. They are typically the unreconstructed goods of high-d enterprises that were produced in Soviet times in the conditions of a closed economy and a sellers' market. Instead, effort must be expended on maintaining good relations since the enterprise needs relational capital in order to continue to sell soft goods.

5. We assume that the director supplies a fixed amount of effort inelastically. Essentially, we are assuming that maintaining the position as director is so lucrative compared with other alternatives that directors supply as much effort as possible. Hence we can ignore the question of the level of effort and focus on its composition.

The effort it takes to produce hard goods depends on the enterprise's level of d. An enterprise with high d—for example, most enterprises that inherited their physical capital from the Soviet era—will be hard-pressed to produce hard goods. It is more costly for such an enterprise to shift to production of a new marketable product than it is for a low-d enterprise. The high-d enterprise will have a comparative advantage in producing soft goods. If the enterprise has sufficient relational capital, it will be able to sell such goods. For such an enterprise the return to devoting effort to producing soft goods will be greater than for hard goods. Hence, *ceteris paribus*, we should expect that the ratio of effort levels would depend on initial conditions: e_h/e_s is negatively correlated with d/r.

Effort levels do not represent the only difference between the two types of output. They also differ in the price received by the enterprise. Goods sold for cash incur monetary tax liabilities not just to various levels of government, but also payments that must be paid to rackets, workers, shareholders and other stakeholders, and to price-discriminating monopolies. It simplifies the analysis to think of all the various penalties placed on earning cash as taxes, whether they are formal taxes paid to government, higher prices paid to suppliers such as Gazprom, or a levy from a protection racket. Soft, or noncash, goods are exempt from these extra charges or "taxes." We can then differentiate between the two types of goods in terms of tax evasion (viewed broadly). If p is the market price of the hard good and we let τ be the tax rate, then $p(1 - \tau)$ is the after-tax price of hard goods. A wedge is thus created between the returns to the two types of activities.[6] Hard goods may fetch a higher return, but some of it must be paid in taxes. Soft-goods production allows evasion of this tax, but the ability to undertake such activities depends on the enterprise's level of relational capital.

The existence of the "tax" wedge means that the productive assets of a Russian enterprise will have two prices: one is a market price (when the resources are used to produce hard goods) and the other an informal shadow price (when they are used to produce soft goods). The tax wedge between the prices of hard and soft goods is a key determinant of the composition of the enterprise's output. When taxes are increased on hard goods, there will be a relative shift to more soft-goods production. The converse is also true, but the adjustment occurs with a lag, because agents must be

6. The terminology is not exactly correct. The two prices are not usually for the same good, so technically this is not necessarily a wedge.

sure that the change is not transitory. To move production from soft to hard goods opens the enterprise to more scrutiny.[7]

The tax wedge offsets the standard advantage of monetary transactions over nonmonetary: transactions costs are much lower for the former if both types of receipts are taxed similarly. However, nonmonetary transactions involve greater possibilities for evasion, and hence the after-tax return to such transactions may be greater. The problem for the enterprise manager is thus to weigh both the different effort levels required to produce hard and soft goods and the differing returns to effort for each and then allocate his effort so as to equate the marginal returns between soft-goods production and hard-goods production.

We present a more complete analysis of the director's decision problem in appendix D. Here, we offer a less formal discussion of the results of that analysis. Given a fixed amount of effort, the director chooses to produce a mix of hard and soft products. In choosing how much of each good to produce, the director is guided by the trade-off between the marginal contribution to profits of extra effort in each type of production relative to the effort exerted. Since it is in general easier (requires less effort) to produce the soft good than the hard good, a typical director is undoubtedly inclined to produce soft products as long as there is a market for them. There is a trade-off, however. A director must retain good relations with government and with other enterprises in order to continue to produce soft goods. Hard goods are easier to translate into cash, which may be needed to procure important inputs, but they require more effort to produce. Indeed, Igor's first three rules were all based on the idea of minimizing the enterprise's dependence on such inputs in favor of the barter alternative.

It seems intuitively clear that the director's choice between hard and soft goods is going to depend in part on the enterprise's market distance and its relational capital. That is, no matter how easy it is to produce the soft good, it is worthless to the enterprise (the director) unless it (he) has the requisite amount of relational capital. Similarly, the quantity of the hard good that can be produced and sold for any given level of effort depends on how well that good is suited to the market. In other words, it depends on the enterprise's d.

---

7. If there is uncertainty about the duration of the price change, the supply response may be less than expected. This probably accounts for the rather slow response to the devaluation of August 1998. Relative prices for hard goods rose dramatically, but the response of suppliers was rather weak at first.

The Cash Constraint

The director's decision problem is further complicated by another factor—the ambiguous role of cash in the system. Igor's fourth rule stressed the necessity of earning a certain minimum level of cash. Despite all the effort made to avoid cash, some minimum amount of it is still needed. This is a sentiment echoed by the director of the Tutayev plant (see chapter 2). Some cash is required to procure key material inputs. Cash may also be needed for bribes to officials, something that suggests an interesting relationship between the cash regime and the regime of relationships. However, for many enterprises the main reason to earn cash is to pay workers' wages. That enterprises face an absolute demand for cash, a *cash constraint*, is evident in the fact that they often sell for cash at a loss. Again, recall the remarks of the Tutayev director.

Of course, *earning* cash is not the only way to obtain it. A common method in a normal market economy is to borrow. This, however, is an extremely expensive way to obtain cash in today's Russia, and it is rare. By the end of 1998, credits to the nonfinancial sectors of the economy composed only 3.8 percent of Russian banks' total loan portfolios.[8] From 1993 through most of 1998, commercial bank claims on the private sector in Russia were only about 10 percent of gross domestic product (GDP).[9] Since the economic crisis of August 1998, this percentage has risen (to about 14 percent by the end of 2001), but it remains small compared with around 90 percent in the United States.[10] Even if an enterprise does borrow, of course, it will eventually have to earn cash to pay off the bank loan in the future. For simplicity, in what follows, we assume that the enterprises cannot borrow.

The essence of the cash constraint is straightforward. An enterprise must earn enough cash to be able to pay for those inputs that must be paid for in cash. Formally, we can write it as:

$$p(1 - \tau)f(e_t, d_t, r_t) \geq m_t, \tag{3}$$

where m_t is the amount of inputs that must be purchased in cash during period t. The left-hand side of equation (3) is the after-tax *cash* revenues of the enterprise.[11] The cash constraint is an extra restriction on enterprise

8. *AKDI Press-byulleten*, no. 3 (January 18–24) 1999; electronic version.
9. *Russian Economic Trends*, January 1999.
10. *Russian Economic Trends*, December 2001.
11. This formulation implicitly assumes that all "taxes" broadly defined are paid for in cash. This is easily seen by noting that if we add "taxes" to both sides, the cash constraint says that pre-tax cash revenues must be at least as large as m_t *plus* taxes.

behavior that stems from the fact that there are some vital purchases for which noncash methods are of no value.

How does the cash constraint alter our analysis of the director's decision problem? If the enterprise earns sufficient cash to meet essential needs, the constraint does not alter enterprise decisions. If the enterprise has not yet earned this minimum amount of cash, m_t, the shadow price for assets used to generate cash sales will be high. This means that the enterprise will produce a greater amount of hard (or "cash") goods than it would—given relative prices and its level of d—if it were not so constrained (as was the case for the director of the Tutayev plant). If the cash constraint were relaxed—say, by an increase in the price of cash goods or by a decrease in the tax rate—the enterprise would be able to satisfy the cash constraint at a lower level of cash goods production, and hence its production bundle would shift toward soft goods. This case of a binding cash constraint is analyzed in appendix D.

The enterprise's situation is depicted in figure 4-1, which plots the relative share of hard-goods production as a function of the price of the hard good relative to that of the soft good (ρ).[12] The existence of the cash constraint sets a floor on production of hard goods. There is some level (level $(Y_h/Y_s)_{min}$ in the figure) below which the enterprise cannot go, no matter what the price of the output. "Normally," the enterprise will reduce output of the hard good when its relative price drops—a straightforward example of supply decreasing in response to lower prices. However, if the relative price of hard goods, ρ, falls below the critical value, $\hat{\rho}$, then behavior becomes rather interesting. In this case the cash constraint binds (that is, the enterprise needs more cash to survive), and, as is evident in figure 4-1, the supply curve in that range is *negatively* sloped; an increase in the relative price of hard goods leads to a *decrease* in production of hard goods. The reason is that when the relative price of hard goods is below $\hat{\rho}$, the enterprise is producing more hard goods than it would like in order to earn sufficient cash. An increase in the relative price of hard goods would thus allow the enterprise to satisfy the cash constraint at a lower level of hard-goods production.[13] The enterprise needs to produce *fewer* hard goods to

12. That is,

$$\rho \equiv \frac{p(1-\tau)}{\hat{p}(r)},$$

where p is the market price of hard goods and τ is the "tax" rate (so that $p[1-\tau]$ is the after-tax price of hard goods), and $\hat{p}$ is the price of soft goods, which we assume to be a function of relational capital. See appendix D for details.

13. One event that would raise the relative price of hard goods production is a decline in the real value of the ruble. The real depreciation after August 17, 1998, had such an effect. See chapter 9.

FIGURE 4-1. Relative Supply of Hard Goods

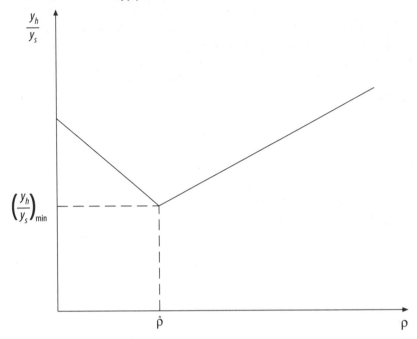

earn the minimum amount of cash it requires. Once it reaches that minimum amount, it stops producing. It is already producing too large a share of hard goods in the sense that it is producing hard goods beyond the point at which it is profitable to do so. It will therefore not respond to the decline in taxes by moving more into the cash sector. For enterprises where the cash constraint is binding—that is, enterprises that still need more cash to survive—a decrease in the tax rate will not lead to increased hard goods production, but in fact have the opposite effect: it will allow the enterprises to survive more easily in the nonmonetary economy.

The implications of this phenomenon can hardly be overstated: good policy produces bad results. In the above case, lowering tax rates causes an enterprise to increase its production of soft goods. The need to earn cash induces the enterprise to produce goods that are unprofitable and to continue activities that ought to be discontinued on efficiency grounds. There are other policy implications that are as bad or worse. Recall that we are using the broad definition of a "tax," which includes not simply formal government taxes, but also money paid to the protection rackets. Consider, then, an effective anticrime campaign, one that reduced the ability of the rackets to extort money from enterprises. For some enterprises whose cash constraint was binding, this would result in less formal market (cash) activity. Whether or not such a case has been or ever will be tested in practice is not clear. What this analysis does suggest is that the response to tax policy will differ from enterprise to enterprise, depending on whether the cash constraint is binding. The aggregate effects will then depend on the distribution of enterprises in terms of this constraint. If a sufficient number of enterprises face binding cash constraints, even the aggregate response to a cut in "taxes" may be perverse.

To make this more concrete, consider two types of enterprises. The first type could be represented by, say, the Severstal steel plant, an apparently successful metallurgical enterprise in Vologda oblast, which exports more than three-quarters of its hard-goods (steel) output. The second type of enterprise is Tutayev, the diesel engine manufacturer. At Severstal, cash sales are profitable at the margin. (For Severstal, the cash constraint is not binding.) What limits its ratio of cash sales to noncash sales are the relative prices of the two. This is determined by the tax wedge. For Tutayev, cash sales are unprofitable at the margin. The enterprise sells for cash anyway because it needs a certain amount of cash for survival. An enterprise like Severstal will respond "properly" to tax changes; the Tutayevs of Russia will do just the opposite.

Regardless of whether the cash constraint is binding or not, the enterprise typically does not follow a pure strategy of producing either hard or soft goods.[14] It chooses instead to engage in a mixture of the two kinds of activities because combining them is more profitable than following either strategy to the exclusion of the other.[15] Technically, this is an implication of assuming that production functions of both types of goods are concave in effort levels. The fact that enterprises follow such a mixed strategy may also mean that it is more difficult to move enterprises completely to the cash economy. An enterprise may wish to pay for some goods with cash, but the seller may refuse to take cash. The former enterprise would then rationally have to retain some production to use for barter even if it otherwise had decided to move to the market.

14. Again, this distinguishes our approach from that of Johnson, Kaufmann, and Shleifer (1997); see footnote 3.

15. The statement that enterprises follow a mixed strategy whether the cash constraint is binding or not is consistent with the empirical evidence reported in Guriev and Ickes (2000). This shows that an enterprise's choosing barter is independent of its financial position. Indeed, no sharp differences across enterprise types explain the use of barter, although barter does appear more prevalent in less competitive industries.

Corporate Governance

An improvement in the manner in which companies are managed and controlled—so-called corporate governance—amounts to an increase in the tax rate on soft goods. Most outside shareholders of a company are likely to have no interest in production of soft goods. Soft goods yield no formal profits, the only kind of profits that can benefit outside shareholders. In companies where the shareholders have only weak power to monitor the director's behavior, where the director has little or no accountability, the very existence of the outside shareholders' claim on formal cash profits is an incentive for the director to shift to noncash production. The shareholders "tax" the cash production while leaving noncash production untaxed. Weak corporate governance is thus essential to the director's ability to divert cash flow to his own use.

In a regime of good corporate governance, power shifts. The shareholders continue to lay claim to their share of cash profits. In addition, they can penalize the director for any actions he may take that divert the resources of the company from its goal of generating visible profits for the shareholders. Production of soft goods is likely to constitute such a diversion. The penalty to the director for production of soft goods can be thought of as a tax on that form of production. Hence, good corporate governance amounts to a change in the relative price of hard and soft goods. The "after-tax" return to production of soft goods declines relative to that of hard goods. Depending on how severe the penalty is perceived to be, it may outweigh any possible benefit from continuing the production of soft goods. Thus improved corporate governance—transparency and the ability to demand accountability by management—will reduce the relative advantage of remaining in the r regime and thus induce a shift toward cash-generating production of hard goods.

Dynamics

The basic principle we have elucidated is that policies that raise the cost of producing soft goods relative to hard goods will lead directors to alter their effort mix toward market (cash) activities. So far we have examined the static decision problem of the enterprise; that is, how to divide effort between production of hard goods and of soft goods at any given moment. However, the complete decision problem for the enterprise is even more complex than this, since decisions made today may determine the conditions the enterprise will face in the future. An enterprise's location in r-d space is not the immutable relic of the past. It depends on the path of enterprise investment decisions. The decision to invest in relations and/or in reducing distance will affect the relative payoffs of these survival strategies in the future. Because these decisions have lasting effects, the enterprise's decision problem depends on expectations of conditions in the future. Hence we must analyze how today's actions affect the choices of action in the future.

The enterprise director's problem is to determine how much to invest in reducing distance and how much to invest in relational capital so as to maximize the value of the enterprise or the expected discounted value of future profits.[16] A formal analysis of the director's investment choice, the dynamic optimization problem, is included in appendix D. That analysis first models how a unit of investment in r or d in the current period is expected to affect total profits in the following period. It then compares the increase in profits generated by each type of investment. The optimal investment mix—the one that maximizes the present value of future profits—will be such that the marginal returns from investment in both directions are equal.

Our approach is to distinguish between the effectiveness of investment and its rate of return. *Effectiveness* of investment refers to the impact of an investment on the enterprise's location in r-d space. For example, when the enterprise invests in the current period with the goal of reducing distance, how much does that actually reduce distance in the next period? The *return* to investment refers to the impact of the improved state (the improved location in r-d space) on profitability. For instance, assuming that the enterprise did reduce its distance, how much would that reduction in distance raise the next period's profits? (Analogous questions can be posed for investment in r.) The payoff to investing clearly depends on both its effectiveness and its rate of return—in fact, on the product of these two factors.

In making the investment decision, the director must cope with uncertainty over future variables. One type of uncertainty regards the effectiveness of investment. To simplify the analysis, we assume that the

16. Of course, the director must also decide whether to invest internally at all. Thus the return to investment must exceed the discount rate. We have ignored any opportunity cost of funds, but there may be outside investment opportunities available to the director. Clearly GKOs were a superior alternative to internal investment at many enterprises before August 1998. Nevertheless, the ability to invest *externally* may require cash, which implies that the opportunity cost of investing in distance reduction may differ from that of relational capital. The question of alternative uses of resources is discussed in the section "Opportunity Cost of Investment."

director knows the impact of the investments on future productivity. (Technically, we assume he knows the form of the investment functions.) However, even this knowledge is not enough to fully eliminate uncertainty, since unforeseen events could influence the outcome. For example, distance could rise unexpectedly because of improvements elsewhere in the world economy. Or relational capital could fall next period due to a crackdown on tax offsets. Essentially, these disturbances affect the effectiveness of investment in r or in reducing d. But if we assume that these kinds of events are random disturbances with zero mean, then the director's investment decision ultimately depends on what he expects relative prices—in the broad sense that includes taxation—to be in the future.[17]

Our analysis relies on important assumptions about how the effectiveness of such investments depends on the current location of the enterprise in r-d space. It seems clear that a higher current value of d reduces the effectiveness of investing in distance. If an enterprise is very far from the market—if it produces the wrong thing in the wrong way—then investments aimed at reducing distance may have little effect. The market still does not want the product. In that case, only a large investment, one sufficient to change the whole scheme of production, could reduce distance for the enterprise. The case of relational capital is likely to be different. It probably is sensible to assume that the level of relational capital does not alter the impact of investment on the stock. That is, no matter how much or how little relational capital the enterprise has in the present period, an investment in r will make the same (positive) contribution to its future stock of relational capital.

Analysis of the director's dynamic optimization problem allows us to answer the critical question of exactly how an enterprise's current state (location in r-d space) may bias its investment decision in one direction or the other. As far as d is concerned, the conclusion is straightforward. Because higher d means that investment in distance reduction is less effective, the greater the enterprise's current distance, the less likely it is to invest in distance reduction. Therefore, all else constant, the low-d enterprise will invest relatively more in d than in r, while the high-d enterprise will tend to invest more in r.

---

17. Strictly speaking, a director would ignore these sources of uncertainty only if he were risk neutral. If the director is risk averse, then changes in the variance of these disturbances—more uncertainty—would influence his decisions even if the mean were unchanged. Increased uncertainty over the effectiveness of investing in relational capital, for example, would bias investment toward distance reduction, all else held constant.

FIGURE 4-2. Three Enterprises in *r-d* Space

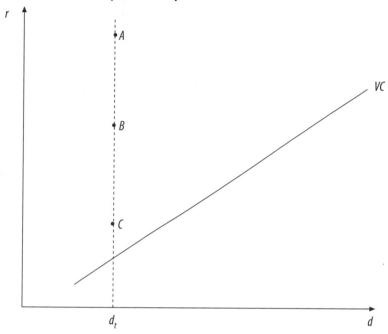

The question of how investment varies with *r* is more complex. The complexity derives from an assumption made already in the static decision problem: *r* affects both soft and hard goods production, since greater relational capital makes it easier to procure inputs, which helps any type of production, including that of hard goods. The effect on total profits of an investment in *r* will differ depending on the current level of *r*. An enterprise with low relational capital will benefit little from investment in relations. It will not be able to find purchasers of soft goods, nor will it be able to obtain inputs through informal means. There is a hurdle that must be overcome before the enterprise can appropriate the benefits of informal activity. Once *r* achieves this critical level, the returns to investing in relational capital will increase. This suggests that at very low levels of *r*, investing in reducing *d* may dominate. As the stock of relational capital increases, the returns to investing in relational capital will increase.

We can further understand the dynamics by returning to the *r-d* space diagram. Our concern is to understand the trajectory an enterprise will follow given some initial conditions for *r* and *d*. Figure 4-2 illustrates three possibilities that differ only in the value of their relational capital in the initial period (enterprises located at points A, B, and C).

To see how the decisions of these three enterprises differ, assume that investment in relational capital or distance reduction in one period simply changes the enterprise's r or d in the next period by an amount equal to the investment; this means that effectiveness of investment is constant for both types. (See appendix D for treatment of a more general form of the problem.) Since our concern in figure 4-2 is with the direction of motion, we consider the changes in distance and relational capital (Δd and Δr, respectively). If we represent investment in d as i_d and investment in r as i_r, we can write:

$$\Delta d = -i_d$$
$$\Delta r = i_r \tag{4}$$

Note that Δd is movement in a negative direction—to the left—on the d-axis, or "west" in r-d space, while Δr is positive movement on the r-axis, or "north" in r-d space. Now consider an enterprise located at point C in figure 4-2. Its relational capital is very low. Analysis of the optimum investment decision (see appendix D) shows that the return to investing in relational capital is likely to be very low for an enterprise at point C. An enterprise with low relational capital will be unable to appropriate the benefits of informal activity for the reasons mentioned above: it does not have buyers of its soft goods, and it cannot use relations to acquire inputs without cash. Hence, for such an enterprise, investing in r is likely dominated by distance reduction. Therefore, to equate the marginal returns from investment in both directions, the enterprise will invest more in distance reduction, driving down the marginal return until it is equal to the marginal return to investing in relational capital. This means that $-\Delta d > \Delta r$ for such an enterprise. The enterprise faces a greater attraction to the west than to the north.

Now consider the enterprise at point A. Relational capital is very high. Hence, the return to investing in relational capital is higher than at point C. If r is sufficiently high, then in order to equate the marginal returns, the enterprise will have to invest more in relational capital than in distance reduction. Hence, for an enterprise like A we would have $-\Delta d < \Delta r$: the enterprise is pulled more to the north than to the west. Continuity suggests that some intermediate location, such as point B, exists where the optimal investment decision pulls in both directions equally. Hence at point B we have $-\Delta d = \Delta r$. We can consider this level of relational capital, r^c, the critical level.

To complete the analysis we now ask how the critical level of relational capital, r^c (that is, the level of r such that $-\Delta d = \Delta r$), varies as the level of d

FIGURE 4-3. The Restructuring Boundary

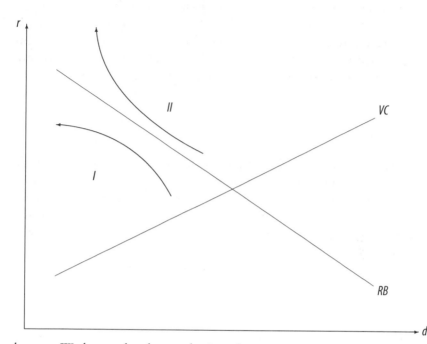

changes. We know that lower d raises the return to investing in distance reduction for any level of r, but it leaves the return to investing in r unchanged. Consider some enterprise, B′, which has exactly the same r as enterprise B ($r_{B′} = r_B$), but whose d is slightly smaller ($d_{B′} < d_B$) by some small increment, δ. The marginal returns to investment cannot then be equal at B′ if the enterprise invests equally in each direction (as at point B). Hence, at B′ we must have $-\Delta d > \Delta r$. This means that the critical value r^c that causes $-\Delta d = \Delta r$ must increase with lower d. If we then let d vary, we obtain a line we call the *restructuring boundary*, labeled *RB* in figure 4-3.

The restructuring boundary divides r-d space into regions where the forces of attraction are stronger to the north and those where they are stronger to the west. Hence, in the region labeled I in figure 4-3, enterprises are pulled more strongly to reduce distance. In region II, in contrast, the pull is greater to further investments in relational capital. The arrows in the diagram suggest the trajectories that enterprises will follow based on their levels of r and d.[18]

18. Notice that even though the *RB* line extends below the *VC* (viability constraint) line, enterprises located under the *VC* line are, by definition, not viable. Hence, they disinvest (loot) rather than invest, and their direction of motion is to the southeast.

Successful economic reform would induce enterprises to reduce their d, not to enhance their r. One can consider policies to be effective if they move enterprises from quadrant II to quadrant I. Even though enterprises in quadrant II invest in reducing d, they invest even more in r. True reform thus requires that these biases be reversed. Only when distance reduction predominates over investments in relational capital is the enterprise truly on its way to becoming market oriented.

Irreversibility

We have, to this point, ignored the implications of irreversibility for the investment decision.[19] If once an enterprise leaves the r-regime it is hard to go back, then an enterprise must consider the cost of changing its overall investment strategy in making decisions. Our arguments have suggested that investing in distance reduction may involve sunk costs that cannot be recovered if the decision is reversed. For instance, once the enterprise engages in more public activity that is associated with distance reduction, it may be difficult to go back to informal pursuits. This may have important implications for the investment decision.

When investments involve sunk costs and when there is uncertainty over future outcomes, there is an *option value to waiting*. In the absence of sunk costs, investments can be undone; hence delay involves only costs—deferred profits—but no benefits. With sunk costs, however, *timing* is crucial. It might pay to delay an investment in distance reduction until more is learned about the likely outcomes. Meanwhile, the enterprise would continue to invest in relations. Investing in relations may turn out to be the best hedge for an enterprise unsure about the future.

Opportunity Cost of Investment

So far we have discussed only the benefits of investment and the choice between the two strategies of distance reduction and relational capital. However, there is also a cost to consider. The opportunity cost of investment

19. An investment is fully irreversible when it cannot be undone—in other words, when negative investment is impossible. When sunk costs are present, investment is at least partially irreversible, since one cannot recover the sunk costs associated with investment. It may be possible to sell a machine tool, for example, but even in a competitive industry the sale price will be less than the purchase price, since the machine tool will be excess capacity to another firm. The literature on irreversible investment has grown rapidly in recent years. The classic reference is Dixit and Pindyck (1994).

is, of course, the alternative use of the resources. Rather than invest in the enterprise at all, the director could invest in financial securities—for example, short-term government treasury bonds (GKOs) before August 1998—or he could send funds abroad. Investing in foreign currency during the early period of Russian transition earned a very tidy return compared with what might be obtained from investing in the enterprise. Consideration of these alternatives might seem relevant only for determining the level of investment in r or d, but in fact it affects the type of investment as well. The reason is that the opportunity cost of investment depends on the form in which the investment must be made; that is, whether hard or soft goods.

Most investment in Russia is self-financed, but even when it is not, it is likely that the investment requires cash profits.[20] Investment in moving to the market requires purchase of new equipment, often imported. In other words, it is more likely to require cash. Second, investments in tangible capital are a highly visible activity. Thus the act of investing in distance reduction carries the risk of alerting the tax authorities. Closer scrutiny (and less lenience) on the part of the tax authorities limits the ability of the enterprise to appeal to authorities to allow tax offsets or other forms of income diversion. The decision to invest in tangible capital involves an increase in production of hard goods. In other words, the enterprise is trading off a reduction in its distance to the market against a higher cost of engaging in informal activities. In addition, investment in reducing distance may be irreversible, in the sense that once the enterprise is engaged in such activity, it becomes too difficult to go back to soft-goods production. Hence investment in reducing d reduces flexibility.

Our formulation of the enterprise problem assumes that the opportunity cost of investment is the same for reduction of distance and accumulation of relational capital. This is a very strong assumption that we made only to focus attention on this choice. In practice, the opportunity cost of investment is likely to differ depending on its form. Investments in distance reduction may require hard cash, while investments in relational capital may be feasible in soft goods. This would make investment in distance reduction more costly and would bias investment choice away from what we conventionally call restructuring.

20. When investment is financed externally, the greater the borrower's involvement in noncash production, the greater the moral hazard problem facing the lender. Obtaining external finance requires more transparency. This would suggest that there is a positive feedback in the investment decision. As the enterprise invests in distance reduction (and eschews informal activity), the cost of external funds may be reduced. The opposite, of course, would happen for the enterprise that invests in relations.

Exclusivity

Until this point we have assumed that enterprises could invest in both distance reduction and relational capital simultaneously. This certainly seems to be the case for Igor. It is interesting, however, to consider the other extreme case, one in which an enterprise can invest in either reduction of distance or enhancement of relationships, but not both. This might occur, for example, if investment in distance reduction requires external borrowing and that in turn requires fully transparent economic relations, thus making it almost impossible to cut deals for soft goods production. Conversely, investment in relationships could preclude a visible effort to invest in production of hard goods. For instance, an enterprise director who is lobbying government officials to accept tax offsets in lieu of cash may find no sympathy if they see him at the same time spending cash to import new equipment for the purpose of earning even more cash.

Faced then with the choice of investing exclusively in either r or d, the director will again compare the marginal returns of the two types of investment, but choose only one. That is, the director will invest in whichever activity has the highest payoff, *exclusively*, up to the point where the marginal return equals the opportunity cost of funds. Thus the result is movement not along the diagonal, but straight north or west.[21]

Which assumption—exclusivity or nonexclusivity—is closest to reality in Russia? Can enterprises invest simultaneously in both relations and distance reduction, or do they have to commit to only one? The answer, it would seem, differs among enterprises. As has been the case with so much else, the answer will be determined significantly by the endowment, or initial location in r-d space. Enterprises close to either the southeast or northwest corners will behave most nearly *as if* the exclusivity rule applied. Those closer to the RB line will show a mix of strategies. Igor certainly seems to be of the latter type.

This discussion takes the cash constraint as given and assumes that it will not be influenced by the investment decision. In fact, an important consequence of either form of investment is that each alters the intensity of the cash constraint in subsequent periods. This is especially the case when investment in distance reduction is financed externally. Creditors and shareholders have a strong incentive to insist on transparency, and this means

---

21. In fact, there may be *disinvestment* in r or d—or, at least, failure to keep up historical levels of investment leads to deterioration of existing capital. This applies to relational capital as well as tangible capital. The effect of not maintaining capital is movement to the south (if r is not maintained) and to the east (if d is not maintained).

that informal activity is viewed with disfavor. Hence, for the enterprise that has committed to reducing d, the burden of the cash constraint will likely increase over time.

The *RB* Line and Economic Reform

Figure 4-2 illustrates a way to think about how policy affects the restructuring decision. The important contrast is between enterprises that lie above or below the restructuring boundary. Clearly, a central goal of transition is to encourage restructuring. Since the RB line separates the regions where investment in distance reduction predominates from those where investment in relational capital predominates, the goal should be to shift the RB line up so that more enterprises will lie below it and will therefore invest more heavily in distance reduction. The question is how to accomplish such a shift.

The first thing to note is that shifting the RB line up is different from the notion of tightening an already hard budget constraint. Policies that tighten the budget constraint affect the viability constraint (VC), shifting the VC line up. Such policies make it more difficult for an enterprise to survive in its current state. They increase the intensity of the enterprise's search for survival strategies, but they do not bias such decisions in one way or another. They do force the enterprise to adjust, but for some enterprises the adjustment will take the form of more intense efforts to enhance relational capital. Tightening the budget constraint may, in other words, deter restructuring in some cases. Shifting up the RB line, in contrast, always alters the investment choice toward restructuring. Hence, it is the latter that is the key to successful economic reform. How then can the RB line be shifted upward?

Policies that raise the return to distance reduction, such as cutting taxes on hard goods or improving corporate governance, are one way to shift up the RB line. Of course, such policies must be permanent. For instance, tax cuts that are viewed as temporary will have much smaller effects because enterprises do not want to become visible participants in the monetary economy if they feel that policy is designed only to induce them to reveal themselves.[22]

A weak ruble is another way to enhance the return to investment in distance reduction and thereby shift up the RB line. Essentially, a weaker ruble

22. This appears to be the strategy of the Putin presidency, at least as evidenced by the Ministry of the Economy under German Gref. Whether the tax cuts will be permanent remains to be seen, but the intention seems to be correct.

increases the competitiveness of enterprises in tradable sectors—in effect, it causes the price of hard goods to rise relative to soft goods. Even enterprises in nontradable sectors may benefit from the increased cash earned by exporters for whom the cash constraint is now less binding. The effect is to raise the return to investment in distance reduction relative to investment in relational capital. As in the case of tax cuts, the change must be viewed as permanent rather than temporary.

An alternative way to shift up the RB line is to reduce the return to investing in relations. This is easy to talk about, but hard to implement. One means might be to crack down on the natural monopolies—the "three fat boys"—that are major suppliers of value to loss-making enterprises.

Investing in r

In the virtual economy investments in r are typically made in kind, rather than in cash. For example, an enterprise director will repair a school or invest in worker housing rather than simply offer cash payment to an official. Why is this the case?

An important characteristic of relational capital is that the investment is made today to obtain some future, often unspecified, benefit. Because the benefit often involves evading fiduciary responsibility, it cannot be enforced by contract. The investor thus faces the risk that the commitment will not be fulfilled. Reputation mechanisms, which often are effective in such circumstances, are also not of particular value here. An investment in relational capital in the form of repairing a school creates constituents for future enforcement. Repairing the school helps the local government official whose budget is insufficient to finance the expenditure. It is public information that the enterprise fixed the school, so it becomes common knowledge that the enterprise is "owed" something. This makes it harder for the official to renege on his obligation to the enterprise when the bill comes due. Ironically, then, it is the "transparency" of the in-kind investment in r (as opposed to a covert cash bribe to the official) that may make it a preferable strategy for some enterprises.

A further benefit to investments in r that are made in kind is endemic to the virtual economy. It is often costly to use cash in the virtual economy. An enterprise that is flush with cash is prey not only to the tax authorities, but also to mafias of various hues. By investing in kind, the enterprise may be able to conceal the actual size of its cash flows, and perhaps even signal that it is cash poor.

The Uneven Playing Field

We have analyzed how the director's decision to invest in distance reduction versus relations enhancement depends on initial conditions and on its past choices with regard to such investments. It is important to consider, however, the impact of other enterprises on such decisions. We touched on this issue when we discussed how the fiscal pressures created by the virtual economy hinder restructuring by putting an extra burden on income-producing enterprises. We now turn to another important implication of the virtual economy: the effect of continued operation of loss-making enterprises on market conditions and what this implies for restructuring.[23]

The different sectors of the Russian economy vary in their competitiveness, but there is also variance within industries. That is, the enterprises in any particular sector of the economy differ in their level of d, some being much closer to the market than others. This means that the survival of loss-making enterprises will affect the competitive situation facing profitable enterprises as well. This follows because the infusion of value to loss makers—allowing them to continue production—delays the consolidation of industries that would otherwise take place. Loss-making enterprises are able to keep producing, and this drives down the market price of output.

Consider how the continued survival of unviable enterprises affects the restructuring decision of enterprises that have lower d. The director of a relatively low-d enterprise must contemplate how the market for its output will evolve. He knows that if high-d enterprises are able to survive and keep producing, the market price will be lower in the future, and hence the return to restructuring will be lower. The director of the low-d enterprise may thus choose to invest in relational capital rather than restructuring (so that he can share in the value infusion). If the high-d enterprises were to exit from the industry, then the remaining enterprises would anticipate a greater return to restructuring. The virtual economy thus creates a barrier to restructuring.

Notice that this restructuring barrier imposed by the virtual economy is in addition to the fiscal burden that this system produces. The barrier is created by the differential impact of subsidies that flow to enterprises that are relatively more endowed with or have invested more in relational capital. The virtual economy is essentially acting as a tax on success *twice*: first,

---

23. This effect has been relatively neglected by the literature, though it was emphasized recently by Volgin (1998). Ickes and Ryterman (1993) discussed the impact of intra-industry variation on restructuring.

through its incessant need for cash and second via the depressing effect on prices produced by subsidization of loss makers.

This analysis implies that the operation of the virtual economy inhibits the potential for improved overall national economic performance. Enterprises that could improve their competitiveness choose not to because of the extra competition contributed by loss-making enterprises. One may be tempted to argue that this effect is temporary: if only the playing field can be leveled, then those enterprises with potential will choose to exploit it. Disregarding the difficulty of actually leveling the playing field, this argument ignores the fact that enterprises in the rest of the world are improving their competitiveness. Enterprises that delay restructuring today are thus falling farther behind world standards of competitiveness, continually widening the gap between the competitive and the noncompetitive.

Endogeneity of the Cash Constraint

As the enterprise chooses today between allocating its resources for production of soft goods or hard goods, it is shaping the cash constraint for future periods. To some extent, the enterprise's cash constraint is beyond its control, in part for institutional reasons. There are also macroeconomic factors that affect the cash constraint. Government campaigns to collect more taxes in cash will tighten the constraint for all enterprises. When the economy becomes more monetized—as in the wake of the ruble devaluation that followed the August 1998 crisis—the representative enterprise will be less likely to face a binding cash constraint.

Nevertheless, some elements of the cash constraint are endogenous, that is, they are affected by the enterprise's own behavior. For instance, enterprises that try to reduce d will most likely face greater demands for cash. This will certainly be the case when the enterprise purchases equipment that is imported. If part of the restructuring effort requires borrowing, then the cash constraint will also become tighter in future periods.

In general, the extent to which the cash constraint binds depends on the strength of the enterprise's relationships with other enterprises and with governments. The desire to loosen the cash constraint is, in fact, a major motivation for investment in relational capital. The share of payments that an enterprise must lay out in cash is a function of the extent to which it is engaged in production of hard goods. However, the strength of relationships and/or the degree of involvement in the cash economy are precisely the elements that are being affected by the investment decisions. They are, indeed, the aim of the investments.

The history of an enterprise's economic activity determines how tight the cash constraint will be in various ways. One way is through selection of the labor force. Enterprises that focus on a paternalistic attitude toward their workers, heavily substituting provision of in-kind benefits and social services for cash wages, will obtain a labor force that prefers paternalistic benefits to cash. The labor force may change through recruitment of new workers but especially through the departure from the enterprise of workers who have a strong preference for cash wages or who have greater outside opportunities. The remaining workers are more tolerant of unpaid wages and wages paid in kind. The net result for such an enterprise is that the cash constraint becomes weaker over time. Conversely, an enterprise close to the market that has recruited a labor force with stronger preferences for cash will have a much higher cash constraint.

In the case of the labor force, the individual enterprise's cash constraint is influenced by other enterprises and by the overall economic environment. Thus an enterprise that commits today to reduce its d and move to the market will need more productive workers. It is likely that an enterprise will have to offer higher returns to skill in order to attract such employees. To put it another way, the enterprise will have a less egalitarian wage structure. This will militate against the use of paternalistic benefits. Paternalistic benefits are not easily differentiated and portioned out in different amounts to different workers; they tend to be uniformly distributed. Hence the enterprise that competes for productive workers will tend to emphasize cash wages over in-kind paternalistic benefits.

In short, distance reduction tightens the cash constraint, not only because of the pressure of operating in an external environment in which other enterprises demand cash, but also because inside the enterprise the labor force tends to demand not just higher wages, but also a higher ratio of cash to noncash wages. This suggests that the decisions enterprises make concerning their involvement in the cash economy today determine the costs and benefits of their involvement in the future. There is persistence in these decisions. The decision to invest in reducing d directly implies a tightening of the cash constraint.

Virtual Economy Traps

Our analysis of the investment decision of the enterprise has focused on the role of inherited values of r and d in making subsequent choices. It suggests that a bifurcation of the economy into market-type and relational-type enterprises is possible, but that many enterprises will follow a strategy of engaging in both types of investment. It is important to consider another effect that may cause enterprises to forsake potentially productive opportunities to reduce distance—the reaction of other players.

Consider the case of an enterprise that sees what appears to be an opportunity to invest to expand production that will allow it to earn more of the cash it sorely needs; in other words an opportunity to reduce d. Let us further suppose that the investment is anticipated to be quite profitable: costs are anticipated to fall and cash flow to increase. Is undertaking this investment the smart thing to do? Not if the enterprise is heavily into the r regime. The unwritten contract with the government (and/or Gazprom) is very likely to be contingent on the volume of cash generated by the enterprise.[24] "We have set up this informal arrangement that stipulates the lowest percentage of cash in taxes (or gas payments) we will tolerate," says the government (Gazprom). "But if you turn around and show us that you actually are earning more cash than you claimed, then the deal's off." The fact that undertaking the d-reducing investment could eliminate the favorable benefits of being in the r-regime may offset the putative benefits of the investment. The enterprise may be stuck in a virtual economy trap.[25]

The virtual economy trap arises because undertaking an investment in distance reduction may alter the way an enterprise's suppliers and customers deal with it. If the enterprise could expect prices and delivery terms to be unchanged, it would undertake the investment because it is efficiency enhancing. In the virtual economy, however, such transaction details are not independent of the enterprise's circumstances. If the enterprise is publicly seen to be able to pay in cash, its ability to use soft-goods production to procure inputs may be weakened. Once it has signaled its ability to pay, the enterprise may no longer be able to continue with its informal activities. This is especially the case if the investment in d is not accompanied by sufficient investment in r to offset the change in circumstances. Hence, an

---

24. This argument follows especially if one assumes that Gazprom engages in efficient price discrimination, as do Woodruff (1999) and Guriev and Kvasov (1999). In that case, the ability to purchase gas at the lower price requires the enterprise to persuade Gazprom that it cannot afford the cash price. Our general argument is that relational capital allows the enterprise to purchase gas at the lower price.

25. Ericson and Ickes (2001) demonstrate the existence of the virtual economy trap in a model in which Gazprom is a price-discriminating monopolist. In that model, enterprises that receive cheap energy on the basis of nonmonetary transactions eschew restructuring opportunities that are *ex ante* profitable if such transactions could continue after the investment. The fact that the restructured firm must pay the market price for energy creates the trap.

enterprise must consider the reaction of its partners before undertaking the investment, and this may prove to be an extra hurdle.

Strength in Numbers

The individual enterprise's situation is affected by what other enterprises do. The larger the number of enterprises that operate in the cash economy, the more difficult it is to engage in noncash production. It is harder to find partners willing to accept barter goods or to tolerate nonpayment of bills since they have more alternative customers who will pay cash.

Governments may also be compelled to reduce their sanctions of this system. As barter and offset chains become less common, governments may find that they, too, must rely more on cash to acquire goods and services. This effect on government is hard to judge, since there are countervailing pressures as well. In situations of extremely low monetization of local economies, and, accordingly, dire cash shortages on the part of government, greater payment of cash taxes by some enterprises could possibly relieve the government's pressure on others to pay in cash. Thus the presence of one or a few important "cash cows" in an economy could actually make it possible for others to keep avoiding cash.

This makes it difficult to assess the status of the virtual economy in Russia by looking only at aggregate figures on the shares of cash and of barter. More cash accruing to a few low-d enterprises might help ease the pressure on high-d enterprises to change and shift to the cash (hard goods) regime. If the government, for instance, collects more cash from the cash cow, the virtual economy enterprises may continue as before and even increase their output of soft goods, all the while increasing their losses. Some of the evidence from Russian industry after the post–August 1998 devaluation is consistent with this story. The devaluation brought windfall revenues to export industries such as gas, oil, metals, and precious stones. As a result, aggregate profits in the economy rose. Yet at the same time (in the first half of 1999), the sum of losses recorded by loss-making enterprises also grew.[26]

However, what happens when many enterprises are in the noncash economy? The cost of engaging in noncash activities is likely to be lower for everyone. For instance, in regions where large numbers of enterprises pay their taxes in the form of barter goods or through offset schemes, local governments establish special companies whose sole purpose is to sell or

26. In chapter 9 we present the case study of Sakha (Yakutiya) as a particularly good illustration of the danger of relying on aggregate statistics.

exchange the barter goods on behalf of the government. As the number of enterprises that engage in noncash activities grows, the costs of these transactions diminish.

In short, the arguments about the general effect of the noncash economy on any individual enterprise's cash constraint are inconclusive. It seems likely, however, that at very high rates and at very low rates of demonetization, enterprises find it relatively more costly to buck the tide. That is, when there is a strong majority in one regime or the other, the pressure is strongest on the dissenters to join them. In a possibly large intermediate environment, however, where the economy is not so thoroughly dominated by either the cash economy or the noncash economy, a change in relative prices of the two kinds of goods can have a significant effect on behavior. This suggests that both the "good" equilibrium (a cash economy) and the "bad" equilibrium (a predominantly demonetized economy) are robust.

r-d Space and Policy Evaluation

An important implication of our model is that the response of an enterprise to changes in its environment—changes in public policy, for example—will depend on its position in r-d space. Heterogeneity in circumstances leads to variation in response to different policy interventions. Consider, for example, a credit expansion that reduces interest rates. In a market economy a lower cost of capital would typically lead to increased investment. Many proponents of such policies in Russia argue that the same effect would occur. However, in the virtual economy the response of enterprises will vary with their position in r-d space. Enterprises that lie in quadrant I of figure 4-3 are much more likely to respond to a credit expansion with the kind of increased investment that proponents expect; that is, they would use the opportunity to improve their market position.

What about enterprises that lie in quadrant II of figure 4-3? For these enterprises, the only reason to borrow cash is to relax the cash constraint. An enterprise like Tutayev sells for cash at a loss. If interest rates fall enough, then a Tutayev may borrow to acquire cash rather than sell below cost. Once its cash needs are met, however, it is not likely to borrow further. Such an enterprise has no profitable way to use additional cash to invest in physical capital (to restructure). Indeed, its only possible need for additional cash may be to enhance relational capital—in other words, to commit itself more solidly *not* to restructure. What would such an enterprise do if given more cash from any source, at any arbitrarily low interest rate, even for free? The answer, of course, is that it would invest in relationships. Free—or low-cost—cash for such an enterprise is merely a way of relaxing the cash constraint. It substitutes for cash production. This makes it easier to exist in the noncash regime today and more tempting to remain there in the future. This is clearly the opposite of what would be intended with a policy to make the Russian enterprise sector more viable in the market economy. For that, the goal must be not to *relax*, but to *tighten*, the cash constraint.

Soft Goods Investment

For the most part, we have assumed that enterprises invest in r to enhance relations, which in turn justify continued production of soft goods by making it possible to barter them or use them for tax payments. Enterprises were assumed to have more than enough capacity to *produce* soft goods. They had, after all, the huge production apparatus inherited from the Soviet Union and its command economy. In a significant number of cases, however, enterprises actually have invested in physical capacity to alter their production profile so that they can produce specific barterable goods.[27] This is another example of how the virtual economy can cause enterprises rationally to undertake activities that are socially inefficient.

To fully incorporate the phenomenon of investment in soft-goods capacity into our model we would need to distinguish two types of physical capital investment: capital investment for distance reduction and capital investment for increasing capacity to produce soft goods. The enterprise director would choose among three types of investment: investment in reducing d; investment in r; and investment in soft-goods capacity. This would greatly add to the complexity of the model: we would have to consider how reductions in d affect the cost of investing in soft-goods capacity. And the return on investing in soft-goods capacity would depend on r. Hence, for simplicity, we ignore this latter type of investment, though it could be considered another form of investment in relational capital and combined with it without altering any important conclusions.

Although soft-goods investment can be safely ignored in our model, the phenomenon itself does have an important bearing on economic performance data, since it renders much more ambiguous all official accounting of capital investment in today's Russia. That is, to the extent that some investment in physical capital is aimed at producing more soft goods, the

27. Cf. the discussion on this point in chapter 2, "Chains of Barter," pp. 32–33.

process of modernization of Russian industry may be even worse than the abysmally low official investment figures suggest. At the same time, if the investment goods themselves are soft goods, then the investment is being overvalued. Our reading of the evidence suggests that soft-goods investment is an important phenomenon in Russia today. An important component of capital accumulation is "investment for investment's sake": using up materials received in barter transactions, but having no positive productive impact at all, or worse. It actually contributes to a "negative restructuring" of industry toward even more production of soft goods.[28]

New Entrants

The discussion thus far has implicitly considered only enterprises that carried over from the prereform Soviet era and their endowments of both physical and relational capital as they entered the period of market transition. What about new entrants to the economy, newly created companies?

Start-ups face the same choice as existing enterprises: they can invest in distance reduction or in relational capital. Precisely because they are new enterprises, however, they are less likely to rely on relational capital as a survival strategy than would enterprises with a Soviet legacy. A start-up would tend to find it costly to invest sufficiently in r to make production of soft goods a profitable strategy. There are exceptions of course.[29] For example, an individual manager may have extraordinary personal or political ties with a local government or even the federal government. Even this may be insufficient, however. The kind of relational capital required usually involves more than just close personal relations between an individual manager and a single influential government figure. It depends on the status of the enterprise itself, its workers, its history in the community, and perhaps its past products (especially if they were prestigious goods, such as defense or space products). Moreover, it is more likely that the individual whose personal (not enterprise specific) relational capital was large enough to ensure the survival of an industrial enterprise would find it much more rewarding to invest that relational capital in a company that produces marketable goods or services, for instance in the financial or resource sector.

Because of these barriers to entry into the r-regime, the distribution of new firms will tend to be concentrated in the southwest region of r-d space.

28. Among the sources supporting this conclusion is Khalin (1999).

29. The most important exception, of course, would be "daughter companies" and other affiliates of existing enterprises that are set up to launder revenues and are not really new enterprises at all.

The typical new firm will produce hard goods and have fairly modest amounts of relational capital. The presumed concentration of new entrants into the southwest quadrant of r-d space represents an important feature of transition. In developed market economies, a sample of new entrants would presumably resemble closely the firms that already exist. In a transition economy, however, the distribution of new entrants differs greatly from that of the incumbents. They are likely to be concentrated in a small number of sectors of the economy—particularly the consumer goods and service sectors, which suffered from underinvestment during Soviet times—and they are likely to be much smaller on average as well.

The fact that the new entrants are low-d enterprises is why some analysts suggest that new entry rather than privatization of existing assets is the key to success in transition.[30] Poland is typically held up as an example of the success of this strategy. The argument is usually couched in terms of the difficulty of changing behavior in enterprises that were previously owned by the state. But this approach takes differences in the initial conditions of transition economies as irrelevant. We say that those differences—especially the relative size of the value-destroying sector—are critical. To support a value-destroying sector of the economy, value-producing sectors—including new entrants—must be taxed. This suggests that the larger is the share of output that is produced by high-d enterprises in any transition economy, the lower will be the rate of new entry. The virtual economy is a major inhibition to new entry. New businesses are not so much an alternative to the virtual economy as a victim of it. To encourage new entry it is thus critical to reduce the virtual economy's tax on value production.

30. See, for instance, Murrell (1992).

CHAPTER FIVE

Evolution of the Virtual Economy

Even though its roots can be traced back to the Soviet era, the virtual economy did not emerge fully developed at the onset of reform. Rather, it represents an adaptation to the changes in the economic environment brought about by the course of economic reform. Understanding the nature of economic reform policies in Russia—in particular the misconceptions that underlay the approach to reform known as "shock therapy"—is thus key to understanding the evolution of the virtual economy.

Shock Therapy and the Nature of Economic Reform

There has been endless debate about the appropriateness of shock therapy versus gradualism in Russia's economic reform.[1] Shock therapy was intended to force a change in enterprise behavior by means of a sudden and sharp intervention into the economy through a package of policy measures that included price liberalization, hardening of budget constraints, and price stabilization effected through tight monetary policies. With hindsight, almost everyone agrees that the results of economic reform efforts in Russia are disappointing, but they disagree about the reasons why. Critics of shock therapy maintain that a more gradual approach to economic reform

1. See Stiglitz (1999) and Aslund (1999) for a recent version of this debate.

would have been better suited for Russia. Shock therapy's proponents counter that shock therapy was never actually implemented.

We do not intend to enter into this debate except to argue that both sides miss a crucial point. While they argue over details, the shock therapists and the gradualists share the same technical approach to the reform problem—namely, they focus on the pace and sequencing of reform rather than on its fundamental nature—and they shared a fundamental misconception: that former Soviet enterprises could be transformed into "normal" firms. Shock therapists, on the one hand, believed that this would be rather easy, as they viewed Soviet-type enterprises as typical capitalist firms encumbered by political controls. The notion was that without government control, and with hard budget constraints, enterprises in Russia would behave like their capitalist counterparts.[2] Gradualists, on the other hand, argued that this would take more time, as collateral institutions had to be created for these "firms" to operate. Neither side questioned that these collections of assets could be successfully transformed into viable companies.[3] The debates were over the modalities of accomplishing this transformation. It thus seems logical that reformers viewed the transition through a technical lens. This induced them to think that the proper way to influence enterprises was through the budget constraint.

Reform Viewed through the Prism of the Budget Constraint

The natural way for economists to conceptualize economic reform, and the effects of reform on behavior, is to focus attention on the bottom line, the budget constraint. The budget constraint stipulates that an enterprise's costs of doing business (including the cost of inputs and supplies, debt repayments, and capital costs) must not exceed the sum of its own revenues plus borrowed funds, or:

$$\text{Revenues} - \text{cost of inputs} - \text{debt repayment} - \text{investment} + \text{borrowing} \geq 0.[4]$$

2. This was articulated clearly by some of the key architects of Russian privatization. For example, Boycko, Shleifer, and Vishny (1995, p. 65) argued: "In our view, controlling managers is not nearly as important as controlling politicians, since managers' interests are generally much closer to economic efficiency than those of the politicians."

3. Murrell (1991) was the notable exception, although his concern was more with the behavioral routines within the enterprise and the difficulty of changing them. He tended to downplay, or dismiss, the issue of fundamental lack of competitiveness.

4. Technically, this is the *cash flow* constraint of the enterprise. Any enterprise that can meet this constraint is liquid and is also likely to be solvent. However, the converse is not necessarily true. An enterprise that cannot meet its cash flow constraint can still be sol-

This view assumes that a profit-maximizing firm will respond to tightening of its budget constraint either by reducing costs or by increasing revenues. The goal of market reform is to force the enterprise to do just that. This presumes that the budget constraint has already been hardened. In Soviet-type economies budget constraints were soft: if revenues did not cover costs, credits were issued, ex post, to cover the difference.[5] Thus to focus attention on the bottom line, the first step in reform is to harden the budget constraint.[6] Formally, this means that ex-post subsidies to bail out enterprises must be eliminated.[7] Once budget constraints are hardened, it is possible to influence enterprise behavior by *tightening* the budget constraint, for example, by raising taxes or increasing the cost of credits.

---

vent if it can borrow against future income, that is, if it has positive net worth—the present value of its assets exceed its liabilities. The problem for Russian enterprises is that underdeveloped financial markets make it hard (impossible) to borrow against future income. An illiquid enterprise thus may not be able to meet the constraint because of current inability to borrow against future income. The illiquid enterprise will then become insolvent because it cannot realize the value of its assets. To speak of insolvency we need to compare the present value of revenues with the present value of expenses. We can write the value of the enterprise as

$$V_t = \sum_{s=t}^{\infty} \left(\frac{1}{1+r} \right)^{s-t} \left[P_s Y(K_s, L_s) - w_s L_s - P_{I,s} I_s - c(I_s, K_s) \right],$$

where r is the rate of interest; P_s is the price of output, Y; K and L are capital and labor, respectively; w_s is the wage at period s; I is investment and P_I its price; and $c(I, K)$ is the installation function. Notice that in this simple formulation there are no material costs of production, though they could easily be added. Solvency of an enterprise requires that the present value in the above expression be nonnegative.

5. See Kornai (1992). Berglof and Roland (1998) note that "hardening budget constraints has . . . not surprisingly, been one of the main challenges of reform in transition" (p. 18). They note that in most of the early literature on transition, "hardening of budget constraints is perceived as a purely exogenous action chosen by policymakers" (p. 19). Following the work of Dewatripont and Maskin (1995), Berglof and Roland focus on problems of commitment. "Hardening of budget constraints thus means creating conditions for a credible commitment not to refinance an agent" (p. 20). This approach emphasizes the role of moral hazard in creating soft budget constraints; if only agents can be induced to supply high effort, the problem will go away.

6. A typical statement is from a World Bank report on Russia: "The first step in transition is to move from the centrally planned regime of transfers and subsidies to one that allows for risk, ensures financial discipline, and creates strong, profit-oriented incentives." World Bank (1996, p. 45). However, as other observers have pointed out, imposing hard budget constraints would result in widespread open unemployment. See, for instance, Leitzel (1995, p. 75).

7. As we will see, budget constraints can be hardened formally yet remain soft in practice if enterprises can find alternative means of survival, via the exploitation of relational capital.

When the budget constraint is tightened, how can the enterprise respond? Several strategies can be pursued to relieve the pressure. First, the enterprise can improve efficiency, which will increase the amount of output that it can obtain from given inputs. Second, it can reduce the amount of inputs purchased, although this may also reduce revenue if the inputs are needed for production. Third, the enterprise may increase sales through better marketing, thus obtaining a better price for output. Fourth, it can forgo investment, but if its capital depreciates, this will have long-run consequences for production, since the capital stock in period $t + 1$ will be lower than in period t. This strategy is clearly popular among many Russian enterprises. Finally, the enterprise can borrow, if credit is available and if the enterprise can transform itself—or give promise of such a transformation—so as to make it more attractive to investors. Borrowing today, however, implies that the cost of repayment of debt will be higher in future periods.

All of the above measures are generally part of "restructuring." The notion of the budget constraint can be amended to account for other positive and negative factors, such as the availability of subsidies and the role of taxes. These other approaches involve actually "softening" the budget constraint. In that case, lobbying to obtain subsidies or failing to pay taxes would be added to the enterprise's repertoire of potential strategies for relaxing the budget constraint. By the same logic, policymakers (reformers) who are interested in forcing the enterprise to restructure can harden the budget constraint by eliminating subsidies and collecting taxes more strictly. They thereby force the enterprise to meet the budget constraint through market methods.

In sum, the essential elements of economic reform in Russia were designed to operate via the budget constraint. Privatization was regarded as an essential reform measure because, by transferring the cash rights of the enterprise to the owners, it would induce the owners to focus on the bottom line. Eliminating subsidies was crucial to induce enterprises to relax the budget constraint by market means. All of these policies that embodied the idea of "reform via the budget constraint" were thus based on the assumption that ultimately there is only one way to survive: earn profits. If the enterprise cannot earn profits, it will not survive. Hence, any policy measures that tightened the budget constraint—thus making it harder to earn profits—would force enterprises to increase efficiency. The idea was that, despite the initial hardship imposed, potentially viable enterprises would survive and be even stronger as a result. The image suggested is that of a vaccine, which introduces minute amounts of a virus in order to trigger the immune system of a healthy organism to produce antibodies so as to protect it in the event of a full-scale exposure to that same virus.[8] The rationale for tightening budget constraints is that it is an attempt to stress the economic organism—the enterprise—to induce it to restructure its behavior to prepare to meet future challenges, thus increasing its long-term viability.

Monotonicity

The type of measure described above will initially weaken *all* enterprises when it takes effect. The assumption is that the potentially most viable enterprises will respond favorably, by restructuring, while the nonviable ones will be wiped out. In other words, the negative effects of the measure on the enterprise are correlated with the enterprise's inefficiency: the less potentially viable the enterprise, the bigger the shock. This is a specific assumption about reform policy that we will refer to as *monotonicity* of reform. Monotonicity was a critical assumption for reformers. It is also a logical consequence of their conventional view that reform (as discussed in chapter 3) is unidimensional: it only involves reducing market distance, d. But when enterprises are viewed in a multidimensional space—as is the case once the role of relational capital is recognized—monotonicity is no longer an automatic property of reform policies. In this case policies may have unintended consequences.

An example is the effect of one classic reform measure, an increase in tax collection, either by higher rates or by stricter enforcement of existing taxes. If reforms are monotonic, this measure is supposed to work as follows. Let $\bar{d}$ be the cutoff point for the viability of an enterprise: that is, all enterprises with $d > \bar{d}$ are not financially viable.[9] A tax crackdown will tighten the budget constraint for all enterprises, reducing each enterprise's competitiveness (compared with the world market), and thus increasing everyone's d. Some previously marginally viable enterprises—ones with market distance d that is barely less than the break-even point, $\bar{d}$—will be pushed into nonviability. These enterprises are the implicit focus of the measures. While all enterprises would feel the pressure, those closest to breakeven would find it easiest to deal with the shock. Proper restructuring would make them viable again, and eventually they would grow stronger as a result of the

8. The danger to be avoided, of course is overprescription. An excessive dose of the vaccine will kill the patient.
9. This implies that reforms are unidimensional; otherwise there is no cut-off level of d.

FIGURE 5-1. Monotonic Reform

1. Shock	Increases everyone's *d*.
2. Reaction	All attempt to reduce *d* (restructure).
3. Result	Bifurcation. Some succeed, are stronger than before (case A). Others die (case B).

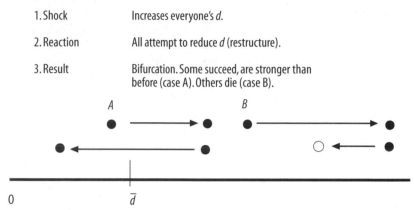

intervention. Meanwhile, more inefficient enterprises would experience a greater shock. The most inefficient might even be wiped out.

This ideal monotonic reform scenario is depicted schematically in figure 5-1. There are two enterprises, *A* and *B*, where enterprise *B* is less efficient than enterprise *A* (in other words, $d_B > d_A$). When the reform measure is implemented, both *A* and *B* are affected negatively; that is, they are pushed to the right. Each responds to the policy by attempting to restructure so as to be profitable despite the negative shock to its bottom line. Enterprise *A* successfully makes it back past the viability cutoff point $(\bar{d})$ and ends up healthier than before the shock. Enterprise *B* does not succeed and dies.

The idea, therefore, is that such a monotonic reform shock has a two-stage effect. The restructuring induced by the shock makes some enterprises even stronger than before the shock. Meanwhile, other enterprises, those that either cannot or do not want to restructure, die. The process also yields double benefits to the economy as a whole. First, the marginally viable enterprises are induced to change themselves to become more robust in the long run. Second, the weakest enterprises are eliminated (bankrupted), freeing up their resources for other uses.

What happens if reforms are not monotonic? That is, what if the reforms do not affect the weakest enterprises most negatively? One way that might happen is if relational capital allows weaker enterprises to survive while stronger ones do not. Suppose, in other words, that we transpose the example in figure 5-1 from unidimensional *d*-space to two-dimensional *r*-*d* space. Suppose further that enterprise *B* has greater relational capital than enterprise A. In other words, $r_B > r_A$.[10] In this case enterprise B's greater relational capital may enable it to avoid or lessen the impact of the reform measure. For example, B may be able to satisfy the tax authorities by using tax offsets. What does this mean? Following Igor's rules 1 and 2 ("Try to have offsets with federal and local governments"), B's director would not want to cease production of his so-called soft goods—the very goods that are responsible for B's large distance to the market. Soft goods can be used to pay taxes, and it is cheaper to produce them than to restructure to produce cash goods and pay taxes in monetary form. The presence of the tax offset opportunity is a disincentive to restructuring, even for the enterprises that potentially could restructure.

Therefore, B does not restructure. Worse: it may not exit, either. As we noted in chapter 3, many enterprises are not merely inefficient—and thus not responsive to changes in organizational incentives—but fundamentally noncompetitive. An enterprise with a noncompetitive capital stock may not be able to restructure.[11] Such an enterprise would prefer to continue to produce soft goods, provided its relational capital is sufficient to ensure a market for such goods.[12]

The key point of this discussion is that in Russia the second dimension—the r-dimension—eliminated monotonicity as a characteristic of reform. Because reforms were not monotonic, survival was not a function simply of fitness along the efficiency dimension. Directors of enterprises that were highly noncompetitive could use relational capital as a means to survive. In this way relational capital subverted the intended effect of the crackdown: the most inefficient enterprises managed to avoid what the more efficient enterprises fell victim to. The inefficient enterprises were not wiped out at all.[13] Instead, completely contrary to intentions, *they* were the ones that adapted their behavior and became more robust.

10. In r-d space, B is located to the northeast of A.
11. Strictly speaking, of course, sufficient investment can make any plant competitive. However, this is not typically a realistic alternative. It may require completely rebuilding the plant, and there is an opportunity cost of resources needed to accomplish this. It would almost always be cheaper to build a new plant than to completely rebuild an old plant. Even though it is always technically feasible to make any plant competitive, it may not be economically practical. The economic consideration is crucial here.
12. Why not just close shop? The reason, as we explain in chapter 7, is that keeping the enterprise open enables insiders to siphon off the cash flow.
13. Moreover, if the marginally viable enterprise also has access to relational capital strategies, it may not restructure either, but may instead be pushed to rely on its relational capital.

Mutation and Resistance

We proposed earlier that the idea of monotonic reform suggested a biological or medical comparison, that the reform measure was supposed to act like a vaccine. The picture we have now given of nonmonotonic reform may suggest a further metaphor from biological evolution. The reform policies created a hostile environment. Enterprises looked for all possible resources to survive. Some found that they had resources that others did not. As a result, they underwent a behavioral adaptation. In other words, the changes in the environment did not reinforce the healthy, market-like behavior, but instead induced an adaptation, or mutation, toward nonmarket behavior. Many of the "mutant" enterprises were those least expected to survive on the basis of market strategies. In the end, they became relatively stronger— contrary to the intent, which was to weaken them.

Furthermore, the mutation process also produced a bifurcation of the population of enterprises. The mutant enterprises were able to produce goods that could be used for barter or for tax offsets but that could not be sold on the market. They could procure inputs at a lower cost because relations allowed them to pay with nonmonetary means. However, because the cost of acquiring these extra strategies was lack of transparency, it was impossible for such enterprises to attract external funds for restructuring. Thus the mutant enterprise found it prohibitive to reduce distance, while the market-oriented enterprise could not engage in virtual survival strategies.[14] In other words, the two "species" of enterprises began to progress along distinct evolutionary paths.

Incomplete Therapy

The biological analogy can extend even further. Incomplete shock therapy failed to wipe out loss-making enterprises. Enterprises that chose transparency were at a competitive disadvantage to those that invested in or had initially high relational capital. Shock therapy was supposed to affect enterprises through the budget constraint, but those enterprises that had invested in alternative means of survival were less affected by the shock. These enterprises were effectively immune from the therapy, even if the therapy was designed precisely to attack them.

The process bears a relationship to the problem of multi–drug resistant (MDR) tuberculosis (TB). MDR strains of TB are never found in the wild.

14. In practice the boundary is rarely so sharp. Recall "Igor's Rules" for successful enterprise management in Russia.

Genetic resistance to particular drugs occurs naturally, but this is diluted by the overwhelming prevalence of drug-susceptible organisms. In the natural environment there is no evolutionary advantage to genetic resistance to antimicrobials that are introduced by man. The presence of antimicrobials provides the selective pressure for resistant organisms to become predominant. Human intervention that introduces antimicrobials creates the selective pressure in favor of MDR. The primary mechanism by which this happens is an *incomplete* regimen of treatment (or poor adherence to a proper regimen). The incomplete regimen wipes out the drug-susceptible organisms, leaving the field for the drug-resistant varieties.

The analogy with enterprise behavior is straightforward. In a competitive environment there is no selective advantage to investing in relational capital. Reducing market distance is the key to viability.[15] Incomplete therapy in Russia, however, did not create such a competitive environment. Rather, relational capital continued to yield a positive payoff in terms of enterprise fitness and survival. For enterprises possessing sufficient relational capital, the opportunity to survive by using virtual economy strategies became a viable option. The burden of therapy was on the enterprises that did not have or chose not to invest in relational capital. Incomplete therapy thus imposed a *relative* burden on enterprises that chose to act in a "normal" manner. Hence, incompleteness provided selective pressure that favored the mutant enterprises, so they proliferate. This is similar to what happens with the tuberculosis virus when patients do not take the full complement of anti-TB drugs or fail to follow a multidrug regimen.[16]

Behavioral Adaptation

In the biological world evolution relies solely on relative fitness. The proportion of mutants is limited by the frequency of mutation. In social evolution, however, change can occur not just through replication but through adaptation.[17] Enterprises can *imitate* behavior that they observe to be successful. If some enterprises are able to survive without undertaking

15. Firms in normal market economies do, of course, invest in relational capital (see chapter 3, p. 62). Hence there must be advantages to doing so. Our point here, however, is that in a healthy economy, attempting to compensate for high d by investing in relational capital is risky. If an enterprise is noncompetitive, investing in relations may bring short-term advantages, but it is a fundamentally unsustainable strategy. Witness the case of Enron in the United States.

16. In fighting TB it is crucial to follow a multidrug regimen because the virus mutates sufficiently that a unitary drug regimen is ineffective.

17. This has been studied in different contexts by Boyd (1997) and Young (1998).

costly restructuring, then other enterprises may choose to emulate this behavior. Thus, once virtual economy strategies appear to be working, the system may rapidly tip.

The speed at which this process unfolds depends on the pattern of interaction among enterprises. Conservatively, one could model the adaptive (imitative) process with the assumption that enterprises were equally likely to interact with any type of enterprise. Payoffs are determined solely on the basis of population frequencies for the economy as a whole. One could argue, however, that enterprises may be more likely to interact with like-minded enterprises. For instance, enterprises in the production sector tend to interact with the same enterprises that they dealt with under central planning. This could lead to further bifurcation. If agents tend to interact with like-minded agents, this may reinforce behavior.[18] The payoff to being a virtual enterprise increases in interaction with other virtual enterprises.[19] This suggests that the presence of nonrandom interactions could strengthen the virtual economy trap.

Policy Ineffectiveness

This evolutionary analysis can illustrate the feedback effects of policy measures designed to induce restructuring. Two examples—improved financial transparency and tight money—make the point. Because these two policies were applied to mutant enterprises, the policies did not merely fail to have the intended effect. They produced results opposite to those intended.

Transparency

An essential element of market reform is that enterprises should make their financial activities more transparent. For the enterprises, there was an implicit bargain here: greater transparency would be rewarded by greater access to credit. Financial markets require transparency, as does foreign investment. Of course, transparency also makes the enterprise's problems more apparent. However, if the only way to obtain external financing is to take the plunge to greater transparency, then the enterprise will choose this costly option.

18. For example, Young (1998, chap. 6) has shown that if agents interact in sufficiently small, closely knit groups, then the expected waiting time until the evolutionary process comes close to its asymptotic distribution is bounded independently of the number of agents or of the initial state.

19. See appendix E for an analysis of the virtual economy as an evolutionary game.

If reforms were monotonic, then policy measures designed to increase transparency would have unambiguously positive results. The move to greater transparency would have the greatest benefits for enterprises that are closest to the market. Hence, the fitness of the most efficient enterprises would be enhanced relative to that of loss-making enterprises. In the virtual economy, where reforms are not monotonic, this is not the case. When relational capital is available for a survival strategy, those enterprises that chose transparency may be relatively disadvantaged, for two reasons. First, since lack of transparency is the veil that protects the value of relational capital, transparency precludes the use of strategies that rely on relational capital. Second, transparency is essentially irreversible. Once the enterprise has revealed its true financial state, it cannot retract the information.

This argument has important implications for discussions of the role of corporate governance. It has become almost commonplace to point out that inadequate corporate governance is a severe problem in Russia, one that inhibits investment, especially foreign investment.[20] This is an important argument, but it is critical to keep in mind that the opposite is also true: the low probability of attracting external finance inhibits the development of good corporate governance. Clearly, enterprises with very high d see little benefit from improving corporate governance. Since the expected return for such enterprises is so low, they are unlikely to attract external financing, no matter how transparent they are. Indeed, transparency works against them. Meanwhile, other enterprises that have somewhat lower d know that transparency is likely to expose them to increased relative tax incidence. Hence they are particularly sensitive to any decrease in the probability (or increase in the cost) of obtaining external finance. If interest rates are high, as they were especially in the early phase of the Russian transition, these enterprises may find that the return to good corporate governance is simply too low relative to the risks.

In sum, transparent enterprises do not receive the intended benefit, but they pay the cost in terms of foreclosing the use of relational strategies. Those enterprises that choose transparency will be more vulnerable than before. Hence, enterprises led by directors who fully understand the connection between good corporate governance and external finance may *choose* not to seek outside investment because the benefits are not sufficient.

20. See, for example, Blasi, Kroumova, and Kruse (1997, pp. 176–81) for a discussion of the problems of corporate governance on the prospects of attracting investment. This issue was also taken up by Stiglitz (1999).

Tight Money

A second example of a policy that is rendered ineffective by the existence of mutant enterprises using virtual economy strategies is tight money. When credit is lax, there is less pressure on enterprises to restructure. Therefore, measures to tighten credit—the argument goes—will force enterprises to reform. Again, however, the existence of relational capital changes this. Enterprises that invest in relational capital insulate themselves against credit shocks. Tight money then has greater relative impact on those enterprises that invested in reducing distance. The "fitness" of the latter enterprises is reduced relatively by the tight money policy.

A key point for Russia is that the importance of relational capital and of networks of relationships among enterprises preceded the imposition of tight money. Thus when tight money was imposed, resort to virtual strategies (use of relational capital) caused the policy to be ineffective. Tight money penalized the wrong enterprises. The transition process was perturbed by the tightening of credit during 1995 and the introduction of the so-called ruble corridor. This induced a mutation in enterprise behavior. In particular, monetary tightening reinforced barter—a phenomenon that clearly preceded the tightening of credit—and gave a relative advantage to those whose relations were sufficient to support barter. Lack of liquidity may have induced enterprises to engage in nonmonetary behavior. Once this mutation occurred, the stability of virtual behavior implied that barter would persist even if the initial conditions that shocked the system were no longer present.[21]

Was There Any Alternative?

Was there any alternative to shock therapy? Perhaps, but it was not gradualism. If it was wrong to practice shock therapy on organisms that had the resources to avoid its consequences, a more gradual introduction of the therapy would, if anything, have facilitated the negative adaptation. Logically, the only alternative would have been a conscious and concerted effort to prevent the adaptive behavior, specifically, to prohibit the use of relational capital. This, of course, did not happen. The reason it did not was a con-

21. This account fits with some recent empirical work that studies barter. Commander and Mumssen (1998) and Morozov, Pinto, and Drebentsov (2000), for example, argue that barter became widespread in Russia in response to the monetary tightening of 1994–95. Yet, as demonstrated in Guriev and Ickes (2000), barter does not seem to be related to the financial position of the enterprise. The latter study also shows that there is a lock-in effect of barter: once enterprises use barter it is cheaper to continue.

straint on economic behavior we call "impermissibility." Impermissibility is key to understanding why relational capital could have the power it does in Russia, and thus why the virtual economy emerged.

Impermissibility

To illustrate the notion of impermissibility, consider one specific aspect of enterprise restructuring: divestiture of social assets. Soviet enterprises were social as well as economic enterprises. They were responsible for housing, child care, health, and many other social activities. It has long been thought that a critical step in restructuring was for the enterprise to divest itself of these assets, either by handing them over to the local government ("municipalization") or by letting the social service organizations operate as independent businesses. Although divestiture policies have been encouraged by the World Bank and other western agencies and officially proclaimed by the Russian government, they have not been successful. Why?

The problem was that once the assets were divested, where would the resources come from to support these services? In principle, the enterprise can be taxed an amount equal to the costs it incurred before divestiture. The actual amount of tax revenues available, however, is unlikely to cover the cost of services. Since divestiture does not immediately cause productivity to rise in the enterprise, it does not raise enterprise profits that can be taxed to support the social assets. Meanwhile, divestiture will entail added up-front costs. A separate new administration must be created for each category of services.

If the economy were monetized and the operation of social assets were paid out of tax revenue rather than via enterprise support, then taxes would have to be levied on the rest of the economy (the low-d sector) to pay for housing, schools, and other services previously provided by the enterprise. Those taxes would likely depress the private sector, eventually leaving even less tax revenue. In short, social assets could not be effectively split off because there would be insufficient resources to keep them operating. Therefore, because total collapse of the social sector was impermissible, true divestiture was impossible. What did happen was the following. Nominally, the assets were divested and handed over to the local government. But governments, starved of funds, were unable to maintain the services. The consumers of the services were the enterprise employees and their dependents. They, more than the community at large, were affected by the failure of the divested social sector. Since the enterprise could not tolerate the failure of the social services, in actuality the enterprise remained responsible for them. In return, the local government allowed the enterprise to credit its social spending against its tax bill. Thus this was not real divestiture; it was only the *pretense* of divestiture. The important principle is that for the enterprise, its work force (and community), and local government, real divestiture was impermissible: it would have led to an unacceptable situation because adequate resources were not available to support the services outside the enterprise itself.

A Different Kind of Constraint

Impermissibility is, as we have said, a limitation on economic behavior, a constraint that affects the outcomes of policies. It is not, however, an economic constraint. In economic analysis, preferences and technology are considered fundamental constraints that govern what is feasible. Our notion of impermissibility is not fundamental in that particular sense. Impermissibility is determined by what is socially and politically acceptable: what society allows. It is about the prevailing values and norms in society, the "rules of the game." Economic constraints are system neutral. Impermissibility constraints are system dependent. Just as with economic constraints, however, impermissibility governs what is feasible. Thus, for any economy, what is feasible is determined by the intersection of three sets of constraints: tastes, technology, and what is socially and politically *permissible*.

Impermissibility must also be distinguished from another form of social/political constraint on policies, which we can refer to as "inconceivability." Certain actions or policies are inconceivable because they are logically inconsistent with other, more highly prioritized policies (or with the system as a whole). An example would be trying to introduce private property in a socialist planned economy. This is not done because it is simply inconsistent *in principle, fundamentally*, with the prevailing system.[22]

There is another important difference between impermissibility and inconceivability. In the latter case, it is the *policies* themselves that are unthinkable. With regard to impermissibility, the policies are not unthink-

22. Usually this fundamental incompatibility is recognized in advance, and therefore the policy is never attempted. There have, however, been occasions when the incompatibility may not have been understood until it was too late, such as East Germany's tearing down the Berlin Wall. Free movement of people between East and West Germany was not allowed after 1961 because it was obvious that it would mean the end of the East German communist system. When free movement was allowed again in 1989, at least some East Germans thought it would be compatible with a "reformed" socialism. It was not, and it instead almost instantly brought about the end of the socialist system in the East.

able. Quite the contrary, they are often fully consistent with the prevailing system. This is exactly the case with divestiture of social assets. This program is fully consistent with Russia's overall goal of privatization and the development of a liberal market economy. Indeed, it was considered to be a necessary step to enhance the market value of enterprises. The social and political *consequences* of this move, however, were intolerable, owing to the inadequate resource base outside of the enterprise to support social services.

Another Example: Privatization

The impermissibility constraint affected other key reform policies. Privatization of state assets was another case in which the intolerable consequences of a policy clashed with its stated intent. In principle, Russia's privatization program was simple. It demarcated the nation's formerly state-owned assets into specific bundles and assigned ownership to them. This was a very different process than privatization of state-owned property in a market economy. In a market economy, even state companies have a market valuation. But in Russia, privatization—redistribution of ownership of assets—was taking place at the same time as liberalization—revaluation of those assets.

When the drive to privatize state-owned property was launched in post-Soviet Russia, few Russians had a clear idea of their own true value in a market economy. A main reason was that, as explained in chapter 3, the Soviet pricing system concealed the true value of production and thus of all the various assets in the economy. This effect was enhanced by the predominance of the so-called shadow economy in the Soviet Union. The cascade of informal, under-the-table payments that had spread through the Soviet system—the loot chain—meant that the income of a typical person was a convolution of formal and informal activity. As a result, most Russians had no idea how they would fare in a liberalized economy. They did not know how liberalization would affect either the formal economy or the loot chain.

As a result of this overwhelming uncertainty about the outcome for each individual, privatization in Russia was tantamount to giving everyone a lottery ticket. People did not know whether they had won, and what they had won, until later. As it turned out, this lottery was to have very few winners and many, many losers. In retrospect, this is not so surprising, because we know that wealth creation in the Soviet economy was concentrated in a relatively few sectors: oil, natural gas, and nonferrous metals were the most prominent. These were handed over to a small number of individuals.

The rest of the citizens received pieces of various other industries, most of which would turn out to have little value.

The Privatization Lottery

A stylized version of the privatization lottery will illustrate this process. Assume that at the point when the privatization program was launched, there was only one company that would be profitable in postcommunist, market Russia: Gazprom. In other words, the lottery has only this one winning ticket. Every other ticket, conveying ownership rights in every other company, is a loser. Suppose further that after the privatization lottery has been held, the government strictly and completely enforces this outcome. That is, the winner's ticket is redeemed, the prize is awarded, and the winner's rights are guaranteed absolutely. Moreover, the government makes no attempt at further redistribution—in other words, the lottery prize is "tax free." The shareholders of Gazprom have all the valuable assets, and everyone else holds assets with no market value. This is a pure winner-take-all model of asset distribution. We will describe it as the lottery distribution, or L-distribution.

Of course, there are many possible alternatives to the L-distribution. The extreme opposite case to the L-distribution of this allegory would be one in which the government broke up Gazprom in such a way that its assets were equally distributed to every Russian citizen. Call this perfectly equal distribution the E-distribution. As designed, Russia's privatization scheme was in principle the L-distribution. However, Russian society was unwilling to accept the consequences of the L-distribution once it became clear what had happened. The revelation had less to do with realizing that the Gazprom ticket was a winner; that was no secret. More important was the recognition that so many others were losers.[23]

Our purpose here is not to offer an alternative scheme for privatizing Russia's assets.[24] Instead we are concerned with the implications of the way privatization was, in fact, implemented. The key point to recognize is that in this process the political and social reality of Russia expressed itself. Two

23. The privatization program was not intended to be literally a winner-take-all lottery. In reality, however, it ended up being nearly so.

24. The basic issue at stake in the difference between the L-distribution and the E-distribution is the trade-off between equity and efficiency. Because the L-distribution reflects the market value of the assets, redistribution of value in the virtual economy represents the postponement of reform. Any method of privatization would have to cope with that trade-off.

things were involved. The first was the prevailing notion of equity in Russian society. The second was the existence of relational capital. Both served to make the L-distribution impermissible. If we assume that some minimally acceptable level of inequity existed among the Russian population, it follows that there were limits on how close to the L-distribution the outcome of privatization would be allowed to come. In real-world terms, there were limits on how much value owners of Gazprom could obtain. As a result, there had to be a mechanism to redistribute some of the value produced by Gazprom among the other holders of lottery tickets. As it turned out, that mechanism was relational capital.[25]

By helping redistribute Gazprom's value to value-destroying manufacturing enterprises, the virtual economy was a way of making Russia's privatization lottery more equitable, a means of paying off on more tickets. It is the outcome of a bargaining game between agents in the economy over the value of the lottery tickets. The reason that this game is played is because it is politically impossible to enforce the L-distribution in a democracy in which equity norms differ substantially from those of that extreme winner-take-all outcome. Consequently, Gazprom must pay off other parts of society to retain some share of the value that is produced. This bargain determines where the economy ends up between the L-distribution and the E-distribution.

The bargain, of course, is purely informal. The manufacturing enterprises have no formal rights at all over Gazprom's value. They can exert their interests only via the governments, federal and local. The ability to do so is the essence of the manufacturing plants' relational capital, which allows them to participate in nonpayments, barter, and offsets—all of which are mechanisms for hidden redistribution of value to the value-subtracting manufacturers, ultimately from Gazprom. Although Gazprom has formal owner's rights over the value it produces, those rights are constrained by the refusal of Russian society to recognize the validity of a full-fledged winner-take-all privatization scheme. But the fact that the deal works is testimony to the efficacy of the impermissibility constraint.[26]

25. Some might argue that the lottery analogy is not appropriate because privatization in Russia took place through shady methods—for instance, the loans for shares deal. However, the main point of the argument above is not the process of privatization, but the *resulting distribution* of assets. Loans for shares and other shady deals do not mean that privatization was not a lottery; they only mean that the lottery was rigged. If anything, that would only strengthen the motivation for a more equitable redistribution away from the winner-take-all result.

26. The notion of the privatization lottery as a model of asset distribution in Russia was first presented in Gaddy and Ickes (1999, pp. 90–91). Although they do not refer to

In sum, privatization of state-owned enterprises as a policy was an essential component of Russia's self-imposed imperative to introduce a free market economy. What was impermissible was not the *policy*, but (some of) the *consequences* of that policy. As the desired policy began to be implemented, it became apparent that it was going to have effects that simply could not be tolerated. In principle, one reaction might have been to reject the policy in toto. That was not done, because rejecting a policy such as privatization (or divestiture of enterprise social assets) would have been tantamount to turning down the imperative of introducing free markets. Therefore, the appearance of the policy was retained while its actual substance was modified.

Why Not Open Subsidization?

For the sake of completeness, we ought also to consider another possible reaction to the case of impermissibility. Since it is the consequences of the policy, and not the policy itself, that are impermissible, might there be a way to implement the policy but correct its unacceptable consequences in ways that are not inconsistent with the policy? Take the case of the privatization lottery. Could not the Russian government have let the winner-take-all L-distribution take place but corrected the impermissible result—extreme inequity—by heavily taxing Gazprom and subsequently redistributing the proceeds? Such a policy would be acceptable in a market economy. In strict accounting terms, the two approaches—(1) "L-distribution + a transparent tax on Gazprom" (L/T) and (2) "L-distribution + virtual economy" (L/V)—could achieve the same final result, namely subsidization of the losers in the lottery. Why did that (L/T) not happen?

First, nearly all segments of Russian society refused to acknowledge the nature of the lottery. They did not want to admit that Gazprom was the only winning ticket. They wanted to believe that the rest of the economy was valuable as well—or at least soon and relatively easily could be made

the virtual economy hypothesis, Shleifer and Treisman (2000, pp. 76–77) make a similar argument about the relationship between Russia's energy producers and the rest of the economy, referring to it as an "implicit bargain." They note that it "continued the subsidization of chronically unprofitable but politically important enterprises and public services without requiring either increased monetary emission or a more effective tax service. . . . The result . . . was an economy of 'zombies.' Thousands of inefficient enterprises, starved of cash or long-term hope of improvement, still managed to hang on in a strange kind of limbo, no matter how clearly their balance sheets indicated that they were in fact 'dead.'" Their explanation for the energy sector's willingness to play: export privileges, tax exemptions, and protection of ownership privileges.

to be. Relational capital, the mechanism that allows loss-making manufacturing enterprises to be subsidized by Gazprom in a nontransparent way, upholds the pretense that many manufacturing enterprises are much better off than they actually are. If there were transparent subsidies (the L/T option), it would be apparent to all not only that Gazprom is supporting the rest of the economy, but to what extent it does so. It would also be evident that *all* of the wealth redistributed from Gazprom is going only to certain loss-making manufacturing enterprises and that, as a consequence, other parts of society get little or none. Lack of transparency makes it easier to maintain the status quo because it hides the fundamental resource transfer that supports the system.

Second, there was again the problem of the loot chain. Individual incomes were such a web of formal and nontransparent informal mechanisms that no one knew exactly how his or her final welfare status was being generated. Therefore, even if the government had wanted to use the L/T option to maintain everyone's status quo, it was impossible to know how to do it.[27]

A final and fundamental reason for not adopting the L/T system was that redistribution of value through its open and transparent subsidization would have been too big a threat to too much *existing* relational capital. In effect, the L/V structure for redistribution was already in place at the time the lottery was held. It was based on production relationships. Inputs, outputs, provision of social services—the entire society, formal and informal, functioned according to these very relations. Cities were based on manufacturing plants; their raison d'être was production. Moreover, relational capital did not belong only to the directors. It—or rather the value it commanded—was shared with workers and with other members of the community, who benefited when the plant maintained the hospitals,

___

27. This argument focuses on the role of uncertainty over the distribution of value in the Russian economy and on the implications of this uncertainty for predicting the individual-specific effects of reforms. The delay in adopting efficiency-enhancing reforms has been studied widely in the economics literature. One important analysis focuses on the status quo bias. This arises from incomplete information about what will happen to the individual once reform has taken place. In this book, we depart from the standard model of status quo bias, where agents know their current incomes but are uncertain of their incomes in the reformed state. We argue that Russia today differs from that case because of the extra degree of noise. Not only is there uncertainty about what incomes would be in the wake of reform, but also agents have only a noisy signal of their current productivity. The loot chain means that current incomes do not necessarily reveal productivities. This adds to the status quo bias because reform will bring about nonmarginal changes.

schools, roads, and so on. Abolishing relational capital would have involved a gigantic, monumental—but involuntary—exchange of assets/value.[28]

Relationship to Rent Seeking

How does this argument relate to the notion of rent seeking? The distinction between value redistribution through open subsidization, on the one hand, and the nontransparent mechanisms of the virtual economy, on the other, is important for understanding the peculiar nature of the virtual economy. It is often argued that the contest for rents in Russia is the barrier to reform. Because the political system has rents to distribute, entrepreneurs focus on influence rather than on restructuring. Rent seeking is destructive because agents undertake activities that waste resources in order to obtain already produced value.

Exploitation of relational capital is a form of rent seeking, but a distinctive form. Like classic forms of rent seeking, it results in wasted resources and is used to redistribute value that is produced elsewhere. The particular difference is that in the case of relational capital the waste of resources is the production, specifically the production of value-destroying goods, that takes place through its use. Relational capital is the continuation of the right to appropriate inputs and the right to dispose of ("sell") output under the Soviet system. Therefore the way relational capital was realized in the post-communist economy inevitably meant that as much of the old structure was preserved as possible.[29]

From the standpoint of the entire system of the virtual economy, the criterion for permissibility of practices is the survival of production of soft goods, which allows the plants to remain in operation. This defines a difference between different types of looting, or corruption. Russian journalist

28. Another way of stating this is that Russians refused to pay for their tickets in the privatization lottery. As it was designed, people were supposed to pay. Citizens were in effect asked to blindly hand over the wealth commanded by their existing relational capital in exchange for a chance at winning the lottery. They did not do that; they accepted the lottery ticket, but did not pay for it in advance. They kept their relational capital (their place in the loot chain). When they saw the lottery ticket was a loser, they threw the ticket away and did not pay for it—that is, they stuck to the old system of distribution of value.

29. Another difference between use of relational capital, on the one hand, and a classic scheme of rent seeking, on the other, is that the owner of relational capital must exploit it before others use theirs; otherwise, all value will be dissipated. Since you may lose your relational capital if market reform succeeds, you need to act to prevent this from happening.

Yuliya Latynina made the classic observation that it is a mistake to think that Russian directors are divided into those who steal and those who don't steal. They are divided into those who steal *from* the plant and those who steal *for* the plant.[30] That is, there is theft, or "looting," that threatens the viability of the plant in the virtual economy, but there are also the necessary forms of theft—illegal appropriation of value—that keep the system going. All of this suggests that it is important to examine the relationship between corruption and the virtual economy.

Relational Capital and Corruption

Russia is unquestionably plagued by extreme levels of corruption, as shown in the latest World Development Report and by events like the Bank of New York scandal. The virtual economy does not pretend to explain the extraordinary scope of corruption in the Russian economy, but there is a connection.

A first and most obvious way in which the virtual economy facilitates corruption is its nontransparency. Virtual accounting—that is, accounts based on bilaterally negotiated and usually inflated prices—offers an ideal situation for looting a value-destroying enterprise.[31] As important as nontransparency is, however, it is still only a technical reason why corruption would be expected to be widespread in the virtual economy. Lack of transparency makes corruption easier. In fact, however, the important connection is that corruption is essential for the working of the virtual economy.

In many ways, the virtual economy and corruption by enterprise directors are inseparable. One could not work without the other. Corruption in this sector could not be sustainable on the scale it has attained without the context of nontransparent transactions and infusion of value into the sector through the virtual economy. In the loss makers, there would be nothing to steal unless the virtual economy continued to operate.

This means that corruption at the micro-level, that of the enterprise, is a necessary part of the virtual economy "deal." Keeping value-subtracting

30. Yuliya Latynina, "Treshchina v brilliante" (The crack in the diamond), *Izvestiya*, October 16, 1997.

31. How can anyone steal if there is value destruction? Whether there is value destruction or even loss making is not the issue, however; *cash flow* is. While it may be extremely difficult for the manager of a loss-making enterprise to receive a large salary, or bonuses, or stock dividends, with virtual accounting (that is, only the pretense of profitability), the only necessity is cash flow. This is true for workers as well. Their wages can remain low or can even go unpaid, but they can be allowed to share in the looting to make up for the unpaid wages.

enterprises in operation through the virtual economy is half of the bargain; letting the directors steal is the other. Neither the corruption nor the non-monetary production activity could exist without one another. Seen from one angle (the director's), the plant is nothing but a vehicle through which the director loots. Keeping the plant going is a means to an end—profits for the manager—but those means can in turn be achieved only via a second means: a flow of cash income that is diverted to his pocket. The director could not have access to that hidden (informal) cash flow unless the enterprise were in the soft goods regime. At a minimum, the soft goods regime justifies the continued existence of the plant and, through that, a powerful constituency (the workers, the community) to protect the director. From the other side (that of the workers, their families, their community), the director's looting is tolerated because it is *for them* a means to an end. The director is the individual who can ensure that the enterprise can participate in the virtual economy. Its participation requires his personal relationships.

The enterprise's relational capital thus comprises two complementary parts: the director's and the enterprise's. The director has both personal ties and knowledge of how the system works. Neither is easily transferable to another individual, except perhaps in part to a person whom the incumbent director may designate as his successor, his "crown prince." Meanwhile, as important as those personal ties and knowledge are, they are fairly useless apart from the specific enterprise. Without the enterprise the director has no negative threat of mass unemployment, no alleged prestige in his products (for instance, defense goods). Thus both the director and the workers (families, community) need the soft-goods production regime for their own interests, But neither can implement that regime without the other. This symbiotic association is a disincentive against the director's laying off workers in large numbers. He will not get rid of so many workers that he loses the justification for his enterprise.[32]

Within the enterprise, there is always a latent conflict over the division of cash. The role of government—especially local government—is to be an arbiter. The workers are almost always in the weaker negotiating position.

32. Why would a director in the soft-goods production (relational capital) regime fire any workers at all? The director of a plant operating in the hard-goods production regime would want to shed nonproductive labor, that is, workers whose presence increases the enterprise's market distance. The r-regime director has a similar motive to fire workers whose activity lessens the value of his relational capital. Examples of such workers might be those who demand transparency or in some other way threaten his control over the company. However, such workers would also be a threat to the rest of the work force, who would therefore be inclined to agree with the director that such workers should be fired.

Their threat, though, is present. The situation is especially tense for enterprises close to the viability boundary, that is, those whose relational capital is barely enough to keep them afloat. Theft of too much cash by directors may undermine relational capital. Such practices carry the risk of alienating the government, either directly, because it does not leave enough cash to pay taxes, or indirectly, because nonpayment of wages contributes to social unrest in the community. The rational response of a director who expects to fall below that boundary would be to follow a loot-and-leave policy, stealing as much as possible without regard for the enterprise's survival.

The implication of all this is that as long as the enterprise remains viable in the noncash, soft-goods production realm, there is an optimal level of appropriation of informal profits by the director. There is, in short, a permissible limit to his thievery. The limit is set by the cash constraint, first of all, but also by equity norms and by the bargaining strength of the various sides involved. After all, what the director takes has to come from what might otherwise be used to pay wages and/or taxes.[33] Thus both the government and the workers have an interest in restraining the director's appropriation of the enterprise's cash. The director's bargaining power lies in the threat that he might abandon the enterprise, leaving it with too little relational capital to survive.

What about the bargaining power of the other side? Under what circumstances might the workers rebel against the director? First of all, strikes and protests are not especially common (nor are they rare) among workers, at least not in view of the prevalence of wage arrears. Fully three-quarters of all Russian workers have experienced arrears, but when workers were asked in the fall of 1998 whether they had participated in strikes or other protests at any time in the past three years, positive responses were in the range of 10–16 percent.[34] Among those who did strike, two-thirds said they did so to protest delays in payment or nonpayment of wages. Almost

33. Recall the Karpov Commission's finding that for major Russian enterprises in 1996–97, gross revenues fell far short of the amount needed to pay both the enterprise's wage bill and its tax bill (table B-3 in appendix B, p. 249).

34. One survey conducted in 1998 found that 75 percent of Russians had received their wages behind schedule at some time during the twelve months preceding the survey. For around half of those, the delay was seven weeks or more. See Rose (1998). In another nationwide survey of around 2,000 adults, also conducted in 1998, 16 percent of manufacturing employees and 10 percent of miners said they had participated in protest actions (political rallies, demonstrations, or other public protests) in the three years before the survey period (September 27–October 12, 1998). Eleven percent of manufacturing workers and 10 percent of miners had gone out on strike in the same period. USIA (1998, pp. 4–5).

none of the strikes aimed to replace the current management.[35] The actions were likely not directed against management at all, but at circumstances beyond the director's control. Above all, this means the government, for not paying its own bills. For enterprises with government orders (mainly defense enterprises), workers' protests are an especially important weapon to be used *by* management. (This suggests that an activist work force could under some circumstances be a positive part of relational capital.) Nationwide, the labor movement has in fact implicitly supported enterprise management on the question of wage arrears. Its leaders have stated that the arrears are the government's fault because it demands more cash taxes from enterprises, a policy that leaves nothing for wages. Russia's trade unions have demanded a change in the law that would give wage payments legal priority over cash tax payments.[36]

The director who might actually be in danger of being the object of protests by the enterprise's workers would be one whom the workers perceived as unable to demonstrate that he has enough relational capital to ensure the survival of the enterprise. Even then, there would have to be a better alternative candidate. The various calls to punish corrupt directors usually are premised on the threat of replacing the director. But who is a candidate to become the replacement for a corrupt director of a loss-making enterprise? What is there to offer? If the enterprise is going to remain in the r-regime, the government would have to guarantee the workers that the enterprise could continue to enjoy the same terms of noncash production, offsets, and so forth, as under the old director. In other words, the government would "grant" the new director relational capital. What about the relationships with other directors with whom the enterprise deals—Gazprom, UES, MPS, and other input suppliers? Finally, how about the rest of the deal, the informal profits that the director would be allowed to appropriate? They would be lower for a new director only if the government decided to penalize the corrupt managers, making it more costly to steal than not steal. In reality, however, the government has little ability to monitor and enforce that. Moreover, the noncash production realm is much more than just relations with the government and the tax offsets deal; it is all other enterprise relations. Those transactions will not be transparent to the government.

35. USIA (1998, p. 13).

36. The unions have support here from the main organization of the directors, headed by Arkadiy Vol'skiy. Vol'skiy also advocates a return to the former practice of legally guaranteeing that a certain proportion of an enterprise's cash earnings must be protected from being used to pay taxes.

If this kind of corruption is rational, then the idea of replacing corrupt managers of loss-making enterprises will be easier said than done. The incentives for managerial behavior remain the same for the new director as for the old one. And yet the calls continue to be heard. Former deputy prime minister Boris Nemtsov, for instance, wrote in a New Year's (1999) essay on Russia's economic prospects about the numerous enterprises (40 percent, he said) that regularly do not pay their workers: such enterprises' "thieving directors [must be] replaced with competent managers."[37]

These are the same calls heard during the regime of Prime Minister Sergey Kiriyenko in the spring and summer of 1998. The new cabinet announced that it would initiate bankruptcy proceedings against directors of state-owned enterprises who failed to "pay wages, keep jobs and pay taxes," in the words of Deputy Prime Minister Viktor Khristenko. They would, said Khristenko, be replaced with "more efficient" managers.[38] In other words, this is a redefinition of the notion of bankruptcy. Contrary to practice in a market economy, bankruptcy in Russia's virtual economy did not mean selling off an unviable enterprise to new ownership that would restructure, cut costs, and make it profitable (a value adder), no matter what it took. Instead, it meant plugging leaks of value from the system. In the terminology of Yuliya Latynina, the reformist Russian government in 1998 was at best proposing to replace the manager who "steals from the enterprise" with one who "steals for the enterprise"—that is, one who does not abuse his position for his own personal benefit at the expense of his labor force and the good of the entire system.

Leakage, "Good" and "Bad"

Viewed from within the virtual economy, the sums that end up in the pockets of the owners of value suppliers such as Gazprom are a form of "leakage" of value: it is value that does not directly serve to sustain networks of soft goods production. Although leakage represents a loss that one would like to avoid, in some instances it is unavoidable. In cases like that of Gazprom, the leakage can be thought of as necessary because it helps keep a critical participant in the game. However, not all leakage of value is necessary and beneficial to the system. Some leakage is damaging, like the

37. Boris Nemtsov, "The Blocked Stream of a Hard Year," *Moskovskiy komsomolets*, January 5, 1999, pp. 1, 3, in Foreign Broadcast Information Service (FBIS)-SOV-99-008.

38. Agence France-Presse release dated May 27, 1998, "Candidates for bankruptcy proceedings to be named Friday."

theft of wage funds by an enterprise director, which makes it more difficult to meet the cash constraint, or a manager's diversion of cash from taxes. There are other ways of distinguishing instances of leakage from the virtual economy. Leakage can be legal or illegal, sanctioned or unsanctioned. The value that leaks out may stay inside the country or may be transferred abroad (capital flight). The most important distinction, however, is whether the leakage is good for the system or bad for it.

Viewed in the context of leakage, the relationship between corruption and economic reform takes on greater complexity. Reducing corruption is typically considered a key element in accelerating economic reform. In Russia's virtual economy, the opposite may in fact be the case. If reducing corruption results in less "bad" leakage from the system, more value remains to support the continued operation of loss-making enterprises. A truly comprehensive anticorruption campaign would thus be a direct attack on the virtual economy, but that is exactly why it will not happen. It falls clearly in the category of policies that violate the impermissibility constraint. That is, it is a policy that can be declared, but whose consequences are intolerable. For this reason, it will not be pursued to its full extent. What might happen is a self-correction of the level of thievery. This means that in Russia today, if corruption is reduced, it will be for the purpose of preserving the virtual economy, not eliminating it.

CHAPTER SIX

A Simple Accounting Exercise

"Barter is a bad form of exchange. It gives rise to illusory, or
'virtual' earnings. This leads to unpayable or 'virtual' fiscal
obligations, which then are settled at nonmarket or 'virtual' prices."
—*Karpov Commission Report*

The preceding chapters have shown that the possibility of using relational capital, or contacts and connections with government officials and other enterprise directors, has allowed the typical Russian manufacturing enterprise to survive without restructuring. Using its relational capital to acquire resources for free, or far below cost, the unrestructured enterprise could continue to produce and exchange goods that were otherwise unmarketable (or marketable only at a loss), so-called soft goods. Our analysis so far has been from the vantage point of the individual enterprise. We now want to illustrate how the enterprise interacts with other actors in the economy. We use a very simple example—an imaginary virtual economy that consists of four sectors that transact with one another using virtual, or fictitious, prices. Our main purpose is to show how pretense is at the core of the transactions that underlie the virtual economy. We will also use the example as a framework for discussing the implications of the virtual economy for economic policy measures—for instance, a campaign to enforce tax collection more rigorously.

A Four-Sector Economy

We assume that the economy comprises only four sectors.[1] Two of the sectors are in industry. One is the core manufacturing sector, denoted M. M produces exclusively soft goods, that is, goods whose market price is less than the value of the inputs used to produce them. M is, in other words, a value subtractor.[2] M is also the only final-goods producer in the economy. The other part of industry is the value-producing sector of the economy, which we denote G.[3] G's output is used as an input by enterprises in M. M's workers and their families constitute the household sector, or H. A government or budget sector, B, collects taxes and distributes the proceeds to H through transfers, which, for the time being, we can think of as pensions.[4] Figure 6-1 lists the four sectors for reference and suggests the basic transactions among them.

The essential feature of this economy is that the value of the inputs used to produce M's output is greater than the value of what is actually produced. In other words, M is a value subtractor, but this fact is masked by the pretense that M actually produces value. A transfer of value takes place, but it is kept from view by the peculiar pricing system of this economy.

There is one important assumption about the operation of this economy. All agents attempt to meet their obligations. No one conceals income. Thus, for example, M contracts to pay G and H the full amount those sectors charge for the inputs (gas and labor) that they supply. All accounting (between enterprises and for tax purposes) is on the accrual basis; that is, income and expense items are recognized as incurred, regardless of when they are actually paid.

---

1. There is an implicit fifth sector, the rest of the world, which purchases output for cash. The discussion in this chapter follows Gaddy and Ickes (1999). We have not developed a complete input-output version of the model. See Götz (1999) for an interesting analysis of the four-sector model of the virtual economy.

2. Note that all we are really assuming is that the sector as a whole destroys value. We could, for example, assume that some enterprises within M produce goods that have value, but that the goods that M delivers to other sectors cost more to produce than they are worth.

3. We choose this label in reference to Gazprom, which is the major value-producing enterprise in the economy. Nonetheless, it is important to recognize that value is produced in other sectors as well.

4. The example is intended to be simple in order to be illustrative, but the reader is cautioned against thinking of the government sector as a unitary actor. There really is no such thing as "the government" in Russia; it is fragmented, not just between the regional and federal levels, but also among different agencies at all levels.

FIGURE 6-1. Interactions among the Four Sectors

H = households

G = Gazprom, a value-adding industrial sector

M = manufacturer, a value-subtracting industrial sector

B = budget, a government sector

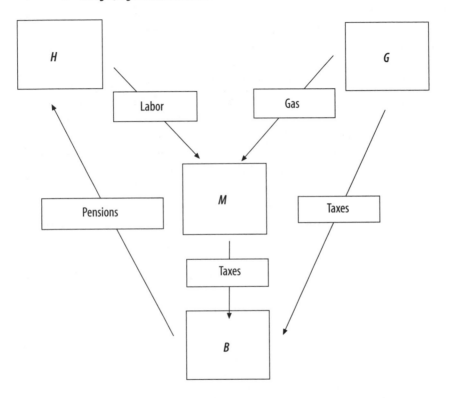

To make the flows that characterize the virtual economy more concrete, we create a numerical example. We suppose that sector G produces 100 rubles' worth of output at no cost, which it supplies as an intermediate good to be used in M's production. Sector H supplies 100 rubles' worth of labor to M. M uses these inputs to produce output that has a market value of 100. Thus, M uses inputs worth 200 rubles (100 rubles of gas and 100 rubles of labor) to produce a product worth 100 rubles; it subtracts 100 rubles of value in the process of producing its good.

To keep things simple, we assume that the only tax in the economy is a value-added tax levied at a rate of 100 percent. All revenues that B collects are simply transferred to H as pensions. B cannot borrow, so unmet expenditure obligations are considered to be debts from B to H (budget arrears or, following the even simpler assumption, "pension arrears").

Generating the Virtual Economy

The critical step to generate a "virtual" economy is to implement the pretense that M is a value adder rather than the value subtractor it actually is. This is accomplished by pricing M's output at a level that exaggerates its value—what the Karpov Commission Report referred to as virtual prices. The actual (market) value of M's output is 100, but if it were to sell at that price, it would be a loss maker. Therefore, M sets a price of 300. At that price, M becomes a value adder. It still uses inputs worth 200, but now it appears to create an additional 100 in value.[5] This pricing implements the pretense if and only if other participants accept this price. Explaining why this pretense is accepted is the critical step in the exercise. Nonetheless, we postpone that until we complete our elaboration of the example.

The "virtual" price of 300 is an arbitrary price that we have chosen to keep the example simple. In fact, though, the rate of overpricing we have used is roughly consistent with what we know about actual practice in many enterprises. In examples cited in the Karpov Commission Report, commodity output used in transactions between enterprises is overpriced by a factor of 2–2.5.[6] When used for the purpose of tax offsets, the goods are typically overpriced by a factor of about two.[7]

We assume that G and B accept this overvaluation of M's goods, but only in a specific way—as soft goods. Three hundred rubles is the soft-goods price of M's output; the monetary price is still only 100. It is critical to keep this duality in pricing structure in mind. To follow the transactions involved in this economy more clearly, let us assume that the inputs (gas and labor)

---

5. M's pricing policy shows that the definition of a soft good depends not on the nature of the good and how it is produced, but rather on the terms on which it is sold. The "softness" of a soft good is determined by the "virtuality" of its price.

6. The Berezovskiy Coal Mine case in chapter 2 (table 2-6, p. 40) is an illustration.

7. See, for instance, remarks by Aleksey Shulunov, first vice president of the Defense Enterprise League, in *Nezavisimoye voyennoye obozreniye*, January 16–22, 1998, no. 2, pp. 4–5.

TABLE 6-1. Claims among the Sectors in the Virtual Economy

	Has claims			Has obligations		
Sector	on sector	For	Amount	to sector	For	Amount
Households (*H*)	M	Wages	100			
	B	Pensions	200			
Gazprom (*G*)	M	Gas	100	B	Taxes	100
Manufacturing (*M*)				H	Wages	100
				G	Gas	100
				B	Taxes	100
Budgets (*B*)	G	Taxes	100	H	Pensions	200
	M	Taxes	100			

are supplied to *M* and production occurs before any financial settlements are made.

We first examine the flows across sectors when everyone pretends that *M*'s output is worth 300. As the output (cash value of 100; "virtually" priced at 300) sits at *M*, waiting to be shipped out, the claims that prevail among the sectors are those shown in table 6-1. *M* has to pay for the gas and labor it used, and it has to pay taxes on its (apparent) value added. *G* also has to pay taxes. *B* will use the tax receipts from *M* and *B* to pay pensions. The exact amounts due are shown in the table.

Financial Settlements

To follow the settlements more clearly, we take each sector in turn, beginning with sector *M*. Notice that because of virtual pricing *M* now reports value added of 100 rubles, so it has acquired a tax obligation of 100 to the budget. This gives it total obligations of 300: 100 to *G* for the gas it used as an input, 100 to its workers (*H*) as wages, and 100 to *B* in value-added tax. We assume that *M* is able to persuade everyone involved to accept the virtual pricing; that is, *M* has sufficient relational capital to engage in this pricing and receive soft goods in return. This means that the value of *M*'s claims will be exactly equal to the value of its output. *M* thus starts dividing its output accordingly. That is, it allocates output virtually priced at 100 rubles to each of *G*, *B*, and *H*. *M* has met its obligations.

Now we turn to the other sectors. *G*, as a (true) value adder of 100 rubles in its gas production, owes a tax of 100 rubles. *G*'s participation in the virtual economy earns it the right also to pay its taxes in kind, but not in its own product (the valuable hard good, gas), but in the soft good that it received from *M*.[8] Thus *G*'s settlements are straightforward. It takes the 100 (virtually priced) units of output it received from *M* and remits them to *B* as its tax payment in full. Because *B* credits *G*'s tax payments at the virtual value, *G* does not suffer from *M*'s overpricing. Since *G* has no direct dealings with *H*, *G*'s accounts are balanced.

What about the budget sector? *B* has now received 100 (virtual) in goods from *M* and 100 (virtual) in goods from *G*. This equals the 200 in revenues that the government's "budget" called for. The government then passes these goods along to the household sector as transfers (pensions).

This is a pure virtual economy, a pure natural economy. It is self-contained. There are only four sectors; none of them conduct transactions outside the system. There is no cash at all in the system. The government budget is balanced: spending equals revenues. There are no arrears, since all wages, taxes, and accounts payable are settled in full. However, it is fairly easy to see that as constructed, the system can continue only as long as *G* is able and willing to inject value into the system. *G* is the value pump that keeps it going.

When Workers Need Cash

The assumptions of this stylized setup are highly simplified. They are also clearly unrealistic, but it is important to recognize where the assumptions most directly clash with reality. The question to ask is, Who will and who will not accept being paid in the form of *M*'s soft goods rather than in cash? Put another way: Who will and who will not accept *M*'s virtual pricing?

As it turns out, of the four sectors, the one with the strongest motives to refuse in-kind payment and virtual pricing is *H*. The simple problem, of course, is that households cannot consume the output that *M* has produced and offers as wages, nor that which *B* has collected in taxes and seeks to distribute as pensions. Households need consumption goods. To incorporate this factor in the simplest manner, we assume that consumption goods are

8. In practice, not all value-producing enterprises can succeed in paying their taxes in soft goods. This depends on their level of relational capital. Of course, Gazprom can, but many enterprises in *G*, especially new enterprises, have relatively low levels of *r*, and they end up being cash cows for the virtual economy, as discussed in chapter 4. We ignore this for now.

obtained through imports, and these must be paid for in cash. Hence we assume that households need 100 rubles in cash as a minimum survival requirement. Later we will see how the level of H's cash requirement influences behavior in the virtual economy.

We continue to assume that G and B go along with the virtual pricing scheme. As before, M pays each its 100 ruble obligation (for gas and taxes) in the form of soft goods. The workers, however, are now demanding cash wages. Therefore, M sells the remaining one-third of its output for cash.[9] Because the market value of M's output is one-third of its virtual value, M's workers receive cash wages of only 33 1/3. M settles its accounts with G and B, but, given the cash demands of the workers, M is not able to fully settle its obligations to the workers, and M ends up with wage arrears to H of 66 2/3. Thus begins the dilemma for M and for the entire virtual economy: even when G and B go along with a three-fold overpricing of M's output (pretending that the 100 rubles' worth of goods are worth 300 rubles), M still ends up with arrears to its workers.

Of course M could try to reduce those wage arrears by allotting relatively more of its total output to pay the workers (H) than to G or B, or both. However, it is easy to see that, under our pricing assumptions, the only way M could fully meet its wage obligation is to pay both G and B nothing at all. There is simply not enough real value (cash value) in M's product to meet all the claims *even though three of the four sectors in the virtual economy are quite willing to go along with the pretense.* The key point, of course, is that virtual pricing shifts value between sectors; it does not create any more value. This also underscores a fundamental dilemma for the virtual pricing scheme to which we will return later: if everyone played along, it would work perfectly; but not everyone can or will.

Let us return to the financial settlements, however, because the wage arrears are not the only problem. Both G and B also have financial claims and obligations to be settled. We assume that the pensioners to whom B owes money are like M's workers: they demand cash and they do not accept the overpricing. B's "tax receipts" may have a virtual value of 200, but their cash value is only one-third of that, or 66 2/3. B owes 200 in pensions (since the government pretends it has 200 in tax revenues, and everything

9. We assume, in other words, that the virtual economy is no longer self-contained. One could assume that a monetized sector exists alongside the nonmonetized virtual economy. It is simple, however, to assume that M exports the output in order to earn the cash. Recall Igor's Rule No. 4: *"Export something to a hard currency market to get cash for essential needs."*

is supposed to be transferred to H as pensions). Therefore, B ends up with pension arrears of $200 - 66\ 2/3 = 133\ 1/3$.

Where does that leave H as a whole—the workers and the pensioners together? They have received a total of 100: $33\ 1/3$ from M in wages and $66\ 2/3$ from B in pensions. On the one hand, this means that H has received only one-third of what it was owed, leaving it with aggregate wage and pension arrears of 200. On the other hand, the 100 (in cash) that it did receive was precisely the amount we initially assumed as H's survival minimum. Thus, even though there are wage and pension arrears, this version of the virtual economy (call it "almost pure") satisfies the feasibility constraint—that H receives 100 rubles—and all accounts are settled.

H's Cash Constraint

The example arbitrarily sets H's minimum survival requirement to make things come out neatly: the amount H needed was exactly equal to the true (cash) value of M's product. In real life, the minimum amount of cash needed for H to survive is not arbitrary. It is determined by the actual social and physiological needs of the population, by real price levels in the cash economy, and, equally important, by the ability of the population to sustain themselves independently of the cash they receive from either M or B.

This is the familiar idea of a "cash constraint," which we introduced for the enterprise in chapter 4. There, it was the minimum amount of cash the enterprise needed to cover certain costs that could not be settled through nonmonetary transactions. Here, we began by introducing a cash constraint only for the household sector. However, that generated a cash constraint for both M and B and thus for the system as a whole.

There are interesting alternative ways to think of how the household cash constraint might be tightened or relaxed. Suppose, for instance, that the household survival requirement were higher than 100. This is more than the total value available for distribution in the system after M's production cycle. The system would be unsustainable unless H were able to earn some cash outside the system in order to survive. Chapter 7 will show that such possibilities do exist and that the management of M typically encourages or even facilitates cash-earning activity by H outside the system.

It is important to note that we have implicitly assumed that only the total of income received by H matters. This simplifies our analysis and lets us focus on the intersectoral implications. It requires us to assume that the household sector will and can redistribute amounts received in the form of wages and pensions to ensure survival of all members of H. There is ample evidence of extensive intrahousehold (and even interhousehold) transfers of cash in contemporary Russia. To the extent that we allow B to choose to fulfill part of its expenditure obligations in the form of in-kind transfers (as in the first version, the pure virtual economy), things are somewhat more complicated, since it is more difficult for H to reallocate those nonmonetary transfers within the household sector as a whole or among workers and pensioners.[10]

The Underlying Real Economy

Earlier sections examined the virtual economy under varying degrees of pretense. In the first case, the pretense was total: everyone accepted the virtual pricing. This version of a pure natural economy "worked" in the sense that there were no unmet claims. The next example relaxed the assumption that everyone accept the virtual pricing by having the workers elect not to accept the virtual pricing of M's output and demand cash wages. Already at that step, problems arose in the form of arrears. What happens if we move to the opposite extreme and assume that no one accepts the virtual pricing? This is a totally nonpretense version. That is, this time, no one, not even M, pretends that M's output is worth anything other than the 100 it actually is worth in market (cash) terms. This example allows us to compare the apparent outcome of the virtual economy with what is really happening beneath the pretense.

Once again, M is a useful starting point. Because the value of its output is really only 100, with nonvirtual pricing M would have to report a *loss* of 100 instead of a profit of 100. It therefore would have no tax obligation. However, with sales revenue of only 100, M could not pay both G (to whom it owes 100 for gas) and H (to whom it owes wages of 100). It would have to apportion between them the 100 it does have.

In the spirit of keeping things as simple as possible, assume now that M pays equal shares to each of its creditors, that is, 50 to H and 50 to G. This leaves M with wage arrears of 50 to H and a debt of 50 to its supplier, G—so-called interenterprise arrears.[11] Meanwhile, G remits to B the 50 it

10. On interhousehold transfers see, for example, Cox, Eser, and Jimenez (1997). A story that we will tell in chapter 7 illustrates how in rural Kostroma province, almost the only cash that circulates comes from pensions. It is then redistributed through extended family networks to others, including workers.

11. Of course these arrears numbers are arbitrary, depending on how M pays its bills. It is important to note that no matter how M's payments are apportioned, the sum of payments will equal 100, as will the sum of the arrears.

TABLE 6-2. Comparing the Virtual and Underlying Real Variants of the Economy

Category	Virtual	Real
Total sales	400	200
Total profits	200	0
Profit rate (percentage)	50	0
Total value added (GDP)	300	100
Industrial output	400	200
Wages		
Accrued	100	100
Actual	33	50
Budget revenues		
Planned	200	100
Actual	200	50
Budget spending		
Planned	200	100
Actual	66	50
Total household income		
Accrued	300	200
Actual	100	100
Arrears		
Wage	66	50
Interenterprise	None	50
Budget	133	50
Tax	None	50
Total arrears	200	200

receives from *M*. Since on an accrual basis *G* owes *B* a total of 100 in tax, *G* now has tax arrears of 50. *B*'s only revenues are what it receives from *G*, since *M* has produced no value added and thus owes no taxes. *B* transfers to *H* the 50 it received from *G*. *B* still has budget ("pension") arrears of 50. *H* survives because it receives 100 (50 from *M* and 50 from *B*).[12]

Comparative Indicators

Table 6-2 compares the economy's apparent performance in the virtual economy regime with its actual performance according to the underlying reality. The table uses one of the versions of the virtual economy presented

12. Again, we note that these proportions could be changed, depending on how *M* initially decides to fulfill its obligations to *G* and *H*. *H* always receives 100. Whatever *M* pays to *G* will eventually be passed on, via *B*, to *H*.

above, the one in which workers must receive wages in cash.[13] Table 6-2 provides some insight into why agents may prefer the pretense of the virtual economy, showing that on nearly all counts the aggregate performance indicators (sales, profits, GDP, output) of the virtual economy look better than those of the real economy.

First, consider the budget. The planned budget in the real variant is only half the size that it is in the virtual variant (100 versus 200). True, the larger virtual budget is accompanied by larger arrears in relation to planned budget outlays. True, households are, in fact, no better off in the virtual economy (the actual value for "total household income" in each case is 100). However, abandoning the pretense of the virtual economy would mean cutting (nominal) pensions by 50 percent ("planned budget spending" is reduced from 200 to 100). Of course, in practice total household income must be the same in both variants, because the value actually produced is identical. In reality, nothing changes, but the pretense is what counts. In response to a proposal to replace the virtual with the real variant, the perception will be: "You want to cut pensions in half!"[14]

Turning to arrears, we have already noted that the picture depends on M's decision on how to allocate payments between H and G. It was assumed above that each received half of the cash value of M's product. In the general case, the proportion used for H's wage payments will be w. Then G will receive $100 - w$. Final household income is always 100 (since that is still the total product that can be allocated). The wage arrears will be offset by budget arrears, since what is paid to G (and passed through B to H) could always be paid directly to H in wages. The greater the share of M's product paid directly to H in wages, the greater the amount of total arrears and the greater the number of sectors that have arrears of one kind or the other. This is evident in table 6-3.

---

13. This is a static comparison between the virtual economy of our simple accounting example and the reality that underlies that economy. Another interesting comparison would focus on outcomes if a full adjustment out of the virtual economy (out of value-destroying activity) were to be accomplished, that is, if agents were to recognize that value destruction could not continue and therefore reallocated resources accordingly. Clearly, that case would enhance welfare. This book, however, aims to show why that adjustment, which represents a potential Pareto improvement, does not occur.

14. In a strong sense this is money illusion. It has been understood, at least since Keynes, that it is much easier to cut real wages by an increase in the price level than by a cut in nominal wages. Workers are much more likely to resist the latter than the former, even though they are equally well off in both cases. The same sense of illusion is present here. With arrears there is at least the possibility that some of the cut is restored, while with a cut in nominal pensions there is no hope of recourse.

TABLE 6-3. Variation in Arrears Depending on *M*'s Allocation of Wage versus Gas Payments
Rubles unless otherwise indicated

Category	Virtual	General	Real $w^a = 0$	$w = 50$	$w = 100$
Total sales	400	200	200	200	200
Total profits	200	0	0	0	0
Profit rate (percentage)	50	0	0	0	0
Total value added (GDP)	300	100	100	100	100
Industrial output	400	200	200	200	200
Wages					
Accrued	100	100	100	100	100
Actual	33	*w*	0	50	100
Budget revenues					
Planned	200	100	100	100	100
Actual	66	$100 - w$	100	50	0
Budget spending					
Planned	200	100	100	100	100
Actual	66	$100 - w$	100	50	0
Total household income					
Accrued	300	200	200	200	200
Actual	100	100	100	100	100
Arrears					
Wage	66	$100 - w$	100	50	0
Interenterprise	None	*w*	0	50	100
Budget	133	*w*	0	50	100
Tax	None	*w*	0	50	100
Total arrears	200	$100 + 2w$	100	200	300

a. *w* = wage.

In the pure virtual variant, there were no arrears. On introduction of a cash constraint for the household sector, arrears problems arose between *M* and *H* ("wage arrears") and between *B* and *H* ("pension arrears"). In the nonvirtual variant, when no one accepted the virtual pricing of *M*'s output, two qualitatively new kinds of arrears problems arose: between *G* and *M* ("interenterprise arrears") and between *G* and *B* ("tax arrears").

The most important difference between the virtual economy and the underlying real variant is that the former masks the nonviability of *M*. In the virtual economy, *M* appears to add value of 100. In the real variant, *M* is a clear loss maker. The virtual economy maintains the pretense that *M* is a productive sector in the economy. To those who hold stakes in *M*—workers, managers, suppliers, and others—this is important. The alternative to pretense, unmasking the nonviability of M, could result in shutting down this sector (or enterprises in this sector, if we had an economy with multiple enterprises). To these stakeholders pretense has its advantages, even though it results in a loss in value to society as a whole.

These differences between the virtual and real economies suggest why it is so difficult to remove the pretense. An attempt to shift from the pretend virtual world to the honest real world would be highly unpopular. It is hard to imagine any politician seriously attempting it. It would mean slashing pensions, irritating Gazprom by branding it as a tax delinquent and demanding more cash taxes from it, aggravating relations between the manufacturing sector and Gazprom, and, ultimately, threatening the bankruptcy of the manufacturing enterprises and devastating losses of jobs and wages for the attached population. Of course, once economic adjustment occurred, the workers and households would be better off, as the resources wasted by M could be redistributed. However, that adjustment is a promise, and the receipts in the virtual economy are, ironically, the reality of the economic situation.

Implications of a Tax Collection Crackdown

The imaginary four-sector economy we have presented in this chapter and the r-d space model developed in chapters 3 and 4 provide a convenient way to analyze the impact of certain economic policy measures. Tax policy is an example. In the pure virtual economy (or even in the modified version that required cash payment of wages), there are no tax arrears (see table 6-2). However, as soon as the government demands that the participants in the virtual economy pay some taxes in cash, there will almost inevitably be tax arrears even if, as the example assumes, no one actually evades taxes. Only in the case that M uses its entire product to pay G and none to pay H are there no tax arrears. This is the "real" case in table 6-3, where $w = 0$, but $w = 0$ means that M pays nothing to its own workers in wages—a clearly unsustainable situation in the longer term.

To begin to understand the complexity of tax reform in the virtual economy, consider the implications of a "tax crackdown" by the government, that is, a campaign to try to secure more cash to the budget. This turns out to be an intermediate variant between the virtual variant first described and the underlying real process. In the end, it would likely be perceived by the virtual economy's participants as worse than both. To see this, assume now the government decides it does not want to continue to accept tax off-sets/barter payments. M continues to price its output at 300 and G accepts that price. M therefore delivers one-third of its output (virtual value 100) to G. As in the original scheme, M pays H the cash value of one-third of its output, that is, 33 1/3. M's arrears to H are 66 2/3.

The key difference is that now B refuses to accept G's and M's offer to each remit 100 (virtual value) worth of M's output as tax payments. B demands that they remit their taxes in cash. M still has a tax obligation of 100, since it continues to price its output at 300. It remits 33 1/3 in cash and has tax arrears of 66 2/3. G will also remit 33 1/3 in cash and have tax arrears of 66 2/3. In the end, the tax crackdown variant will be the same as the real variant except that in addition to all the aforementioned problems, M, too, will have a tax arrears problem. In other words, this scenario is worse in this respect than the real variant.

The situation will also appear to be worse than in the pure virtual econ-omy. After the tax crackdown, the wage arrears remain the same: 66 2/3. The cash value of tax revenues to the budget is the same: 66 2/3. The bud-get arrears to H are the same: 133 1/3. Now, however, there is a major new problem that did not exist at all in the virtual economy: tax arrears. Both producers in the system, the value adder G and the value subtractor M, are declared to be tax delinquents. This despite the fact that the objective of the crackdown was to improve tax discipline!

Of course, if the cash tax collection policy is pursued vigorously enough, the likely outcome is that the budget actually will collect more value from M, but only because M pays less to either G or H, or pays less to both, in order to have more cash to deliver to B. This means increased wage arrears, increased debts to G on the part of M, or both. This is precisely what has happened in the Russian economy time and again as the result of various cash tax collection campaigns.

This outcome was completely predictable because the campaigns did noth-ing to change the fundamental fact of the virtual economy: not enough value is being created to meet all the claims. The tax crackdowns just temporarily shifted the flow of value relatively away from G and H and toward B.

Representatives of Russian labor have explicitly stressed the trade-off between tax arrears and wages arrears. In response to the results of the early 1998 campaign, Mikhail Shmakov, head of Russia's Federation of Inde-pendent Trade Unions, called for an article in the Civil Code that would obligate enterprises to pay their wages before taxes. Vadim Borisov, director of the Institute for Comparative Labor Relations Research, an organization that is helping the unions in their campaign to eliminate wage arrears, said in the spring of 1998 that "the government's recent efforts to squeeze more taxes out of industrial enterprises to pay public-sector workers were only worsening the problem of private-sector wage arrears."[15]

Effects on G

The remarks above were related mainly to the tax crackdown's effect on M. The impact on G may be quite different. If G is earning additional cash on the side—outside the virtual economy—the government's demand that G pay more cash will be tantamount to changing the rules for G's participation in the system: it will be the same as raising the net contribution that G makes. This could be accomplished, but presumably only if the government had a credible threat of punishment or retaliation if G failed to go along (for instance, dispossessing the current owners, whether through "nationalization" or "privatization").

Of course, the idea with the crackdown may be that forcing G and M to pay cash to the budget will force G in turn to refuse to accept the inflated price of M's output. In other words, the true goal is to impose the full real variant. That scenario would have even worse political consequences, including the possible bankruptcy of M. What is interesting is that G can act alone to avert these consequences. All it has to do is tolerate M's arrears, and this is precisely what has happened. As an example of how Gazprom can relieve pressure on the manufacturing sector by borrowing money outside the system, consider this news from May 1998:

> Russian gas giant Gazprom is to press ahead with a bond issue this month worth some one billion dollars as part of a borrowing programme needed to make up for customers' unpaid debts. . . . Further unsecured and convertible bond issues will follow this year to increase the company's 1998 borrowing to two billion dollars, [Gazprom chairman Rem] Vyakhirev said. . . . Last week, Deutsche Bank announced it would lead a syndicated loan to Gazprom worth 230 million dollars.[16]

In other words, the government squeezed Gazprom to pay cash taxes so it (the government) would not have to borrow so much on the bond mar-

15. *Financial Times*, April 9, 1998, p. 2.
16. Agence France-Presse, news release, May 5, 1998.

kets. The government may also have hoped that this would lead Gazprom to squeeze its own customers to pay in cash, and so on. However, what did Gazprom actually do? It turned around and mortgaged future gas exports by borrowing cash, thus refusing to tighten the cash constraint for the enterprises. The result: no change at all!

"Igor's" Reaction

So far we have considered the effects of a tax crackdown on a manufacturing enterprise that produced only soft goods. Imagine an enterprise like Igor's, which chooses between devoting effort to hard goods and soft goods. How is it affected? If the government demands cash, and the enterprise believes that this is a credible policy change, why should it any longer produce soft goods for the state at all? The only reason it did was that it wanted to offset federal tax obligations. Therefore, federal soft-goods activity disappears. What happens to hard-goods production? If the "tax" rate on hard goods is still high, it will depress the incentive to produce hard goods. What we can expect, therefore, is more effort devoted to tax evasion and concealment. The exercise is just the classical one of costs versus rewards of hard-goods production plus concealment. Concealing revenues from the tax authorities is a normal activity in high-tax economies. Such activities require effort that can otherwise be used for value-producing activities. It is only when the cash tax crackdown is accompanied by a reduction in tax rates that an enterprise like Igor's will increase its production of hard goods.

The implications of a cash tax crackdown in the case of an enterprise like Igor's depend on Igor's expectations. If he regards this as a temporary phenomenon, a crisis that has to be weathered in order to stay in the game, he will be prepared to sell some more steel (at a loss) to get some cash. He may borrow to get cash. Because he expects this to be temporary and assumes that the government will have to back off this policy sooner or later, the enterprise director needs to make sure he does not go completely bankrupt before then. In such a case, what we will observe is an accelerated drawdown of existing stocks of value for a certain period. That is, not only wages will be a source of cash, but also other arrears. This, too, is what the accounting example predicts.

When cash collection crackdown is assumed to be temporary, this only intensifies the cash constraint. That is, it forces the enterprise to earn more cash just to survive. However, if the enterprise's cash-earning activity is loss making (value subtracting), the effect is perverse: the enterprise undertakes even more loss-making activity to earn more cash. In other words, if done episodically (enforced and then relaxed), a ban on tax offsets will have very negative effects. Only if done with the full intention to pursue it to the end can it have the positive effect of eliminating some value-subtracting activity for good. Then, however, the government must be prepared to deal with the consequences.

CHAPTER SEVEN

Running Out of Value

"Today, you're better off if you don't work at all.... The less you produce, the less your losses."
—*Russian peasant, quoted by Aleksandr Solzhenitsyn in* Rossiya v obvale

Where is the virtual economy leading Russia? This is the subject of the next three chapters. The virtual economy is an evolving system. It would be inconsistent with our analysis to ignore the likelihood that it will continue to adapt. Exactly what the Russian economy will look like is impossible to predict. However, if we are to understand how the future may develop, we must first analyze the long-run trajectory of the virtual economy. This is not necessarily a forecast of the future of the Russian economy. That will depend on political choices and unforeseen shocks. Instead, we are exploring the dynamic behavior of the virtual economy— how it would develop if left unchecked. This is a necessary prerequisite for any analysis of how the Russian economy will evolve and how agents will react to the virtual economy.

As we have described it, the virtual economy is inherently degenerative. One key part of the virtual economy—the manufacturing sector—is made up of old capital and old labor. Over time these factors can be expected to wear out. Capital replacement in loss-making enterprises is nearly nonexistent. This suggests that the size of this sector will shrink relative to the rest of the economy. At the same time, we know that the operation of the virtual economy depends on the continued infusion of value, most important, from Gazprom, but also from the new private sector and external sources. Arguably there are no serious limits to further infusion of value into the vir-

FIGURE 7-1. Gazprom Running Out of Value, 1997–2010[a]

Gas volume (billions of cubic meters)[b]

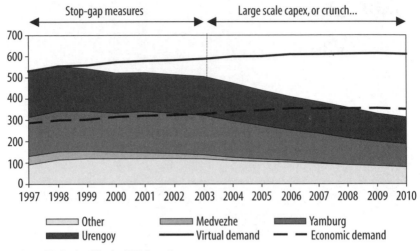

Source: Westhead and Weaving (1999, figure 1).

a. Figures for 1999–2010 are estimates.

b. Shaded areas refer to natural gas fields.

tual economy. After all, as long as actors are willing to support the system, it can persist. However, the capacity of even the most willing donors to contribute value is finite. This is true of all three major suppliers of value: Gazprom and other resource industries, Russian domestic private business, and foreign sources.

Gazprom

Russia's gas and oil sector—the most important source of value in the economy—has suffered from inadequate investment. In a sense, the current operation of this sector overstates true value production, since inadequate investment means that present levels of value creation cannot be maintained indefinitely. Gas industry analysts who have applied the virtual economy approach have estimated the timetable for when Russia will literally "run out of gas." The dilemma is shown in figure 7-1, which compares projected levels of production of gas with expected demand. The higher demand curve represents the amount of gas that would be needed to perpetuate the virtual economy in its current form, while the lower curve reflects the demand for gas under true market conditions.

The analysts explain:

[It] is clear from underlying field decline rates that if current 'virtual rates' of demand are to be met, another major field development will be required by 2003. Whilst there are plenty of candidates (Zapolyarnoye, Yamal, Shtockmanovskoye), the problem is one of finance: will western investors be prepared to offer either debt or equity to finance new gas supplies to an unreformed Russian market? Trade investors might be prepared to, but only in return for access to export markets. Gazprom would have to sacrifice Europe's coveted (and scarce) hard currency revenues.

For the next five years or so, we believe that Gazprom can make do with a variety of "stop-gap" measures: through better utilization rates of existing fields, by placing a modest squeeze on Russian demand, and through allowing more gas to be sold to markets such as the Ukraine (and perhaps even Russia) by the Central Asian republics. These supplies have hitherto been inhibited by Gazprom for competitive and political reasons.

Similar issues are true of UES [United Energy Systems, Russia's electricity monopoly], and by implication throughout the virtual economy in its entirety. On this basis the virtual economy would appear to reach some kind of *"crunch point" within the next five years* or so [emphasis in the original].[1]

New Domestic Private Business

A second source of value is Russia's domestic private sector. Once again, however, the capacity of this sector to provide value to offset loss making elsewhere is limited. The very operation of the virtual economy is a heavy tax on new activity in various ways. In fact, as value from other sources declines, there will be pressure to increase the tax on private business.

The virtual economy has an ambiguous effect on private business, one that flows from its complex relationship with cash and market-based activity in general. Agents in the virtual economy seek to avoid cash, but they cannot reduce their demand for cash to zero. A certain amount is necessary to carry out key transactions. We saw this in the form of the cash constraint.[2] As shown in the accounting exercise of chapter 6, in anything but

1. Westhead and Weaving (1999, pp. 21–22).
2. Recall Igor's Rule 4: Find some way to earn a minimum amount of cash.

the case of the "pure" virtual economy (one in which the workers need no cash at all to survive), there always must be a buyer outside the system who supplies cash by buying enough of M's output at the market price for M to meet its cash constraint. That is, the system is not self-contained; it cannot survive without a parallel monetized sector—either domestically inside Russia or in the world market.

Even as enterprises in the virtual economy depend on small business in the monetized sector to help generate value, the system is hardly supportive of small business. Emerging businesses are an important source of value, but their growth also poses a threat. This is because the modus operandi of the virtual economy is *nontransparency*. This is the central feature of the virtual economy. The anonymity (part of the rule of law) of the monetized market economy is anathema. If transparency becomes the norm, then the virtual economy and all its participants will be ruined.

The virtual economy's continual need for value inhibits the development of the new private sector. Real taxation—taxes paid in money—falls heaviest on this sector, which cannot pay taxes via tax offsets and other machinations. Because the virtual economy needs an infusion of value to survive, it acts as a brake on the growth of the private sector. A functioning private sector is needed as a source of value, but the pressure that comes from the virtual economy circumscribes its potential.

Foreign Sources

In its boom period of 1996–97, the virtual economy relied heavily on infusions of value from abroad, in the form of both foreign investment and loans. In the wake of the August 1998 crisis and the default on short-term government debt (GKOs), foreign investors have been less willing to invest in the Russian economy than before. Portfolio investment into Russia collapsed.[3] It is not clear how long the aftereffects of this shock will linger, but the optimistic scenarios that led to growth in foreign investment in 1996–97 have been shattered.[4]

3. In 1997 portfolio investment into Russia was more than $45 billion. For all of 1998 the inward flow was $8 billion. Since then portfolio investment has been negative, the outflow exceeding the inflow. See *Russian Economic Trends*, 1999, no. 4, table 43; *Russian Economic Trends*, 2001, no. 1, table D26; and *PlanEcon Report*, vol. 15, no. 2, p. 16.

4. Moreover, in the aftermath of the 1998 crisis, the international financial institutions appeared more reluctant to contribute net new resource. They merely kept aid at the level needed to keep Russia quasi-current on debt repayment. (We use the term *quasi-current* because the debt was being rescheduled, although not always formally, in order to keep

Foreign direct investment is another potential source of value. Direct investment into Russia has continued after the crisis, but at relatively low levels of the mid-1990s.[5] Most foreign direct investment into Russia is concentrated in the energy sector, the main source of value in the economy. Given the potential opportunities, actual inflows are rather low. An important reason for this is the constraints that foreign and joint operations face when operating in the virtual economy. Joint ventures present a special case of new companies in the virtual economy. They are subject to the same constraints as all enterprises in r-d space, but they differ from the inherited enterprises of the Soviet period and from new, purely Russian entrants. Most of them can count on only their tangible market capital. They have little relational capital in Russia, though they may try to overcome this by combining with a domestic Russian enterprise. If they are entering the Russian economy in a situation when the virtual economy regime dominates, nationally or locally, they will be regarded as the cash cows, the value pumps. They may be allowed to play the game, on more or less the same terms as Gazprom: contribute value inside the virtual economy in return for a share of the value. What differs for most of them is their own internal corporate governance (and perhaps legal strictures in their home countries), which simply demands too much transparency for them to be effective participants in the virtual economy. Another way to think of this is to ask, "What western company could follow Igor's Rules?"[6]

The virtual economy penalizes Russian small business and foreign joint ventures alike for being in the cash economy. Russian small businesses can adapt to this in their two traditional ways: moving their activity underground or voluntarily restraining their activity (keeping it at a lower level—and thus hidden—than it otherwise could be). Neither of these strategies is attractive to foreign companies. Their own shareholders and home office management will eventually demand that they justify their presence. They cannot just scale back and operate on a survival level indefinitely, but to the extent that they grow, they will be prime candidates to squeeze for cash.

---

this an orderly process.) With the decline in the value of the ruble and the rise in international oil prices, Russia has more recently been in a position to cease new borrowing altogether. This may not continue to be the case.

5. For direct investment, which peaked in 1997 at more than $4.8 billion, the inflow was $2.7 billion for 2000 and $2.9 billion for 2001. See *Russian Economic Trends*, 1999, no. 4, table 43; *Russian Economic Trends*, 2001, no. 1, table D26.

6. For an interesting and informative discussion of the problems of investing in Russian enterprises, see Fox and Heller (1999) and Black, Kraakman, and Tarassova (2000).

The stories of some western companies that have attempted to get involved in Russia's most lucrative, cash-rich sectors are illustrative. For most foreign companies, the most serious obstacle to more investment is the way they are taxed. The Russian government is quite capable of collecting taxes from foreign companies, precisely because they tend to be transparent and law abiding. One of the most widely publicized ventures, White Nights, which was operated by the U.S. company Phibro Energy Production, Inc., abandoned its Russian operations in November 1998, after eight years. A former Phibro executive succinctly expressed the problem of the profit-making firm that tries to operate in Russia without adequate relational capital: "The Russian government absolutely strangled the life out of [the] nascent joint venture right at the beginning." When the venture began, the Russian government levied only three taxes on the business. By the end, the number had risen to twenty. "There weren't enough dollars left in the barrel," concluded the executive.[7]

To one extent or another, every foreign direct investor in Russia has had to decide how to deal with Russia's virtual economy. It is usually not a matter of whether to deal with it at all; remaining completely outside is hardly an option. Instead, it is how deeply to become involved. Some of the largest western investors have had long histories with the Soviet Union. In that past, much of what they did was a form of barter (countertrade). They have in effect accumulated a substantial amount of relational capital. Some western companies have taken the approach of becoming a partner with an existing Russian company for the express purpose of negotiating the Russian bureaucracy.[8] The western companies that have least been able to handle this have been the new players, especially smaller ones. They expected to enter a "normal" market economy. The virtual economy, with all its byzantine mechanisms, was not what they bargained for. They may have expected to have to deal with excessive regulation, corrupt officials, and so on, but they probably did not anticipate having to choose between receiving no payment at all for sales and accepting 70–80 percent of sales in the form of barter, between being subjected to marginal tax rates of more than 100 percent and agreeing to pay taxes in kind. The choice between seeing all profits (and more) taxed away and engaging in a form of virtual accounting that no one in the home office could accept was too much.

7. Reuters, March 16, 1999. "Giant Russian Oil Sector Withers for Want of Cash," *Russia Today* online: www.russiatoday.com.
8. Such behavior may be considered an investment in a secondary market in relational capital.

Crowding Out Private Business

The crude tax squeeze is the most obvious response of the virtual economy to private business in Russia, both domestic and foreign. The virtual economy handicaps market-oriented businesses in other ways, too. Policies adopted in Krasnodar kray (province) provide an example. As described in box 7-1, the Krasnodar regional government has prohibited public-sector institutions, schools, daycare centers, hospitals, and so on from contracting with private farms for produce because doing so clashes with a virtual economy scheme of tax offsets with the large farms. Big farms are allowed to pay their taxes in kind, that is, in the form of food delivered to public-sector institutions. For this to work, however, the government cannot allow the budget institutions (those organizations that receive funding from the provincial government) to deal with private suppliers. This system effectively supports those large, formerly Soviet farms at the expense of the new private sector. The result? Inefficiency (large farms are much worse at producing vegetables than private family farms); poor quality food delivered to institutional consumers (the vegetables will be collected and deposited in Soviet-era central warehouses before being redistributed); and private farms pushed closer to bankruptcy.

This is an example of how the virtual economy "crowds out" the real market and real private enterprise as the administrators of the virtual economy facilitate expansion of soft goods production by loss makers. The Krasnodar measures are an example of how the local government—the local administrators of the virtual economy—dictates to M that it must resume production of a soft good that it had abandoned. Vegetables produced by collective farms can be thought of as a soft good—a nonprofitable, low quality product. Vegetables produced by the private farmers, on the other hand, are profitable. There was an increase in social efficiency when the big farms abandoned their production and let the small farmers do it. Now, however, the administrators of Krasnodar's local virtual economy are going to reverse that.

Adjusting to Less Value

Whatever the levels of infusion of new value, the virtual economy still redistributes it in an inefficient manner, since value is lost in the process. First, value is destroyed in production by M. Second, many types of exchange that are characteristic of the virtual economy—such as barter—by their very

BOX 7-1. Krasnodar Kray:
How the Local Virtual Economy Strangles Private Enterprise

In mid-1998 the Krasnodar kray (province) government banned sales of produce by private farmers to government-financed ("budget") organizations. The reason is that it needed this market for offsets with former state and collective farms to repay their loans from the government (commodity credits).

Until then, in Krasnodar as elsewhere, most vegetables were produced by households and by the small private farmers (*fermery*). In 1997, 77 percent of vegetables in Russia were grown on plots. The big farms considered vegetable production too costly and labor- intensive and had abandoned it.

By 1998, private farmers in Krasnodar kray had established excellent sales relationships with many budget organizations—kindergartens, schools, hospitals, and local army bases. They delivered produce 20–30 percent cheaper than the big farms and the former state food procurement networks; they did not charge for transport costs; and their produce was fresher and of better quality.

One farmer, for example, had over a three-year period developed her relationship with the city gerontological center to the point where she specifically grew the types of vegetables and herbs that the center's medical staff needed. She had a similar relationship with the local army base. The new government decree suddenly barred her and other farmers from these markets—or, rather, prohibited the government institutions from buying from the private farmers.

The result will clearly be economic injury to the private farmers. Public-sector consumers will also suffer, however. They will be forced to take more expensive, old, low-quality produce that first has been delivered to a central warehouse and then redistributed to consumers, just as in the old days. The old state farms will again take up the loss-making vegetable production.

The chairman of the Krasnodar Private Farmers Union, Anatoliy Chizhov, correctly concluded: "This decree will have a negative impact on private farmers, city residents, and most of all on the budget organizations. . . . The food served in the budget institutions will be poorer and more expensive and there will be less of it."

Source: Tat'yana Kovaleva, "Kubanskiye chinovniki opyat' obizhayut fermerov" [Kuban bureaucrats again offend private farmers], *Krest'yanskiye vedomosti*, 1998, no. 27, p. 1.

nature involve substantial transactions costs. Third, value is leaked from the system. Some is the leakage necessary to keep value adders in the system (the "good leakage"); other is unnecessary, a form of looting.

The virtual economy thus wastes value, and this process continues even when the level of value produced in the economy varies. When the overall level of value shrinks,[9] the picture is one of waning sources of value to be pumped in, continued loss of value inside the system, and leakage of value to the outside. Clearly, there is some margin for adjustment in all of these. Slowing the loss of value, on the one hand, and increasing the infusion, on the other, would allow for greater sustainability of the virtual economy. We will examine these possibilities later on. To begin with, however, let us assume that the present trend of at least gradual decline in available value prevails and ask the question, What happens as the system runs out of value?

A decline in value may occur at the aggregate, national level, but it is more likely to occur first at the local level if there is less nationwide redistribution of value than is now the case. A handful of Russia's regions have their own value pumps (producers of fuels or energy or export industries), but most do not. The regions that lack their own internal sources of value and that do not receive redistributed value from elsewhere will find that fewer enterprises can be sustained through a virtual economy scheme. Some enterprises therefore will have to be excluded from the barter chains and tax offset arrangements that hitherto have provided them with hidden subsidies. They will in effect be pushed out of the virtual economy, but only in rare cases will they be pushed into the market economy. Most will try to hang on and survive on their own. There will be little or no investment in these enterprises. Such enterprises will increasingly operate at the subsistence level. This is the trend that is already dominant in Russian agriculture. We suggest that it may take on more prominence in industry as well. While the overall volume of economic activity may contract, there may be less value destruction overall, because fewer enterprises will be subsidized.

Another trend that may assert itself as value becomes more scarce is that some governments, especially local and regional governments, will take a more activist attitude toward their local virtual economies to make them more sustainable. These governments will take a number of steps to reduce the internal inefficiency of the virtual economy, specifically, to keep unnecessary leakage in check and to reduce transaction costs. For instance, by assuming the role of "coordinators" of production and distribution, gov-

9. In chapter 9 we deal with the impact of an increase in the level of value, brought on by the depreciation of the ruble and the expansion in oil exports.

ernments will attempt to make the virtual economy's transactions more efficient on their own terms. The example considered earlier from the Krasnodar region (box 7-1) could serve as a paradigm for local government "coordination" of economic activity. However, such measures to reduce or eliminate loss of value will be for the sake of perpetuating a third form of loss of value: destruction of value by inefficient, noncompetitive manufacturing industries that continue to be subsidized.

Local governments will want to protect their local economies not only against the private sector, but also against other regions' economies. This rivalry has contributed to the economic fragmentation of Russia. While some local governments will play a more active role in managing the virtual economy, the size of government, in terms of the real value of goods and services provided by the public sector, will in fact shrink. This will be especially true of the central government. The most vital functions it should perform—national security, public health, and environmental protection—will suffer greatly. This topic will be discussed in the next chapter.

A Shift in *r-d* Space

What kind of future is there for a loss-making enterprise when there is less value available to support it? Examining the relative position of such a plant in $r\text{-}d$ space as time passes will help to answer that question. In chapter 4 we analyzed the effects of investment in distance reduction and relational capital on an enterprise's state—in other words, the effect of the enterprise's own decisions on its current state. But the state of the enterprise will also be affected by events external to it. A loss-making enterprise will, in particular, suffer over time in both the d and r dimensions. It will in effect be pushed toward the southeast corner, further away from viability in both directions.

First of all, consider the d dimension. Chapter 4 showed that for many enterprises, especially those with poor prospects, investing in relational capital and distance reduction are mutually exclusive alternatives. The loss maker that concentrates on investing in r will do so by sacrificing investment in reducing distance d. The enterprise is assessing the relative payoffs and concluding that it has a better chance of survival by investing in relations. The problem, however, is that firms in the rest of the world (and perhaps in the domestic economy) are not resting on their laurels. As frontier firms increase their competitiveness, the distance d for the enterprises that fail to restructure will increase. That is, even without changing their own behavior, enterprises will be further and further from market viability. Their own equipment will grow older and less productive. Their human capital may depreciate as well.

Now look at r. As the value available for redistribution runs out, the relational capital of any given enterprise depreciates, thus moving it further to the south in r-d space. Why? With less value available for redistribution, the relative price of this value, in terms of existing connections and relations, must increase. As relational capital is the ability to appropriate value produced elsewhere, the measure of the value of relational capital, therefore, is how many resources it can appropriate. As value in the economy becomes scarcer, the contribution to enterprise survival from any given level of connections is reduced. The enterprise is pushed closer to the viability constraint.

Let us take a concrete case, such as the story of the Kostroma linens (pp. 37–38). This is an example of the application of relational capital in fairly modest amounts. The three-way personal connections between the director of an impoverished rural clinic, the director of a local textile mill, and the financial officer of the regional government allowed a deal permitting a quantity of fabric delivered to the clinic to be offset against a portion of the mill's local tax obligation. The payoff from this particular deal was, perhaps, quite low. The value of enough fabric to produce sheets for a few dozen beds in a rural clinic, even if virtually priced at many times its market value, is still an extremely small amount. Hundreds of such petty deals would be needed to have a significant impact on the mill's output. More important, however, the textile mill still could not survive unless it simultaneously had enough relational capital to facilitate arrangements that could infuse value to the mill from suppliers of raw materials, gas, and electricity—deals that require a good deal more relational capital than the sheets-for-taxes agreement. If, increasingly, the mill has to compete with other enterprises for dwindling supplies of valuable inputs, its relational capital may eventually not suffice for it to continue to participate in long barter chains or to negotiate the all-important tax offsets. Ultimately, it may find itself cast off from existing networks, forcing it to rely on itself and on direct connections with the retail sector.

In other words, the enterprise that has previously chosen to emphasize relations over distance reduction now faces a decline in the return to its relational capital because of the general decrease of value in the economy. Such an enterprise would find itself pushed further toward the southeast corner of r-d space, perhaps even below the viability constraint. In figure 7-2, for example, enterprise A was viable before the shock, owing to its relatively

FIGURE 7-2. Depreciation of Relational Capital

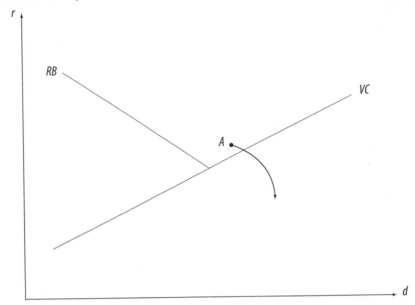

high level of r. A reduction in value resulting in depreciation of the relational capital stock causes the position of enterprise A to shift below the viability constraint (VC). By definition of the viability constraint, the enterprise would be shut down. In expectation of this, the director might engage in looting of assets before the enterprise was closed. Indeed, if the redistribution of value is reduced in the next several years, many enterprises will doubtless fall into this trap.

The trajectory followed by enterprise A in figure 7-2 is toward eventual closure. We know, however, from the paucity of bankruptcies in Russia that closure is not the only potential outcome for a loss-making enterprise. Indeed, a more likely result may be that the enterprise transforms and contracts its activities so that it can continue to survive outside the virtual economy once the external infusion of value has ceased. We refer to this behavioral path as *shrinkage*.

Shrinkage

Rather than cease production, Russian enterprises on the verge of bankruptcy may radically reorient their activities to survive. This may involve complete alteration of production lines and may at first glance seem to be desirable restructuring. However, the shift in products is not the primary characteristic of this type of adaptation. Instead, the key characteristic of the shrinking enterprise is increasing withdrawal from the market—in both the conventional (monetized) and virtual economy (demonetized) dimensions. That is, it ceases to participate in any form of complex exchange economy. In ideal restructuring, the enterprise replaces loss-making exchanges with profitable ones, but it retains the complex production chains. In shrinkage, the enterprise consumes capital as a substitute for purchased inputs.

The way this happens is as follows. As the enterprise sees the value of its relational capital dissipated, it ceases production of soft, value-destroying goods. The enterprise has no use for them outside the network of relational capital; it is relational capital that gives them value. At the same time, given that its distance to the market has increased during transition, the enterprise has virtually no opportunity to shift to producing hard goods (marketable products). Of course, with a large enough infusion of external finance, presumably any enterprise can be restructured sufficiently to produce hard goods. However, there is an opportunity cost involved, and enterprises that have migrated toward the southeast corner of r-d space are the least likely to be able to attract any external funds, let alone a sufficiently large amount. To survive, the enterprise must continue to insulate itself from market forces. Since it can no longer participate in virtual economy barter chains, it will turn inward and reduce dependency on the outside. For instance, it will use its capital stock to produce goods that require little or no purchased inputs. The enterprise focuses its activity increasingly on the pure survival of its workers.

There are several characteristics of this form of industrial activity. The primary form that this survival focus takes is more small-scale production, less specialization, and production that is simply more primitive.[10] Ironically, in a purely technical sense it is *more efficient* than the previous situation. Before, the plant was attempting to produce, on as large a scale as it could, a soft good that in fact destroyed value. The more of such a soft good the plant produced, the worse the result for the economy as a whole. Now, because the plant uses little or none of the valuable inputs that it previously used, its activity is less socially harmful. Indeed, the enterprise may now be even adding value, but it is doing so on a drastically reduced scale of production.[11] The cessation of value infusion clearly leaves the workers

10. Andrei Volgin (1998) has termed this process the "primitivization" of production.
11. Note the implication for economic statistics: a drastic decline in output represents a rise in value added.

TABLE 7-1. The Effect of Shrinkage on *M*, the Virtual Economy Manufacturing Plant

Benchmark category	*M* in the virtual economy	A "shrunken" *M*: cast out of the virtual economy
Gas	100	0
Labor	100	20
Value of output, real prices	100	25
Value of output, virtual prices	300	Not an option
Value added, real prices	− 100	+ 5

and managers worse off—the smaller scale of production reduces their remuneration. The gains from the elimination of waste are felt elsewhere in the economy.

We can cast this discussion of shrinkage in terms of the four-sector model of chapter 6. Recall that the manufacturing plant *M* purchased an input (gas) for 100 rubles to produce a product whose market value was 100. The only way it could appear to justify its continued existence was to substantially overprice the product. (We more or less arbitrarily chose a price of 300.) Consider now the case illustrated in table 7-1, where *M* is cast out of the virtual economy. That is, *G* no longer gives it gas, and *B* no longer accepts tax offsets. *M* responds by a radical change: it abandons its former production, in which it consumed 100 rubles' worth each of gas and labor to make a product worth 100 rubles. It now produces a new product that uses no gas at all and only 20 rubles' worth of labor.[12] This new product is worth, say, 25 rubles. What is the result? Gross production in real, nonvirtual prices falls by 75 percent (and in virtual prices even more: by 91.5 percent). Nonetheless, as the final line in the table shows, by shifting to a product that requires no purchased inputs, the enterprise transforms itself from a value destroyer to a value adder.

This may seem like a completely hypothetical discussion. But consider a real-life case of such an enterprise: the Kvarts enterprise in Siberia (see box 7-2), which has already regressed to something close to the shrunken state illustrated above. Where it once produced industrial goods, it now produces vegetables, chickens, bread, and pasta. Kvarts started as part of the Soviet defense-industrial complex, although only a rather insignificant part. It apparently had been created in the 1970s as a jobs program for a remote

12. The reason the labor force falls so much in this example is that the smaller scale of production affords less employment. At such enterprises much of the work force has been whittled away over time. The remaining component may also increasingly engage in household production.

area of Omsk oblast. For a defense plant, in other words, Kvarts had only modest relational capital to begin with. With the collapse of the USSR, it experienced severe cutbacks in its defense orders. At the same time, its civilian product—black-and-white television sets—had extraordinarily bleak prospects in Russia's new open economy. Therefore, with no government demand for its defense goods and no market demand for its television sets, what little relational capital Kvarts possessed had vanished—or the enterprise has simply lost the capacity to invest in relational capital (or distance reduction) over time as conditions worsened—while its market distance was vast. It was in the extreme southeast corner of *r-d* space and would have seemed a guaranteed candidate for bankruptcy and extinction. Nevertheless, it has survived by shrinking its level of output almost to the level of only sustaining its own work force at a subsistence level and, more important, by reorienting into directions completely inconceivable before. It has also written off most of its physical capital.

At the shrunken level of activity, Kvarts could not employ its full labor force. Eight of every ten left the plant. Nevertheless, those who did remain were willing to fundamentally abandon all previous assumptions about the nature of their plant and its products. Through the self-organization of their activity, the remaining workers survive, even though survival means converting industrial production facilities of relatively recent vintage (for Russia) into a greenhouse to grow vegetables.

One should be careful before dismissing the Kvarts story as merely an isolated example in one small town in Siberia. There are numerous towns in Russia roughly comparable in size and structure to Tara, the town where Kvarts in located. Many enterprises were created for the same reasons as Kvarts. Nor should one rule out that considerably larger plants might return in this way to something out of the preindustrial era.

The Cost of Shrinkage

Several important aspects of the Kvarts example are worth discussing. First, shrinkage allows the enterprise to limit its interaction with the rest of the economy. Since the enterprise does not participate in large barter chains with other enterprises, it does not require as much relational capital. The more self-sufficient it can become, the better it can cope with the drop in relational capital.

Second, shrinkage involves a write-off of the capital stock. The write-off is typically not a formal step, but in effect the capital stock that was

BOX 7-2. The Kvarts Plant

Tara (population 26,000) is a town in a remote district of Omsk oblast in Siberia, located 300 kilometers north of the capital city of Omsk. The town's main factory is a former defense plant, a branch of the Omsk enterprise Kvarts, which made components for black-and-white television sets and defense electronics.

Founded in the 1970s, the plant's heyday was in the late 1980s, when more than eight hundred people worked there. The Russian government terminated the defense orders in 1992. Demand for Kvarts's civilian product, Russian-made televisions, collapsed at about the same time. Most of the employees quit voluntarily or were laid off, leaving only 156 workers by 1998. The plant now produces neither TV components nor defense goods. Yet it continues to operate. What do the workers do? As reported in an article in a leading Russian economics journal, they:

—bake bread, up to 3,000 loaves daily in the summer and 1,000 in winter;

—make pasta;

—repair television sets and, using cannibalized parts, even assemble some 10–15 sets a month;

—log and cut trees from forests on the plant's territory to produce lumber;

—repair boilers and heating units in the rural villages and in other public institutions;

—grow green onions and other vegetables by converting one entire assembly building into a greenhouse;

—raise baby chicks in an incubator of their own construction which they have set up in another assembly shop.

All of these goods and services are sold to the local population, some for cash.

The article describing this situation summed up: "In general [plants like Kvarts] are looking for any and all ways just to survive. And in this sense *the fate of the Kvarts plant is an excellent illustration of restructuring in Russia's industry* [emphasis added]."

Source: Shcherbakova (1998).

designed to produce TVs is now used as a greenhouse. One could assign a value to the capital assets of the enterprise based on the plant's estimated production of TVs under the assumption that the TVs could be sold. This value would be much greater than that of a greenhouse, since the greenhouse activity uses so little of the enterprise's actual capital. However, it is precisely the fact that Kvarts cannot sell the TVs that explains why the plant has now become a greenhouse. Therefore, the difference in the valuation of the assets in these two lines of activity represents the write-off of capital that is associated with such developments.

The write-off of assets involved in shrinkage is both rational (after all, it is just a recognition of the overvaluation of the capital based on previous bad investments) and efficient. Less value is destroyed in the new activity. However, there is another side to this development that is less propitious for the country's economy. Shrinkage may also involve a write-off of human capital, and that does represent a waste to society.[13] Human capital accumulated for the production of industrial goods may be wasted if the enterprise is transformed into a greenhouse. This may represent a permanent loss to the economy from the desperate struggle to survive the loss of relational capital.

The social cost of shrinkage is an ironic result of Soviet industrialization strategies and the course of Russian economic reform. The Soviet system accumulated human capital to a very high degree, primarily in the sectors that were most dependent on Soviet demand, notably defense production. As the economy has been transformed, the demand for this output has fallen dramatically. Enterprises in such situations had two alternatives: either restructure to radically reduce d, or else invest in relations to avoid what might be a difficult and costly process. We know that many enterprises faced with this choice opted for the latter. Relational capital allowed the enterprises to postpone painful restructuring. However, they could not post-

13. The extent of the loss of human capital is critically related to the distinction between job-specific and general human capital. Human capital that is not job specific may not be lost *if* workers can move to a new job, a process that is often difficult owing to the lack of labor mobility and housing, not to mention wage arrears. More important, much of the human capital in question was specific to the associated physical capital. Hence, this human capital is likely to be lost as shrinkage takes place. In fact, this process is very similar to what we described in chapter 3 with regard to the divergence between inherited and newly installed capital (p. 51). Much of the human capital inherited from the Soviet period was developed for a specific industrial structure. As the economy transforms, the rate of return to investment in new human capital may be very high even as the value of the inherited capital shrinks toward zero. Just as in the case of physical capital, the longer the necessary restructuring of human capital is delayed, the greater the loss to the economy.

pone it forever. The imperative to restructure eventually did assert itself. That imperative did not come early, when the physical and (especially) the human capital of Russia's manufacturing sector were more intact, but only after the enterprise's *relational* capital was exhausted (at least depleted to less than viability levels). By the time restructuring eventually did occur, a great deal of resources had been wasted. Had such enterprises restructured early in the transition period, when d was lower than it is today, it might have been possible to save some of the human capital. Conversion of a missile producer to production of sanitary milk containers may not fully utilize the skills of the physicists and engineers employed at the plant, but it still involves production of industrial goods. Forgoing this alternative, ending up shrinking like Kvarts, implies that the ultimate loss of human capital is much greater.

Shrinkage thus represents a reduction in the amount of specialization in the economy. Division of labor is reduced, and self-sufficiency is enhanced. The need to engage with external actors is pared to the bare minimum.[14] As specialization decreases, the value of human capital decreases at a faster rate. This represents an important loss for the economy. The process demonstrates how fragile is complex economic organization and how costly is the virtual economy path onto which so many Russian enterprises have been pushed.

Agriculture as a Paradigm

It is no accident that a prominent part of the activity of the restructured, "primitivized" Kvarts is food production—bread, pasta, vegetables, chickens. Food production is the ultimate self-sufficient activity. It follows that the agricultural sector proper may have special lessons for the future of other parts of the economy. For the most part, agriculture in Russia today represents something close to a self-sufficient economy in its pure form. In that sense, it is a disturbing paradigm for the rest of the economy.

The Soviet Union's old collective and state farms (which Russians still refer to by their old names, *kolkhozy* and *sovkhozy*, or sometimes just *krupkhozy*—"big farms") are the *M*s in the nearly self-contained virtual economy that is Russia's agricultural sector. The distinctive feature of Russian agriculture is how little value is needed to keep the system going. Very little value is being infused by a *G*. Instead, almost all value comes from *H*,

14. This process is characteristic of what Ericson (2001) refers to when he speaks of the feudal nature of the Russian economy.

the peasant households, and from consuming (cannibalizing) the endowment of physical capital (including land improvements).

The Bobino farm in Kirov oblast (box 7-3) is an example of how farms operate under such conditions and how much their behavior resembles that of a classic virtual economy manufacturing enterprise (*M*). Like Igor's enterprise, Bobino is able and willing to engage in tax offsets with the local government because it can continue to provide goods and services for many of the same social-sector institutions it previously had built or owned (day-care centers, schools, roads). Like the Tutayev diesel engine manufacturer, Bobino consciously sells some of its output below the cost of production because it is so desperately in need of cash to meet its cash constraint.

Is Bobino unusual for Russian agriculture? Yes, but only because it is *better off* than most farms. It is relatively monetized. At the time described (1997), it was only three months behind on its wage payments. Producing any marketed surplus at all places it in the elite of Russian farms. In general, the agricultural sector is far more plagued by losses and overwhelmed with debt and arrears than even manufacturing. Because of their massive debts and arrears, nearly all farms are effectively barred from any credit whatsoever. Their bank accounts are blocked. If they earn a single cash ruble, it will be appropriated by the tax authorities. The responses by the farms have been the same as those of industrial enterprises. Barter, of course, is one reaction. The farms have also responded by turning over more and more of the farm to the households. Land and animals are given to the families, who grow food for themselves first and foremost.

The result is a dramatic decrease in the marketed surplus of agriculture (that is, the food sold off-farm in the city stores and markets). This illustrates a big difference between the old Soviet planned economy and today's virtual economy. In the old system, the state appropriated output for redistribution. In effect what this meant, especially in the harshest periods of Soviet rule, was the total subordination of the peasantry to the urban population. Meeting the food needs of the nonagricultural population was the "first commandment for the kolkhozes." The peasants' requirements for seed grain, not to mention their own consumption, were met only on the "residual principle"—that is, they had to take whatever was left over.

Now the tables are turned. The farms meet their own needs first. Only then do they see how much is left to be sold off the farm and how much of that is for cash. In the post-1991 period, rural households in Russia eat more food than urban households, something that was not the case under the Soviet Union. Survey research by Russian scholars shows that the aver-

BOX 7-3. The Bobino Farm, Kirov Oblast

The Bobino farm is one of the largest farms in Kirov oblast, with 5,600 hectares (about 14,000 acres) of arable land and a herd of 2,130 dairy cows. This is a "reformed" "private" farm. As part of its reorganization, it divested its so-called social assets to the local (district) government. That just meant that it now has the problem of paying taxes and fees to the government to maintain those very same social services. The farmers' weekly, *Krest'yanskiye vedomosti*, writes that Bobino has found "a simple solution. Basically, [the farm and the district government] have agreed on mutual offsets. Bobino supplies the day-care center and the school with food, performs necessary repairs, etc."

The newspaper also provides the following revealing discussion of the role of that same farm's cash sales:

"Bobino's main products are livestock, potatoes, and grain. The first of these is basically unprofitable. The cost of production of a liter of milk is 1,200 rubles; the selling price is 800–900. The oblast provides a subsidy of 95 rubles per liter of milk (the only oblast subsidy to farmers), but as you can see this does not cover the difference. The same thing is true for meat: the cost of production is 16,000–18,000 rubles [per kilo], and it is sold at 10,000. People on the farm were saying: 'Let's give up livestock altogether. Let's keep

age rural resident eats over 50 percent more calories than the average urban resident. They also eat better. For instance, rural Russians on average eat 28 percent more protein than urban residents.[15]

Of course, the other side of this process is that the self-subsistence farms have almost no interaction with the urban industrial economy—a typical feature of shrinkage. They do not deliver food to the cities, but they also do not receive industrial goods from them. Table 7-2 shows how the level of inputs purchased by agriculture has dropped down close to zero. The picture for other inputs such as fertilizers and seeds is hardly better.[16] This is another big difference between today's virtual economy and the previous Soviet command economy. The Soviet economy's top-down command sys-

15. Ovcharova, Turuntsev, and Korchagina (1997).
16. In addition to table 7-2, see Kukharenko (1998, pp. 87–90).

only our grain production.' But we calculated that we could live comfortably from the profit on grain for only three months out of the year. So, unless we have four grain harvests a year, we need to get help from our livestock operations. On the whole, [livestock] is unprofitable; nevertheless, it provides a small stream of [cash] revenue every day. It gives us the bare minimum we need to solve all the little problems that crop up. Also, the farm has a sawmill. We barter sawn timber or rights to standing timber for spare parts and fuel."

The article concludes with a description of the agricultural household sector's attitude toward this near-complete virtual economy:

"The farm is about three months behind in its wage payments. It would have been possible to reduce that gap, but the general director persuaded people to invest the money in finishing up the harvest. The people agreed to be patient, in the meantime receiving their wages in the form of milk, butter, and meat. So that's the way things balance out: there's a downward pull from the government's economic problems, but an upward pull from the farmers' own feeling of self-preservation and an attempt to organize their labor in a new way."

Source: Yevgeniya Kvitko, "Vyatke ne khvatayet tol'ko feodalov. Natural'noye khozyaystvo tam uzhe yest'" [All that's missing in Vyatka are the feudal lords. The natural economy is already there], *Krest'yanskiye vedomosti*, 42 (20–26 October) 1997, p. 6.

tem has been replaced by a bottom-up (voluntary) barter system that is more limited in scope and continues to contract. The disincentive to use money and, more important, the draining reserves of value will push an ever larger part of the economy away from transacting altogether. The Soviet economy used to sustain an elongated chain of transactions between industry and agriculture. Now, there is nearly none.

Agriculture in Russia is thus already an extreme example of the kind of shrinkage discussed above in the case of Kvarts. The farms have increasingly withdrawn from the market in any form. They receive almost no inputs from other parts of the economy. They are not replacing their physical capital. They produce only for their own workers' households. At present, perhaps as few as 500 of Russia's total of around 25,000 farms would be needed to produce nearly all the agricultural sector's current marketable surplus.

TABLE 7-2. Decline in Major Industrial Goods Delivered to Agriculture, 1990–97
Units delivered in 1997 as a percentage of those delivered in 1990

Tractors	2.6
Trucks	2.6
Combines	7.1
Ploughs	1.0
Sowers	2.1

Source: *Krest'yanskiye vedomosti*, no. 41 (1998), p. 2.

Because of the dominance of farms like Bobino and those much worse off, rural Russia—which comprises forty million people, or more than one-quarter of the Russian population—is in an extreme state of demonetization. Predictably, the household cash constraint in agriculture is rarely binding. The average farm wage in January 2001 was less than 25 percent of an industrial worker's wage.[17] Households cope by earning modest amounts of cash outside the system, but mainly by producing their own food on household plots. In an increasing number of self-subsistence farms and the regions around them, the only cash that circulates at all originates not from wages or other earned income, but from government transfers such as pensions and child benefit payments. The story told by one native of Kostroma oblast, a rural province about three hundred kilometers northeast of Moscow, poignantly demonstrates that no matter how successful households appear to be in providing for their basic needs without money, there is always a need for a critical minimum amount of cash. Without it, the effects can be devastating. Under the heading, "Why the Russian Countryside Has Fallen in Love with Its Old Folks," a Moscow weekly newspaper related the comments of one Kostroma resident who worked as a health clinic nurse on a *kolkhoz* (now a joint-stock company). Because her *kolkhoz* had long ago stopped paying its workers, she also worked in the fields. Neither she nor her fellow *kolkhoz* members had seen any cash at all in the village for half a year.

The only time we see cash is on the rare occasions when the old folks receive their pensions. And when that does happen, they are immediately surrounded by affectionate relatives. The absence of cash has led to the resurrection of all formerly lost family ties and put an end to intrafamily feuds. Without cash, you can't buy a notepad for a school

17. "Average monthly wage per worker in Russia, by sector," *Interfax* (2001, no. 31–32, table 10).

child or a bottle of medicine for a sick person. Both the middle and the younger generations crowd around their elderly relatives. Pensioners have become important figures in the village . . . if they've been paid their pension.[18]

Effect on Households

Shrinkage, if it continues to affect industry the way it has come to dominate agriculture, may define a new split within the Russian economy. We have emphasized the division between market-oriented and loss-making enterprises. Shrinkage—withdrawal from the market—suggests a further division in which some loss makers remain inside the virtual economy, while other enterprises, or even entire sectors and regions, are excluded from it but continue to exist in a multitude of highly localized, self-contained (household-community) economies. One way to think of shrinkage is as a process of moving self-protective activity to ever smaller units. Survival becomes more and more localized. This suggests that a critical factor for the sustainability of a shrunken virtual economy is its effect on the most localized unit of all, the household. How do households deal with the cash constraint?

As it evolved during the 1990s, the virtual economy pushed all its participants to minimize the need for cash. The ultimate burden, however, ended up with the households. Households had to either acquire cash outside the system—apart from what they were receiving from their official jobs or from government transfers (from M or B)—or they had to acquire goods without the use of cash. When the process first started, the shift to nonmonetary transactions—reducing the amount of cash necessary for everyone's survival—proceeded smoothly. It seemed so especially because it all happened at the individual, personal level. But the marginal returns to this process of "personalization" of economic activity were diminishing. Households substituted goods and services obtained by barter for those acquired through cash transactions and substituted nontraded (self-produced) goods for traded goods. In both cases, there was a loss of efficiency, and that loss grew as the percentage of noncash activity grew. Take, for instance, households' substitution of home-grown food for store-

18. "Pochemu v russkoy derevne polyubili starikov" ["Why the Russian countryside has fallen in love with its old folks"], letter to the editor of *Obshchaya gazeta*, December 11–17, 1997, p. 15, from Yekaterina Stepantseva, librarian.

bought. The huge share of food that Russians grow in their family gardens, as opposed to the official farms, is well known to most observers of Russia. The share of home-grown food as a percentage of total agricultural output grew from 32 percent in 1992 to 57 percent in 1999.[19] For certain categories of food, the limits of home production seem to have been reached. Since 1996, for instance, family plots have accounted for more than 90 percent of all potatoes grown in Russia, reaching a share of 92.6 percent in 2001.[20] The nearly 30 million tons of potatoes that ordinary Russian families grow in their backyards and dacha (vacation home) plots is more than the amount produced by all the farms, big and small, of the United States and Great Britain combined.[21] Self-production of food on the scale seen in today's Russia is an example of extreme primitivization. It reflects both shrinkage and loss of human capital. If the labor of the scientist is more valuable in the potato field than in the research laboratory, then there is a serious problem in the economy.

Other Coping Mechanisms

Individual coping mechanisms to relax the household cash constraint are not restricted to agriculture, of course. Particularly widespread is the phenomenon of moonlighting, or part-time secondary jobs, by industrial workers. Virtual economy enterprises typically tolerate and sometimes explicitly encourage and help organize the participation of their employees in the cash economy in order to supplement their incomes. An example of how moonlighting in the cash sector complements the virtual economy comes from a Russian sociologist's 1996 study of a large manufacturing plant in Siberia, the PO Vega company near the city of Novosibirsk. In the Soviet era Vega was a producer of defense-related electronics, and it had a work force of more than 11,000. By the mid-1990s, a well-organized system had emerged in which the Vega management sanctioned and even facilitated the moonlighting activity of the plant's employees. In many cases, the pay rate workers received for the extra jobs was several times higher than they received from Vega.[22]

The Vega example shows how individual moonlighting workers live a shared existence in both the virtual economy and the monetized private

19. *Russian Statistical Yearbook 2000*, table 15.3, "Structure of agricultural output by category of producer."

20. *Interfax* (2001, no. 52).

21. *Russian Statistical Yearbook 2000*, tables 15.13 and 25.25.

22. Arsent'yeva (1997).

economy. However, the intertwining of the virtual and market worlds is still more complicated. Even when an individual works full time in the monetized economy, he or she cannot be assumed to be completely outside the virtual economy. To the extent that such a person's household has a shared budget, the cash earnings from outside the virtual economy will still be used to help meet the cash constraint of the rest of his or her family, which may still live in the virtual economy.

These examples remind us that Russians' participation in the monetized part of their economy—whether as full-time workers or moonlighting part-time workers—is not in itself evidence of households' leaving the virtual economy. The reduction in the size of Russia's industrial (mining and manufacturing) labor force may not reflect a correspondingly reduced importance of the virtual economy and enhancement of the cash economy. Some of the alternative employment has been part of the adjustment of the virtual economy's household sector so as to be able to survive and *continue* the existence of the virtual economy. Private cash-earning activity is not a threat or an alternative to the virtual economy; it is a means of making the participation in the virtual economy affordable for the households involved.

Finally, the role of family strategies to share income from various sources underscores the difficulty of policy approaches that might be aimed at separating the virtual and monetized economies. The household is a key channel for transmission of cash from the money economy into the virtual economy. The willingness of the households' most productive members to subsidize the least productive members' continued participation in the virtual economy is another method of value infusion into the virtual economy.

Personalized Safety Nets

The most important thing that happens as the cash constraint presses tighter is that people spend more time and effort looking for a way out. Households survive wage arrears and loss of benefits by insulating themselves as much as possible from the cash economy. As a rule, society becomes more atomized, as each group or even each family looks for its own solution. The result is a phenomenon that can be described as the "personalization of the social safety net." The following letter from a village in Arkhangel'sk, entitled "We Want a Normal Life," illustrates the issue:

> We live in a forestry *posyolok* [company town]. The main employers here are logging and farming enterprises. They pay their workers

poorly and rarely. You might say that people work in the state farms for free. My husband, for example, hasn't been paid for 6–8 months.

We survive thanks only to our household plot: We have a garden and some cows. We *ourselves* have enough to eat, and even some left over to sell. We sell sour cream, milk, and *tvorog* [cottage cheese] much cheaper than you can buy them in the stores. We live from one day to the next: If we sell something, we can buy something. If we don't sell anything, we have nothing to buy necessities with. When things become unbearable, I bake our own bread. I put two bread pans in an oven we made under our hot-water heater in the bathroom. That's the way we live. Everyone finds his or her own way. Necessity is the mother of invention.

But can you imagine: because we have a couple of cows, we're considered wealthy! And yet there are times when we don't even have the three or four rubles [10 cents] you need to buy a loaf of bread. All our so-called wealth consists of the calluses and manure that cover our hands.

When in the world is our government going to give those who are willing and able to work a chance for a normal life?[23]

There are many such personalized solutions available, and as long as there is time for adjustment, the margins are still there for the overwhelming majority of the people and enterprises. To put it bluntly, there is still a long way left before reaching the rock bottom of Kostroma's rural residents or the workers of the Kvarts factory in Siberia. While one should be very cautious in forecasting limits to the ability of families to adjust, it is bad economics to ignore the cost involved.

23. Letter to the editor of *Krest'yanskiye vedomosti*, no. 48, 1999, p. 4, from Galina Mezentseva of Shipitsyno settlement, Kotlasskiy district, Arkhangel'sk province.

CHAPTER EIGHT

The Virtual State

As the preceding chapter illustrated, a shrinking virtual economy has far-reaching negative effects. It exacerbates the fundamental problem of much of Russian industry—its lack of competitiveness—and it puts an increasingly heavy burden on households. The most immediate detrimental consequences, however, are on the public sector. The continued operation of the virtual economy inflates the apparent size of government while in fact hollowing it out; it reduces government employees themselves to nonproductive, survival-oriented individuals; and it fragments and weakens the state at all levels, but especially at the national level. All of this is a vicious circle. As the government fails increasingly to play its role, more of society turns away from the public sector altogether, ignoring it when it can and actively undermining it if it must in order to protect itself.

The virtual economy has helped create a virtual public sector, a "virtual state," in Russia. This condition results from the inability of government to collect enough taxes to meet approved levels of government spending. The problem is not that the tax base is too small; it is that relational capital means there is less value for the state to get its hands on. The value-destroying manufacturer (M) pays only in soft goods. Therefore the actual receipts to the government are far smaller than if the real source of value (G) had been taxed directly. To be explicit: when G shifts 100 rubles of value to M, M's taxable income should rise by the same amount that G's falls. However, M uses the value to produce soft goods and pays its taxes in this form. Hence what M pays to the government is worth much less than if G had delivered the 100 rubles directly to the government in cash.

When taxpayers are allowed to pay in the form of soft goods, with prices set on the basis of the taxpayer's relational capital, this creates an additional problem as it demonetizes government budgets. Direct government transfers to households—such as government workers' wages, child benefit payments, and pensions—cannot, with rare exceptions, be paid in kind. Other budgetary outlays do consist to a large extent of in-kind payments: direct provision of public goods such as education, health care, roads, and so on. This is true in normal economies. However, budget *revenues* are another story. In a "normal" economy, the fact that budgetary income is in the form of cash is what allows the government to purchase precisely the public goods and services that the society has decided on. Because cash allows full freedom and flexibility in meeting the needs as defined by the budget, it makes possible maximum efficiency and equity. In the Russian virtual economy's demonetized public sector, this is not true. The Chelyabinsk subway is a good example.

The Chelyabinsk Subway

In March 1998 the governor of Chelyabinsk oblast (province), Petr Sumin, declared the construction of a subway system in the capital city of Chelyabinsk to be one of the most important construction projects in the region.[1] The story of how that subway project came into being is a good illustration of how public policy priorities become shaped by the rather fortuitous existence of tax obligations by certain companies. Construction companies in Chelyabinsk were deeply in arrears on their taxes to the local (city and oblast) governments. Unable to pay in cash, the companies offered to start construction of a subway system in this city of more than one million residents—a project that had been discussed for years, but shelved for lack of funds. At the same time, the federal government had a few years earlier pledged to financially support a subway in Chelyabinsk, but did not make good on its pledges. In other words, the federal government "owed" money to the oblast and its capital city. The local government was more or less forced to accept the construction companies' offer of a big construction

---

1. "Chelyabinsk Builds New Subway System," *Russian Regional Report, RRR-Internet Edition* (April 2, 1998), by correspondent Igor Stepanov in Chelyabinsk.

project in lieu of the debts, while the federal government canceled the companies' tax arrears in place of the federal contribution to Chelyabinsk. Therefore, by building the subway, the construction companies are making good on their debts to the three levels of budgets. By granting the companies the right to offset their federal taxes in this way, the federal government is making good on its "debt" to the region.

The fact that the *federal* government is also involved in accepting the construction work as a tax offset is an interesting example of how local companies and local government can collude to extract a concession from the federal government. One might ask, How can a company providing a "local government good" use that to pay federal taxes? In this case, it is as if the subway construction work were "delivered" to the federal government as payment for federal taxes, and then the federal government in turn "delivered" that work to the city and oblast as payment for the money it had promised them earlier.

In Chelyabinsk, the political weight—the relational capital—of the large construction enterprises in town ensured that they would be able to pay their taxes in the form of soft goods. The result is a subway—or at least, subway construction activity for an undetermined number of years. It does not matter if the city and oblast have more pressing needs. When goods are delivered in kind as tax offsets, it is a seller's market. Enterprises dump on the government whatever they happen to produce—whatever is easiest, cheapest—not what society (the citizenry) says it wants and needs.

The Chelyabinsk subway story illustrates a worst-case scenario of public-sector development. Not only are individual taxpayers determining the amount of the taxes they pay, but they are also deciding what goods or services government delivers to the population—in effect rewriting the local budget. The example also shows how government comes to be inflated in size (it is virtual). The deliveries to the government are overpriced—by exactly how much is of course never clear to the outsider.[2] But studies such as those by the Karpov Commission leave little doubt that there is a pattern of overpricing and that there is substantially less in the government budgets than appears to be.

---

2. Of course, the problem is not just general overpricing, but arbitrary overpricing. This is what relational capital is all about. In her crime novel *Okhota na izyubrya* [Deer Hunt], a fictional account of some essential features of the virtual economy, Russian journalist Yuliya Latynina observed: "How much you pay [in taxes] depends on your weight in society. . . . You see, that's the beauty of the nonpayments system: the amount you pay depends on your status."

Reduced Efficiency

Efficiency clearly suffers when taxes are paid in kind. The goods and services delivered in tax offset schemes are not necessarily the ones that citizens want. To the extent that it is possible to exchange those goods and services for other, more desired ones, much is lost in transaction costs. Other schemes offer somewhat less inefficiency. Take, for instance, the practice of tax payments in the form of *veksels* (promissory notes) by a natural monopoly such as Gazprom or UES, the electricity producer. When these companies pay their taxes in *veksels*, the government at least has some choice of where to redeem the *veksel* for goods. All local enterprises that use gas or electricity and have debts to Gazprom or UES will accept the *veksels* as payment.

In rare cases, this can work reasonably well on a local basis. The town of Zarechny in Sverdlovsk oblast provides a rather ideal example.[3] In this town more than 90 percent of the 1997 municipal budget was nonmonetary. The biggest taxpayer is a nuclear power plant whose *veksels* serve as a limited form of local money. The power plant's *veksels* (colloquially known as "electro-rubles") can be used by any city government body to pay electricity bills. More interesting, the power plant also functions as the mediator of in-kind payments by a long list of other local companies. When the power plant presents its *veksels* to the city, it also gives the government a list of the enterprises that owe it money for electricity. The city then can turn to those companies and redeem the power plant's *veksels* (the electro-rubles) for goods. The companies in turn use the *veksels* to pay off their electricity bills. In effect, the scheme becomes similar to one in which there are "participating merchants" in a voucher scheme.

Zarechny's situation is extraordinary. Not only does it have a local "value pump," but it has one whose interests coincide with those of the city government. Zarechny is a true company town. It is a cohesive community, nearly all of whose residents are connected to the agency to which the power plant belongs, the Ministry of Nuclear Power ("Minatom"). However, even Zarechny's arrangement has negative consequences. Not surprisingly, the power plant *veksels* are very much "virtually" priced, with a cash value that is perhaps only 60–70 percent of the nominal value. More important, because the electro-rubles are restricted in their application to companies that have debts to the power plant, their use isolates the region's

3. Information on Zarechny from interview material and unpublished data provided to the authors from town officials, 1998–2000.

economy from the rest of the nation.[4] This is in fact a general problem with the practices of tax offsets and other nonmonetary settlements with budgets. They lead to a fragmentation of the Russian economy and state. Local governments are pitted against the federal government, region is pitted against region, ministry against ministry, all the way down to individual agencies of government.

Region versus Region

Fiscal transfers are an important element of public policy in federations such as Russia, where economic performance differs substantially across regions. Interregional fiscal transfers are used to offset differences in economic performance and to smooth welfare. These transfers typically take the form of disbursements of revenue by the central government on the basis of some allocation rules.[5] The central government redistributes resources from better-endowed regions to poorer areas. An important concern about fiscal transfers is that they can have negative incentive effects: if regions that perform well are taxed to support lagging regions, the incentive to reform is weakened.[6] Our concern in this section is different. Most discussion of fiscal transfers assumes that they take place in the conventional way: a portion of the cash taxes paid by wealthier regions is collected by the Center and then reallocated to poorer regions. In Russia, however, the virtual economy opens up an alternative channel for fiscal transfers, with consequences that distort the intended policy. This alternative channel arises because in the virtual economy the donor region often is able to effect the transfer in kind, delivering its own output to the recipient region. The donor region itself, not the federal government, ends up determining how much wealth is redistributed and to whom.

A particularly egregious case of a region's dictating the terms of society's spending in this way concerned Samara, a large oblast, and Mari-El, a much smaller and poorer region; see box 8-1.

As reported by Ivan Dakhov, from the government watchdog agency, the Federal Audit Chamber, Samara was allowed to fulfill its obligation to one

4. Indeed, this seems to be the whole purpose: by sanctioning the use of a surrogate currency such as the electro-ruble, the local government protects its own soft-goods producers against competition from outside the region.
5. There has been considerable discussion concerning the determinants of these transfers across regions. See, for example, Narayan (1999).
6. See, for example, Shleifer and Treisman (2000, chapter 6), and Zhuravskaya (2000).

BOX 8-1. The Samara Toxic Chemicals Story

"Last year, the Employment Committee of the Republic of Mari-El was supposed to receive subsidies [*dotatsii*] of five billion rubles from the federal [unemployment compensation] fund. At the same time, the Russian Ministry of Labor permitted Samara oblast, which is a donor region [a region that makes a net contribution to the federal budget], not to pay its federal share to the Russian Federation State Unemployment Fund in money, but instead to deliver to Mari-El for that same amount goods which had been received from [enterprises] that had debts to the unemployment fund. . . .

"However, goods worth only 2.4 billion rubles arrived in Yoshkar-Ola [the capital of Mari-El]. Moreover, for all their skills, the locals were able to make use of only one-third of those. The rest, to put it mildly, were not in huge demand among the unemployed in Mari-El. You would think someone might have figured that out back in Samara before they were loaded and shipped out. For instance, one item being offered as a subsidy to Mari-El was ten tonnes of toxic chemicals [*yadokhimikaty*] from the Middle Volga Chemicals Plant that they claimed were worth almost 400 million rubles [$80,000]."

Source: Ivan Dakhov [auditor of the Audit Chamber], "Za vnebyudzhetnymi fondami" [Behind the extrabudgetary funds], *Ekonomika I zhizn'*, no. 16 (April 1998), p. 8.

of Russia's important "extrabudgetary funds" by shipping goods to another region of Russia instead of paying cash to the federal center. Nominally, Samara was settling a R5 billion obligation. In fact, it appears that the value of the goods it actually delivered to Mari-El was at the most R0.8 billion. Large amounts of essentially worthless output from Samara were shipped hundreds of miles back up the Volga River to be dumped on the unemployment office in Mari-El. Not only were factories in Samara being allowed to discharge their obligations to the unemployment fund by delivering junk, but they could also chalk up that much more in "increased industrial output." The toxic chemicals that the chemical plant in Samara oblast tried to palm off on the unemployed in Mari-El had absolutely no value at all. For the chemical plant, however, their production served its purpose of earning informal profits for the enterprise. They are the epitome of a "soft good" circulated within the virtual economy.[7]

By most measures, Samara is one of the small number of Russia's regions that are net contributors to the federal budget. It thus appears that Samara is transferring resources to poorer regions. But the virtual economy allows Samara to reduce the real cost of these transfers. It does so by shipping output to satisfy its debts. Samara is able to ascribe value to worthless output—up to the limit of its debts to the federal government—and use this output to pay its taxes. For the unfortunate recipient, of course, the story is different. Poor regions, desperate to receive any transfers at all, take whatever they get. This means, however, that the actual value of what they receive—and hence, of the services they can provide their citizens—is far smaller than the nominal budget suggests. As a consequence, the picture of interregional transfers is distorted as compared with the official statistics. More important, policies that were actually intended to enhance social welfare end up wasting society's wealth.

Fragmentation of the State

The situation of the government sector in the virtual economy is complex. For reasons of efficiency, budget authorities would prefer taxes paid in cash rather than in goods and services, which are almost always overpriced and often random in structure. Frequently, however, governments must either accept taxes in kind or collect nothing at all. Faced with this choice, they typically accept offsets; some tax receipts are better than none. This is not the only source of offsets, however. Offsets often arise out of a conflict between different agencies of government or between different levels of government. That is, with not enough value being collected, offsets (payment of taxes in kind) may "tie" budget receipts to one particular recipient to the exclusion of others.

7. The Samara toxic chemicals story also highlights the importance of the extrabudgetary funds for the practice of offsets. These funds, which are of the same order of magnitude as the federal budget itself, are federal funds, but, in contrast to the federal budget, they are managed locally. That is, they have their own regional ("territorial") structures. While the funds are not formally subordinated to the regional governments, they may be de facto under their control, since the officials who make the critical decisions about permitting offsets and so on are residents of the local communities. Formally, they are federal employees—in other words, they receive their (very miserly) salaries from the federal government—but they depend on the regional and local authorities for office space and other more valuable perks. The latter is true even for officials of the Federal Tax Service.

When the resources of government are inadequate to meet all its obligations, tax offsets provide a way for individual agencies of government to meet their own needs at the expense of other, competing agencies or government entities. In the fragmented state produced by the virtual economy, each entity acts independently, trying to survive. The basic rule is: find a way to appropriate taxpayers' value that cannot easily be taken away from you. It depends on the ability to "get to the taxpayer first." Local governments shift more tax collection to offsets of services—for instance, repairing the school roof—which, unlike cash tax receipts, are immune to appropriation by the federal government. Ministries or even individual budget–financed institutions may try to locate taxpayers who have a product or service that only they can use or that they have been the first to ask for.

In both cases, that of local versus federal government and that of one ministry versus another, tax offsets are a means for one particular government entity to continue to acquire resources at the expense of others when there is insufficient revenue to support the expenditure of all. For a government agency (or a local government) to prefer such a policy of offsets to a policy of cash revenue and cash outlays, it is only necessary that the agency's individual valuation of the soft good be higher than the cash value of the budget allocation it can realistically expect to obtain.

Consider the case of a conflict between ministries. When the ministry of finance restricts the budgets of an important ministry (say, the defense ministry), rather than reduce purchases, the defense ministry may continue to order output from a military producer even though it knows it does not have the means to pay. This will result in government debts to the enterprise. Through the combined influence of the enterprise itself and its sponsoring ministry, the government's debt can then be canceled in lieu of the enterprise's tax obligation.[8]

There have been repeated campaigns to stop this practice. Especially when the ruble was strong and oil prices were low, and hence rubles were in short supply in the economy, these efforts inevitably failed. In an interview in December 1998, Tat'yana Nesterenko, the head of Russia's Federal Treasury [kaznacheystvo], described how, despite efforts to establish a treasury system as a centralized bookkeeping department that could monitor all payments from the budget, government agencies still managed to illegally appropriate funds for their own uses. Even the Treasury is defenseless, she

---

8. Unapproved orders to defense enterprises and ex-post use of tax offsets to those enterprises were the first significant use of the tax offset system.

noted, when suddenly some government agency concludes a contract not provided for in the budget.

> The scheme works as follows. The [contracting] agency cannot pay for the services stipulated in the agreement. Under the terms of the Civil Code, the contractor issues a collection notice, goes to court, and as a result the sum in question is charged to the account of the Treasury. . . . We [at the Treasury] raise a hue and cry: "How dare you?! There's no provision for this payment in the Budget Law. You're violating the rights of other budget-financed agencies." They just point to the Civil Code.[9]

Local versus Federal Governments

Russia's system of taxation is one of tax sharing as opposed to tax assignment. Regions and cities do not have separate revenue agencies that collect specific provincial and local taxes. Instead, the federal government's revenue body, the Federal Tax Service, is a single federal agency, with territorial branches throughout the country. The federal legislature provides for a list of taxes to be collected nationwide, and it prescribes a specific percentage of revenues from each tax to be remitted to the center while a portion is kept in the region. In principle, this should mean that tax revenues are first collected and pooled and then shared according to the formula. In practice, what happens is quite different. Under conditions of the virtual economy, the tax sharing system provides a big incentive for regions to collude with enterprises to make tax payments in kind rather than in money.

The local government seeks to maintain a "natural" economy, while the federal government is more inclined to a monetary economy.[10] The local government wants to keep as much income as it can within its jurisdiction, to maximize what it can capture. That is best done by collecting taxes in a form that the federal government cannot, or does not want to, appropriate.[11] Many of the in-kind payments involved in noncash production activity are precisely of this nature. To take the archetypal case: taxes paid

9. *Ekonomika i zhizn'* (Moscow edition), 1998, no. 30, pp. 1–2.

10. This paragraph and the next follow closely Gaddy and Ickes (1998).

11. Why can the federal government not compensate by reducing its transfers to a region that behaves in this way? Doing so would clearly be ineffective in relation to the donor regions, which by definition are net payers. Meanwhile, reducing transfers to the poorer, net recipient regions would be impermissible, since it would deprive them of the minimal amounts of cash their residents need to survive.

by a local enterprise in the form of roof repairs on the neighborhood school remain in the community, no matter what the formal rules for dividing taxes.

The tax-sharing system has encouraged a bifurcation of Russia's federal economic system: local governments are relatively more demonetized than the federal government. This relative difference has persisted, and possibly even grown, since August 1998, despite an increase in cash payments at all levels of government in the past two years. In principle, the key to ending this bifurcation is straightforward. The federation's tax system should be changed to one of revenue assignment—separate and distinct taxes levied by the national and local governments—rather than revenue sharing. If regions and cities can be assured that they can keep a share of the cash generated by the economic activity that takes place on their territory, the logic goes, they will then have an incentive to promote the growth of monetized local economies. The problem is not the logic; it is the poor initial position of so many regions that are burdened with value-destroying enterprise sectors. Moving enterprises to the formal sector requires large restructuring expenditures when market distance (d) is large. It is not clear who would pay for those investments or whether they would even make economic sense. In the absence of such payments, however, why would the local government monetize and give up its ability to appropriate value through local tax offsets? If the enterprises are shut down, local governments bear the economic and political burden.[12] The federal government can wean local governments from their virtual economy policies only if it can insure them against a net loss in their welfare as a result. However, Russia's federal government lacks the revenues for that.[13]

Consequences for Local Government

Because Russia's local governments are so heavily committed to virtual economy practices, that level of government manifests the most extreme symptoms and bears the greatest consequences. Below, we present a few concrete examples: how the virtual economy inflates the size but reduces

12. In chapter 10 we consider the political economy of restructuring when there are significant differential effects on regions.
13. The discussion in this section makes clear that regions differ in their endowments of relational capital and market distance in much the same way as do enterprises. This suggests an analytic approach to local government behavior analogous to that we have presented for enterprise behavior. We outline the principles of such an analysis in appendix F, "Regions in r-d Space."

efficiency of local government, how it upsets public policy priorities (with the health and education sectors suffering especially), and how it leads to a form of "personalization" of the public sector as government employees sacrifice to maintain minimum levels of service.

Government Size and Efficiency

It can be argued that "government is too big" in Russia. However, those arguments make sense only when "government" is measured by the size of its budget, the number of its employees, or the extent of its regulatory interference in the economy, not by the actual output of the public sector. Detailed studies of actual performance give a very different picture. Consider the results of a study of the public sector in one of Russia's largest regions, the Republic of Tatarstan. Much of the public sector there has been transformed into a vehicle for household survival. While the local government sector is quite large when measured by employment, it falls far short in services provided. The public sector is being used as a way to hide unemployment, a sort of work sharing. The study showed that in the past seven years the number of budget-financed institutions in the republic had grown by 20 percent, but the number of employees by 50 percent. It is common to see the same worker filling 1.5–2 slots (and getting paid for them), but this means that efficiency suffers.

Some findings from their study:

—Kindergartens and day-care centers have decreased enrollment but maintained the same employment. There are now 17,500 extra staff positions due to this phenomenon.

—During the seven-year period, hospital beds were down by 3,429 units, while staffing was up more than 20,000 workers.

—In 1989 Tatarstan had eight large museums with 312 staff positions. By 1998, it had over sixty museums with more than nine hundred staff positions. Many of these are not museums at all. They have no space and no displays; they have only a roster of employees.

—The "dead souls" syndrome is rampant. For instance, in order to qualify for having a public librarian in a rural area, the library needs a minimum of five hundred patrons. Patrons are defined as card holders. The enterprising librarian therefore issues cards to every resident in all the villages, including infants. Some people listed as patrons have not checked out a book in ten years.

—Rural cultural centers are typically open two hours a week, for disco dances. The manager receives a full-time salary. "Rural movie houses essentially do not operate at all. With 12–17 staff positions in the rural district movie network, they show 3–4 films a month. Ticket sales do not even cover the cost of gasoline to drive out with the film from the district center to the villages."[14]

Tatarstan's government has announced a policy of reducing this overemployment. The plan is to use the money saved by reducing staffing to raise salaries (or actually pay them) to the best-qualified workers. As with most policies, it is not clear whether these measures will ever be implemented. It is important to note, however, that they are likely to entail a redistribution of transfers at the expense of the region's rural residents.

Whether intended or not, the system described above is much more important as part of the social safety net for the countryside than it is for the cities. This jobs program is presumably a major source of cash in the rural economy. To the extent that relatively more jobs are eliminated in the villages, rural Tatarstan will be demonetized even more. No matter how Tatarstan resolves its particular problem, the key point is that when local government policy is dominated by the virtual economy, the efficiency of the public sector declines. Government services deteriorate and the size of government is mismeasured.

Reprioritization

When public sector priorities are determined from the bottom up, and not through formally adopted budgets, provision of public goods is likely to be haphazard. In some cases, remarkable initiative and perseverance on the part of government employees can produce minimally acceptable results in spite of the system. Chapter 2 related the story of how the director of a small rural hospital in Kostroma bypassed the regional government by organizing the delivery of cotton bedsheets from a local textile mill. Newspaper accounts from Russia have been full of similar stories in recent years. One example occurred in the local blood bank in the southern city of Rostov. The regional budget there grew short of cash and in 1998 disbursed only 30 percent of the budgetary funds allocated for the blood bank:

> Faced with a chronic shortage of funds and blood, the blood bank staff came up with a barter scheme that solved their problem. [The chief financial officer of the blood bank, Yelena Pavlova] and her colleagues approached local factories that had no money to pay their

14. A. Shishkin (deputy minister of finance) and M. Zakharov (deputy department head in the finance ministry), "Ne chislom, a umen'yem" [Not number but ability], *Ekonomika i zhizn'*, no. 25 (1998), p. 29.

taxes and asked them to donate food packages to the blood center. In exchange, the local tax inspectorate agreed to write off their tax debts to the regional budget. "I take this food and pay the donors with it," Pavlova said.[15]

It is no accident that the health system suffers greatly in this system. It is near the bottom of the totem pole in priority, lower even than education, a service used by a large segment of families at any time and thus one to which many people are sensitive. Teachers' strikes, for instance, usually do bring results, simply because working families cannot tolerate them. Hospitals are a public good that is used by only a small proportion of the population at any time. Their leverage is not great.[16]

The Kostroma hospital director was able to negotiate bed linens because that was a soft good. The producer benefited from delivering them to the government institution, the rural clinic, in lieu of taxes. Another example of a taxpayer's attempting to negotiate the right to engage in tax offsets had an outcome that was far less happy. The story of what happened in March 1999 at a hospital in the Siberian city of Prokop'yevsk (see box 8-2) illustrates the fragility of a situation in which budgets are negotiated on a case-by-case basis: in the maze of individually negotiated deals, the weak will lose.

Personalization

Owing to the demonetization of local budgets, a large proportion of the time of government employees is spent not on providing public goods at all, not even inefficiently; it is spent on earning money, or growing food, or other activities, to finance sheer survival. This is because even if services can be provided in kind—schools painted or roads repaired—government workers themselves cannot be paid this way. They are therefore forced to work for their own survival. In some cases, government agencies have become the

15. Bronwyn McLaren, "Blood Banks Both Winners and Losers in Crisis," *Moscow Times*, Saturday, October 31, 1998.

16. Determining who ends up literally as the bottom priority in the virtual economy is difficult. Health, especially mental health, would certainly be a candidate. So would the penal system. Consider then the following news from the town of Achinsk in Krasnoyarsk region in January 2002. A hospital for the criminally insane with more than 100 inmates was left unguarded when the guards walked off the job in protest against not having been paid for eight months. According to a news account: "The hospital's medical staff say that they cannot guarantee that the inmates will not stage a mass escape." "Mental hospital for criminals left unguarded after pay dispute," RIA-Novosti in Russian 0433 GMT 31 January 2002 (FBIS Report).

BOX 8-2. The Prokop'yevsk Hospital

"Three Die over Hospital's Unpaid Power Bill," by Richard C. Paddock

"The three patients lay unconscious last week in the intensive-care unit, kept alive only by the Siberian hospital's life-support system. Two were elderly; one was 39. None of them could know that the greatest threat to their lives was an unpaid bill. On Wednesday, the hospital in the town of Prokop'yevsk received a telegram from the local power company, Gorelektroset, warning that it would shut off the hospital's electricity the next day if it did not pay its debt of $95,000.

"At 6 a.m. Thursday, the hospital's power went off; 40 minutes later, all three patients were dead.

[. . .]

"As part of the national power grid, Gorelektroset, the local company, has itself been under pressure from its supplier to pay for electricity it has distributed to homes and enterprises in Prokop'yevsk, a town of 240,000 in the impoverished coal-mining region of central Siberia.

"One of its biggest debtors is the hospital, which has not paid its bill since 1994. The company briefly cut off the hospital's electricity several times before but always telephoned ahead to warn doctors so the power would not go out in the middle of an operation. [Hospital director Anatoly] Shutov said the telegram he received from the util-

bureaucratic analogues of self-subsistence farms. Employees use government assets (real estate, for instance) and government time to earn enough to keep themselves alive. Little or nothing is left to serve the public.

Virtual economy practices thus mean inefficiency on three counts. First, deals emerge like the Chelyabinsk subway: wrong choices for spending. Second, the time of public employees is wasted as they try to earn income. Third, the resources of the public sector are misused: they are used to finance survival of public employees, not to provide service. The final stage is when public-sector employees work for free, or beyond: they pay for the public sector from their own pocket. An open letter to a newspaper from a group of teachers in a rural region in Pskov illustrates the ultimate shrinkage of Russia's public sector. See box 8-3.

ity Wednesday ordered the hospital to pay 2,187,202 rubles ($94,931) or 'the electricity supply will be cut off March 11.' The hospital heard nothing more before the power went off promptly at 6 a.m. the next day.

"Gorelektroset chief Pavel Pichugin acknowledged sending the telegram but insisted that the company had not carried out its threat. The timing of the power outage was a coincidence, he said. Pichugin said he issued the warning in the hope of triggering the kind of mutual cancellation of debts that has become commonplace in Russia's barter economy.

"Gorelektroset faces power shortages of its own, he said, because it cannot pay its supplier, the much bigger Kuzbasenergo. Because Kuzbasenergo owes money to the Kemerovo regional government, and the regional government owes money to the city, and the city owes money to the hospital, a debt swap could wipe Gorelektroset's obligations off its books.

"Such explanations are lost on the families of the three victims: Filipp Salnikov, 82, who was recovering from stomach surgery; Zoya Gasanaliyeva, 69, who was being treated for poisoning; and Alexander Gart, 39, who was recovering from a knife wound to the chest. Some of their relatives blamed the hospital; some blamed the government."

Moscow Times, Tuesday, March 16, 1999.

Disappearance of the National Public Sector

The fragmentation (both personalization and regionalization) of the public sector is a logical consequence of an untrammeled virtual economy. It is the attempt of individual units—municipal and regional—to survive. Some have their own value pumps, and they want to keep the value at home. Others are triaged. They shrink. The national institutions are left to suffer. This threatens national security, indeed, national survival. In a poor rural region such as Kostroma, the regional government is serving as little more than a rubber stamp of the bottom-up arrangements, but this is neither acceptable nor sustainable at the level of national (central) government. By default, more of government responsibilities devolve to regions, with potentially

BOX 8-3. "A Cry from the Soul: Rural Teachers Work for Free"

The teacher's life in rural Russia today is "unbelievably difficult." In addition to the teaching job, they keep a minifarm: "We have cows, pigs, sheep, chickens, and we tend our plots."

"We are up at 6 a.m., run out to tend the livestock, then run to school, then again to the animals. After that we take care of our own children, and then stay up until midnight correcting papers and preparing classes."

"What, you ask, compels teachers to run all over the place, trying to cope with school and farm chores? The answer: the complete demonetization [*pol'noye bezdenezh'ye*]. [Without this coping activity] we simply would not be able to survive. We haven't seen a salary for eight months now. The same goes for our husbands [most of the teachers are women]. But we still have to buy firewood, pay for electricity, buy medicines and at least some clothing and shoes. Besides that, we teachers need notebooks, paper, pens, textbooks, journals, books, and even just newspapers and magazines, if we aren't to revert to being Neanderthals."

"We're giving 100 percent at school—both teaching class and supervising extracurricular activities—because we cannot do otherwise. And we do it all for free. Despite the government's promises to give us our back pay, our pockets are still empty. But it's worse when our souls are empty, too—from unfulfilled promises and a life of hunger and humiliation. What then do we have to give the children?"

[Letter signed by Lidiya Belugina, Valentina Meshcheryakova, and eighteen other teachers from the Ushchitskaya Secondary School in Kun'yinskiy rayon of Pskov oblast.]

Source: *Krest'yanskiye vedomosti*, no. 5 (1999), p. 6.

dangerous consequences. Consider the important federal government function of providing for national security.

For several years, regions in Russia have quietly been taking over more and more responsibility for the national defense. This has been most prominent and farthest reaching in support of defense industries. Some of the leading defense industry oblasts have had an arrangement with the federal government whereby orders to the plants were financed by taxes collected locally—another example of earmarking taxes for a specific purpose not necessarily agreed on in the federal budget. When the overall budget revenues fall so short of plan that no one receives what they are due, some agencies still manage to get more than others. The governor of Sverdlovsk oblast, Eduard Rossel, explained in a November 1998 interview that his oblast had succeeded in concluding a "tripartite agreement" between the oblast, the Ministry of Defense, and the Ministry of Finance on financing the state defense order for defense enterprises in the central Urals at the expense of taxes collected locally in Sverdlovsk oblast. Rossel explained: "This agreement allowed us to settle up with the defense enterprises through a facilitated procedure (*bypassing the Moscow authorities* [emphasis added])."[17]

This system was later suspended, but Rossel, along with officials of the defense ministry, continues to lobby hard to have it restored. A regional leader like Rossel is a much better ally for the federal defense ministry officials than their colleagues in the federal Ministry of Finance. Note how this works. The regional government of Sverdlovsk oblast is given the right to dispose of federal budget obligations to defense enterprises as it sees fit. In practice, this means that the output of local enterprises that can in one form or another be used by the defense enterprise will be accepted in lieu of federal taxes up to the amount owed to local defense enterprises for their defense order. Who benefits? Clearly, the defense enterprises do: they are legitimized as producers. The other enterprises in the oblast that can supply inputs to the defense plants also come out ahead, since they deliver some of their output as payment of federal taxes and are accordingly relieved of paying cash. The federal Ministry of Defense is happy, since it will receive weapons and other defense goods from the Sverdlovsk plants. The Sverdlovsk regional government wins: it is going to be able to get credit for federal taxes collected and remitted to the center. In addition, it finds its local enterprises supported—both the defense plants and the others whose goods are used for offsets.

Who loses? Other intended recipients and beneficiaries of government spending. The offset must come at someone's expense. It must reduce the amount of cash to the federal budget and perhaps to the regional budget as well. This, as always, most directly affects government employees, whose

---

17. Interview with Eduard Rossel by Aleksandr Kerdan, "Eduard Rossel: In the Hardest of Times, Russian Eyes Have Turned to the Urals," *Oriyentir* (Moscow), November 1, 1998, no. 11, pp. 4–8. Translated in *FBIS-SOV-1999-0311*.

BOX 8-4. The Submarine *Bryansk*

Captain Viktor Andreyev is relieved: He just received a truckload of vegetables from his hometown in southern Russia and now his subordinates on a strategic nuclear submarine, which carries 16 ballistic missiles to sea, will have some food to help survive the arctic winter.

"I have meagerly provided for my crew," he said by telephone from the Northern Fleet base in Skalisty, in the Murmansk region. "Officers' families will not be hungry, for which I thank my fellow townsmen in Bryansk."

[. . .]

Andreyev said that three years ago his division commander gave an assignment to all captains as they headed home for vacation: to find patrons for their ships. So when Andreyev went to his native Bryansk last year, he met with regional governor Yury Lodkin and other local officials and invited them to visit the base, which is north of the Arctic Circle and one hundred kilometers from the Norwegian border. When a group of Bryansk city officials arrived at Skalisty last October they were shocked by the condition of the sailors' barracks on shore and by the number of ships rusting in their docks.

"My eyes popped out of my head," said Igor Kaplunov, deputy chairman of the Bryansk city council and a retired strategic rocket forces officer.

While Andreyev's Delta 4–class submarine is one of the most combat ready in the fleet, the crew's barracks had bare walls and no basic furniture such as stools, Kaplunov said in a telephone interview from Bryansk.

wages will not be paid, though other types of government activity may also be affected.

Conditions have gone much further than local financing of defense industries. Box 8-4 describes how, for well over three years, local governments in Russia have assumed responsibility for providing the basic needs of even the most advanced units of the Russian armed forces—the nuclear submarine fleet. Things are worse even than that. There is a "householdization" of the army. The national weekly television program *"Sluzhu otechestvu"* ("I serve the fatherland") presented the story of a young artillery officer and his fam-

The city council shipped $10,000 worth of goods to Andreyev: construction materials for the renovation of the barracks, as well as furniture, a computer, a VCR, and videocassettes for the sailors to watch at sea. Andreyev boasted that with the donated materials, he was able to turn the barracks into the best on the base.

Two other submarines in Skalisty were adopted by Tula regional governor Vasily Starodubtsev, and they were renamed last year: one to "Tula" and the other to "Novomoskovsk," an industrial town in the region south of Moscow.

This gave Bryansk authorities an idea, and earlier this year Andreyev's K-117 became "Bryansk."

The latest call for help was for food. Although sailors are fed pretty decently by Russian army standards, Andreyev said, officers, who make up two-thirds of his 145 men, were last paid in July, and most of them couldn't even leave the arctic town for vacation.

At ten rubles a kilogram, even potatoes were out of the officers' reach, the captain said.

Earlier this month, a truck with about twenty tons of potatoes, cabbage, carrots and beets arrived in Skalisty from Bryansk.

[. . .]

The city government gathers the supplies for the sailors from local companies that have no money to pay their taxes, Kaplunov said. In exchange for erasing their tax debts, the companies provide goods for Andreyev's submarine.

Excerpt from "Sailors Put Their Subs Up for Adoption," by Andrei Zolotov Jr., *Moscow Times*, Friday, October 30, 1998.

ily who described how he, a regimental commander, had to receive money from his parents just to survive. "How do you live on that salary," asked the reporter. "We don't live," he said. "We survive." In another family, that of a flight mechanic, the officer's wife reported that their neighbors regularly donated food and clothing. "Even the pensioners help us. They know that we are worse off than even them."[18]

18. "Ne zhivyom. Vyzhivyom" [We don't live. We survive.] The program was broadcast on Sunday, March 28, 1999, on RTR.

This chapter has shown that the virtual economy weakens the effectiveness of government at all levels. The deterioration of services provided by local governments causes citizens to lose faith not only in local governments, but in all levels of government. The conflict between levels and regions and the resulting inefficiencies and waste breed cynicism in the Russian population and undermine faith in the Russian state. For a leader—like Vladimir Vladimirovich Putin—whose goal is to strengthen the Russian state, the virtual economy creates a fundamental dilemma.

CHAPTER NINE

Mr. Putin's Dilemma

"Originally, I had hoped that economic growth and the development of democratic institutions would halt this process [of national collapse]. But life and practice showed that this did not happen."

—*Vladimir Putin,* Ot pervogo litsa

Granting the virtual economy hypothesis, an optimist might nonetheless argue that this is merely a detour along the road to the market. All that is needed is time to escape. Indeed, for some observers the performance of the Russian economy since the August 17, 1998, financial crisis is taken as evidence that this positive development has already begun. Not only did the Russian economy in these years record significant growth of gross domestic product (GDP) for the first time since transition began, but there was also a break in the trend of demonetization, as barter declined and cash transactions increased. As one report put it, Russia in 1999 showed "a positive reversal in all the indicators of the so-called 'virtual' economy."[1]

Our goal in this chapter is to show that, contrary to such views, there is reason to believe that the Russian economy has not yet begun to escape from its trap. The virtual economy persists, and the analytical framework presented in the preceding chapters remains the best way to understand economic developments, including the post–August 1998 recovery. Analysis shows that the recovery was not the result of desired restructuring, but rather the predictable result of the large devaluation of the ruble. In purely technical terms, the devaluation provided a window of opportunity for reform, but the opportunity has hardly been used. In spite of some rhetoric,

1. Breach (1999, p. 3).

serious reform was never—and could not be—on the policy agenda in this period. The reason why this is so, which is the second major topic of this chapter, has to do with the interaction of the virtual economy with Russia's overall stability. Reform serious enough to weaken the virtual economy would threaten social stability, precisely because society has so thoroughly adapted to the virtual economy. In Russia's present political and security circumstances, the "will to reform" is insufficient. Incremental reforms will not move Russia out of the virtual economy, and true comprehensive reforms threaten social stability and even national security.

Security concerns may seem an afterthought, or a topic deemed necessary for discussion only because of the identity of Russia's new president. However, integrating security concerns is really consistent with two earlier themes in this book. The first is the biological, evolutionary metaphor. In natural history, changes in the macro environment altered the course of evolution. Climate changes, for instance, led to the extinction of the dinosaurs. If the virtual economy represents an adaptation of behavior to what would otherwise be an unsustainable environment, this suggests that the way to escape this trap can be discerned by examining this broader environment itself. The second theme we revisit in this chapter is impermissibility. Russia's resistance to intolerable stress to the system created what we call Russia's "impossible trinity." The impossible trinity is a specific, more fundamental notion of the impermissibility constraint introduced in chapter 5.

The Devaluation and Its Effects

Before applying a specifically virtual economy analysis to the post–August 1998 performance of the Russian economy, let us make a few, more conventional observations. We can begin with an examination of the real devaluation of the ruble that occurred in the wake of the crisis. Thanks to a nominal depreciation that exceeded the ensuing inflation, the real value of the ruble at the end of 1998 was only about 36 percent of its immediate pre-crisis value. This exchange rate shock hugely increased the ruble value of exports. Hence, even without any behavioral changes the balance sheets of exporters improved significantly.[2] Their ruble revenues increased sharply, while their costs did not rise nearly as much.[3]

2. The effect of the devaluation on the balance sheet of enterprises depends on the structure of their assets and liabilities. To the extent that the enterprises had foreign-denominated assets, devaluation increased the value of their liabilities. For exporters this may not be a problem because assets are also more valuable. Importers, however, especially those with large foreign-denominated debt, may find that devaluation seriously

FIGURE 9-1. Russian Hourly Dollar Wage Costs, January 1996–January 2002

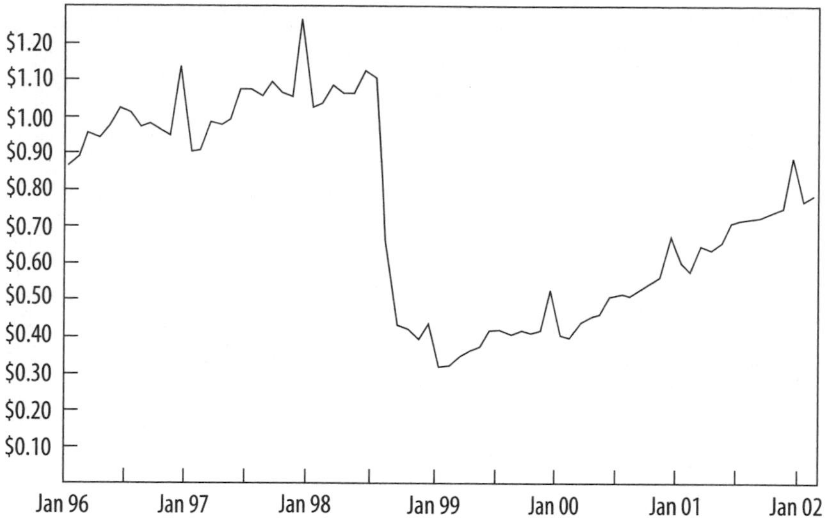

Source: Authors' calculations from monthly data on average wage and ruble-dollar exchange rate in *Russian Economic Trends*, various issues.

One way to view this impact of devaluation is in terms of producers' wage costs. Figure 9-1 shows the path of the dollar wage during this period. In January 1999 the dollar wage was $0.32, only 29 percent of its July 1998 level of $1.11. By July 2000 the dollar wage had climbed back to about $0.51, which was still less than 46 percent of the July 1998 level. At least as far as these costs are concerned, Russia thus experienced a dramatic change in its external competitiveness, solely due to currency depreciation. It should thus hardly be surprising that Russia showed signs of recovery. The surprise is instead why the response was so small.

One important mitigating factor slowing recovery was that the increase in competitiveness coincided with a dramatic fall in household incomes. In

jeopardizes their solvency. Debt service becomes more costly at the same time that domestic purchasing power declines.

3. The devaluation led to large current account surpluses. At dollar exchange rates the current account surplus in 1999 was nearly 15 percent of GDP. In 2000 it was more than 18 percent of GDP. (IMF, *International Financial Statistics*, October 2001.) Is this is a sign of recovery? An economy in transition with serious needs to rebuild its infrastructure should be importing capital, not exporting it. Of course, given Russia's need to finance its external debt, it must earn these surpluses, but this is a result of foreign investors' unwillingness to invest in Russia. The fact that Russia still negotiates for debt restructuring given the size of these surpluses is, perhaps, the most telling fact about Russia.

FIGURE 9-2. Russian Machinery Exports, First Half 1997–First Half 2000
Billions of U.S. dollars

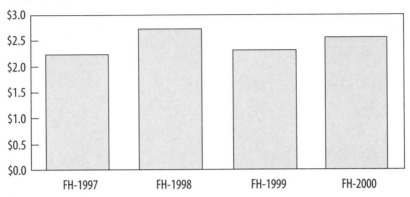

Source: *Interfax* (1998, no. 35; 1999, no. 36; 2000, no. 37).

1999 incomes were roughly only 75 percent of their 1995 level. This decrease in real incomes depressed domestic consumption. The increased competitiveness of domestic manufacturing caused expenditures to switch in favor of domestically produced goods, but the extent of this import substitution was constrained by the decline in real incomes. The real depreciation of the ruble caused a massive improvement in the trade balance, due largely to the fall in imports. This decrease in turn was due primarily to the fall in consumption rather than import substitution.

Perhaps the more important reason for the limited response to the real depreciation is that the incentives to undertake costly restructuring activities remained weak. This is because the underlying factors were perceived to be temporary. The devaluation did not eliminate the value of relational capital, and it did not reduce the costs to enterprises of operating in the open environment. Hence, enterprises continued to operate as before, taking advantage of the windfall that resulted from real depreciation, but not undergoing the restructuring that would be needed to take full advantage of the improvement in their external competitiveness. An indication of this can be seen in figure 9-2, which compares exports of machinery and equipment from 1997 to 2000. Despite the huge improvement in the terms of trade, Russian producers were exporting *less* in 2000 than they did before the financial crisis.[4]

4. An example of how complex the Russian economy is as a result of the persistence of the virtual economy: a decline in some exports might in some cases have been a favor-

Another factor that weakened the response to the devaluation is that it penalized some of the companies that before the crisis had chosen to move most aggressively toward the market—in other words, companies that had attempted to reduce their market distance, d. Before August 17 such firms, especially in the retail food industry, realized that in order to be competitive against foreign products, they would need western higher-quality inputs and machines. To do so they incurred dollar debt, or ended up with current costs in dollars. Although their modernization effort was a desirable form of d reduction under the circumstances that prevailed when they undertook the programs, the devaluation of the ruble hurt such companies badly. An example is the packaged fish plant IRIS-1 in Sakhalin, which had been a success story of domestic Russian business. It imported plastic for its vacuum-wrapped packaging from South Korea. The company had budgeted $40,000 for plastic; after the devaluation this amount more than doubled in real ruble terms. Similarly, the spare parts for its machines that the company was required to import from Europe rose in price. These inputs were not available inside Russia. "As a result, we've nearly been stripped naked," lamented the director.[5]

Reduction of Barter

Barter declined significantly as a share of industrial sales in Russia after the August 1998 crisis. As indicated earlier, this fact was widely interpreted as a sign of a healthy behavioral change on the part of manufacturers, even as an indication of the demise of the virtual economy. Such conclusions are misguided. One need only reflect on the effect of the real ruble depreciation on barter to understand what was happening. Any ruble depreciation will make the export-oriented part of Russia's economy (which is predominantly value adding and cash based) larger in ruble terms relative to the dinosaur part of the economy (which is largely value subtracting and noncash based). Hence the nonmonetary transactions needed to subsidize production at value-destroying enterprises shrink in ruble terms. However, this does not reduce M's demand for value infusion. Resources are still being destroyed.

---

able development. Consider "Igor's" steel exports. To meet his cash constraint, Igor—a high-cost steel producer—was exporting steel at a price insufficient to cover his costs (see chapter 3). Reducing that steel production is positive.

5. *Ekonomika i zhizn'*, no. 8, 1999, p. 4.

Real depreciation will necessarily reduce the dollar value of the value-destroying sector. In principle, large enough ruble depreciation would shrink the dollar value of the virtual economy to zero, but that would still not end value destruction as long as the industries responsible continued to operate. If there is no behavioral change, then resources are still being destroyed. The fact that a large real depreciation can make economic performance look strong without any change in behavior is a rather simple point, yet it seems to have been missed in discussions about Russia's performance after the crisis. Hence, it may be worthwhile to consider a simple accounting example.

One Way to Explain Growth and Remonetization

Imagine an economy (which we will identify as a "pre-August" economy) that appears in terms of the recorded value of output/sales to be half barter and half monetized. Assume further that the monetized sector can be divided into two equal parts: one part is export based, for dollars; the other sells domestically for rubles. The barter sector is exclusively domestic. The total economy produces for 100 rubles at officially recorded prices. This means that the breakdown between the sectors is as shown in table 9-1.

Let us now subject this economy to an "August 17-like" event. That is, we devalue the ruble against the dollar by a factor of four, and let domestic prices double.[6] This means that the cash export sector's output is now worth 100 rubles instead of 25; the domestic cash sector's sales are priced at 50 rubles instead of 25; and the barter sector's recorded sales are 100 rubles instead of 50.[7] Table 9-2 shows the new ruble values and the percentage of the total economy that each sector now represents:

Finally, let us deflate these values to account for inflation (the deflator is 2.00). That is, the barter sector's inflation-adjusted output is 50 rubles, the domestic cash sector's is 25, and the export cash sector's is 50 (table 9-3).

Table 9-3 presents the postdevaluation outcome in predevaluation rubles (or "table 9-1 rubles"). Comparing table 9-3 with table 9-1 shows two positive effects: (1) total output in the economy grew from 100 to 125,

6. These assumed figures are not too different from reality. From July 1998 to the end of December 1998, the ruble's value against the dollar dropped by a factor of 4.3. Meanwhile, the producer price index rose by a factor of 2.07 in the same period. Calculated from *Russian Economic Trends*, September 2000 monthly update, tables.

7. This ignores the effect of real depreciation on the price of import substitutes, which would presumably rise in response to the increased price of imports. If these goods were primarily in the domestic cash sector, then taking this into account would only enhance the effects described in this example.

TABLE 9-1. The Pre-August Economy

Category	Barter sector	Cash sector			Total economy
		Domestic cash	Export cash	Total cash	
Rubles	50	25	25	50	100
Percentage	50	25	25	50	100

TABLE 9-2. The Post-August Economy, Nominal

Category	Barter sector	Cash sector			Total economy
		Domestic cash	Export cash	Total cash	
Rubles	100	50	100	150	250
Percentage	40	20	40	60	100

TABLE 9-3. The Post-August Economy, Adjusted for Inflation

Category	Barter sector	Cash sector			Total economy
		Domestic cash	Export cash	Total cash	
Rubles	50	25	50	75	125
Percentage	40	20	40	60	100

meaning there was 25 percent real (inflation-adjusted) growth; and (2) the share of barter in the economy dropped from 50 percent to 40 percent.[8]

The important point is that in this example both positive effects—the growth in sales (output) and the growth in the cash sector—come solely from the increased real value of exports resulting from the devaluation. *Both growth and "remonetization" in this stylized economy involved no change in behavior of the enterprises.*[9] All the enterprises in all of the sectors continue to produce exactly what they did before, in the same

8. The positive results reported here are actually understated because they do not take into account the "virtual component" of the officially reported figures. That is, the barter sector's sales are overpriced. If they are overpriced by a factor of 3, then the true relative percentages of the sectors in the predevaluation economy would be: 25 percent barter and 75 percent cash. Postdevaluation, that would change to: 18.2 percent barter and 81.8 percent cash. The true total output of such an economy would have grown from 66 2/3 to 91 2/3, or a growth rate of 37.5 percent.

9. This is in contrast to the conclusion of a 1999 report on the Russian economy by JP Morgan, which stated that the postdevaluation performance "proves that the Russian economy—albeit not yet fully functioning as a developed market—is responsive to changes in prices and costs." In our accounting example, the enterprises did not "respond" to anything. JP Morgan (1999).

amounts—absolutely and relatively—and sell it to the same customers as before. They use (and perhaps waste) the same physical amounts of inputs as before: gas, electricity, steel, labor, and so on.

In fact, the positive effect of increased value of exports could even off-set (but hide) negative developments elsewhere. For instance, the barter sector could grow in size (in terms of physical volume of goods produced and traded) or the domestic cash sector could actually shrink. However, if the growth of the export sector—thanks exclusively to the devaluation—were large enough, the overall figures could still show net growth and net remonetization.[10]

The real point of this exercise is to underscore again that *barter is not the essence of the virtual economy*. Barter is not the main problem of the Russian economy; it is a symptom of the problem. The essence of the virtual economy is enterprise behavior that exploits relational capital to protect and maintain value-destroying activity—soft goods production. Barter is important because it facilitates that behavior. The real question for the actual Russian economy is, What happened *to enterprise behavior* as a result of a positive cash shock and a shift in relative prices between hard and soft goods production? This stylized example shows that simply looking at figures on the percentage of barter in the economy says nothing about behavior.[11]

There is another important lesson here. It is that aggregate statistics can often hide underlying reality. While the virtual economy permeates the Russian economy, it does not do so in a uniform way. Often real insight into its operation requires looking at specific regions or industries. Unfortunately, our ability to do this in a systematic way for Russia is severely limited by the inadequacy of official statistics on barter.[12] However, a case study of

10. It should be obvious that we could achieve as high a growth rate as we liked, and we could simultaneously reduce barter to as low as we liked, if only we depreciated the ruble enough. Depreciate by a factor of 10, for example, and the model economy illustrated here could have growth of 225 percent while reducing barter to 15 percent.

11. There is admittedly one respect, however, in which a devaluation causes behavioral changes that contribute to a decline in barter. The extent to which enterprises use money or barter is an economic decision. Because barter is costly, enterprises used cash for some transactions even when use of barter was at its peak. Enterprises traded off the transaction cost of barter against the cost of using money. In the current Russian environment, that cost is primarily increased visibility, which in turn implies greater tax liability. When cash is more plentiful, the margin between using barter and using money shifts. Real depreciation thus shifts behavior toward greater use of money. This is a behavioral change, but it does not constitute restructuring.

12. The situation is better in Ukraine, where data on the share of transactions conducted with nonmonetary assets are available at both the regional and industry level. According to the Ukrainian State Statistics Committee, the proportion of settlements for

one (admittedly extreme but not unique) case, the Republic of Sakha (Yakutiya), illustrates the point that aggregate statistics concealed critical aspects of the nature of the recovery (see box 9-1). Sakha has one giant value source, the diamond exporter ALROSA. In the first half of 1999, ALROSA exported the same volume of diamonds as the year before. Thanks to the devaluation, however, the dollar revenues translated into four times as many rubles as before. Since ALROSA alone accounts for 69 percent of all industrial output in the republic of Sakha, the overall figures for the region looked extremely positive. Much more cash also was collected by the budget, but nearly all came from this one source. The profits picture tells the whole story. Aggregate profits in the republic were 5.4 billion rubles. ALROSA's profits alone were 5.6 billion rubles.

Investment Growth

The most important positive sign of recovery during 2000 and 2001 was growth in investment. Capital investment grew at annual rates of around 17 percent and 9 percent, respectively, in those years. This was from an extremely low level, however. Real expenditures on new construction and equipment in 2000 still remained below the level of 1995 and 1996.[13] Meanwhile, the average age of the capital stock in industry had risen from 10.8 years in 1990 to 16 years in 1998.[14] The post-1998 rise in investment was insufficient to make a serious dent in this trend. Moreover, direct foreign investment in 2000 was still lower (by 17 percent) than in the precrisis year of 1997.[15]

Investment is not a sufficient condition for growth, especially under Russian conditions. Indeed, much of the investment in the Soviet period was

---

delivered industrial products (services) that was conducted by barter in Ukraine fell to 19.3 percent in the first seven months of 2000 from 33.3 percent in the same period of 1999. Yet barter remained quite high in some industries: for example, at companies producing industrial carbon (80.1 percent), in the synthetic dye industry (79.3 percent), the cement industry (78.0 percent), porcelain and earthenware industry (73.8 percent), silk industry (73.2 percent), cotton industry (69.2 percent), sugar industry (56.9 percent), and in wooden construction materials and wood-based board (60.5 percent). Barter was also quite high in certain regions: 39.7 percent in Rovno region, 32.5 percent in Lugansk region, 29.3 percent in Ivano-Frankovsk region, and 26.8 percent in the Crimea. *Interfax* (2000, no. 41, p. 420).

13. *Russian Economic Trends* (September 2000, table 1); *Interfax* (2000, no. 12); *Interfax* (2001, no. 12); PlanEcon Report (2002, no. 1, p. 8).

14. *Russian Economic Trends* (May 2000, p. 8); and *Rossiyskiy statisticheskiy yezhegodnik* (1996, p. 509).

15. *Interfax* (2001, no. 12).

BOX 9-1. Sakha: A Regional Case Study of Appearance and Reality

Russia's government statistics office published the following figures for the performance of one region, Sakha, for the first half of 1999:

—Industrial output was up 80 percent in constant prices (160 percent in current prices)

—Gross regional product was up 1 percent

—Fixed capital investment was up 30 percent in constant prices

—Corporate profits were up 1400 percent

—Budget: revenues were 21 percent over target; spending 38 percent under target

—Tax revenues were up 120 percent. Cash revenues were up 300 percent. Cash in the first half of 1999 composed 85 percent of budget revenues (compared with 48 percent in the first half of the previous year).

One could easily imagine that this is a regional example of the postdevaluation Russian economy that various observers claim is so successful, one that is growing, monetized, and modernizing. Nevertheless, other facts raise some questions. For instance, the percentage of loss-making companies rose from 57 percent to 63 percent. Only

wasted. What is needed is restructuring—which may involve investment, but almost surely involves closing down some enterprises and reducing activities elsewhere. What investment figures do indicate is the extent to which Russian industry has not kept up with developments abroad.

The real question, however, is not the volume of investment, but rather what this investment was being used for. Chapter 4 pointed out that enterprises choose between investing in r or d, or a combination of the two. While some enterprises did use their export windfall to make necessary changes to increase competitiveness, others used it to create breathing room to *avoid* having to make such changes. Those enterprises continued to invest in good relations with officials and workers rather than in better productive processes. An illuminating discussion of the ambiguity of increased investment in a virtual economy environment came from an analyst's report on reform in one important Russian region, Perm:

[Some enterprises view the devaluation] as the latest removal of a hard budget constraint and an opportunity to recreate the firm [sic]

14 percent of enterprises were technically solvent. The nonpayments problems were also getting worse.

How can this be reconciled? The answer is one word: "diamonds." The region's biggest enterprise, without comparison, is ALROSA. It accounts for 69 percent of all industrial output. When we learn that the region's industrial output, measured in rubles, was up 80 percent, we also need to notice that the physical volume of output barely increased at all. The reason is that ALROSA, which exports nearly all of its diamonds for dollars, was making four times as many rubles on the same volume of exports as before.

Putting ALROSA into the corporate profits picture tells the story: aggregate net profits in the republic in the first half of 1999 were R5.4 billion. ALROSA's net profits were R5.6 billion! This means that taken together, the region's other 19,300 corporate entities had a net loss of -0.2 billion! Thus, the increased ruble value of ALROSA's diamond exports alone—its positive cash shock—accounts for the region's higher profits, increased industrial output, and improved fiscal performance. There is little to indicate that anything else changed in the region.

Source: *Interfax* (1999, no. 33).

which existed before the collapse in production. They are reinvesting in social assets and to create a better environment for their workforce, and see their major task to increase production to pre-transition levels with little thought to efficiency or profitability. The General Director of Uralsyazinform, one of Russia's most successful and potentially promising regional telecoms, in the same breath mentioned that he was planning to sell 8 percent of his company in the form of American depository receipts (ADRs) to increase liquidity (perfectly laudable) and that his number one aim for investment was to improve the quality of his firm's social assets, which included hospitals and kindergartens.[16]

The general director of Uralsyazinform was investing, but not necessarily in reducing the competitive disadvantages of his enterprise. Instead, he was investing in relationships. This may have been advantageous to the

16. Nash and Lissovolik (2000, p. 11).

director—and even to the enterprise in negotiations with officials. It almost certainly helps the workers as well, at least in the narrow sense of providing social benefits, but it does not reduce d for the enterprise. Consequently, it does not help the economy as a whole to escape the virtual economy trap.

In the end, the occurrence of d reduction, whether on the enterprise level or on the aggregate level, is not in itself a clear sign of overcoming the virtual economy. For an enterprise to move out of the virtual economy, its investment must cause it to move in r-d space to lower d and lower r, that is, movement in the southwestern direction. Movement that maintains the current balance between r and d—that is, moving along the restructuring boundary (the RB line)—does not change the virtual economy. Only the kind of investment that moves the enterprise in a direction that will take it across the RB boundary is a sign of real progress toward elimination of the virtual economy.

A Costly Recovery

The squeeze on households was an important element of the post-1998 recovery. If there was pressure to change anywhere in the economy, it was on households more than on enterprises. The rise in profits came largely at the expense of a decrease in real wages. There is an often-expressed glibness about the effects of the virtual economy on Russian households. Despite statistics on poverty, and so on, there has been a continuous sigh of relief that no matter what happens, "Russians can always cope." This attitude was especially prevalent after the financial crash of August 17, 1998.[17] However, the resilience of the population did not prove that ordinary Russians are immune to financial breakdowns and macroeconomic conditions. On the contrary, close examination shows that those who bear up the entire virtual economy—the workers and their households—were badly hurt.

The increase in the cost of living brought about by the devaluation of the ruble tightened the cash constraint. Barely two months after the crash, the purchasing power of the average worker's wage had been reduced by one-third, and it continued to drop as inflation remained high and nominal wages stagnated. We can illustrate the tightening of the cash constraint for the workers by comparing a worker's wage in January 1999 and what that wage should have been for the worker to be able to consume the same bas-

17. A common line used by U.S. administration officials to downplay the effects of the crash was the following: "Before August 17 the bad news about the Russian economy was that 60 percent was barter. After August 17, the *good* news was that 60 percent of the economy is barter."

ket of goods for that money that he or she had six months earlier, before the August crash. The gap between the two was huge. The average worker, earning a wage of about 1,000 rubles a month before the August financial collapse, would have needed a pay raise to 1,915 rubles a month by January 1999 just to stay at the same level of purchasing power. In fact, the average monthly wage rose to only 1,075 rubles, leaving the "missing" 840 rubles to be made up by the wage earners by again turning to outside sources of subsistence, including moonlighting at extra jobs. The devaluation-created wage gap represents the extra amount that families have to earn outside their virtual economy workplaces (the Ms) just to be able to afford to stay there.[18]

The important point is that whatever else the devaluation may have accomplished, because of the tightened cash constraint that resulted from the real wage cut, it did not induce households to move toward the market. The virtual economy is a protective mechanism. When it prevails, further pressure merely tightens the cocoon of protection against the market. The greater the hardship, the less likely people are to leave it.

Summing Up

We can recapitulate the postdevaluation results. The huge amount of extra value injected into the Russian economy by the devaluation of the ruble in August 1998 (and subsequently by high world commodity prices) represented a pure windfall for Russia's raw materials exporters. They did nothing different, but they earned four times as much cash. It was a massive, positive cash shock for these enterprises and for local economies based on them. Tax revenue also increased, and wage, pension, and tax arrears all fell as a result. The devaluation also had modest benefits for a small sector of the economy that gained a price advantage relative to foreign imports. These benefits came at a high cost. Incomes fell drastically, and they remained down. The poverty rate rose by nearly 50 percent.

18. For the economy as a whole, the aggregate wage gap due to the devaluation was enormous. In absolute terms, from October 1, 1998, to October 1, 1999, the cumulative difference between the actual wage and a hypothetical wage adjusted to the cost of living for the entire economy was 661 billion rubles. As a percentage of GDP, this "real wage cut" amounted to just about 18 percent over the twelve months. The size of the pay gap puts the post-August reduction of wage arrears in perspective as well. Between October 1, 1998, and October 1, 1999, wage arrears were reduced by 38 percent. The amount repaid (33.5 billion rubles), however, was still only 5 percent of what workers lost in the real wage cut (661 billion rubles).

In purely economic terms, the real depreciation of the ruble, followed by the rise in commodity prices on the world market, gave Russia a window of opportunity to alter the course of its transition. This could have provided the cushion needed to begin extricating Russia from the grip of the virtual economy. The next chapter will show that ruble depreciation is a necessary part of true reform of the economy, but it is only a precondition. In isolation, it achieves nothing, and under the circumstances of the continuing virtual economy, it will inevitably be used in the wrong way. This window opened at great cost to the Russian population, and now it is starting to close.

Why did enterprise behavior not respond to the real depreciation? Why was the window of opportunity not used? The direct answer is that the structural factors that generated the incentives facing enterprise directors did not change appreciably. Moreover, real depreciation actually increased the liquidity of export-oriented value producers. Increased tax payments made possible by increased monetization of the economy meant that more value was available for transfer to loss-making enterprises. With government budgets enhanced by larger tax receipts, officials had more to offer in exchange for investments in relational capital.

Of course, real depreciation could have weakened the virtual economy, but this would have required that relational capital no longer yield benefits for loss-making enterprises. Without the value infusion that their relational capital commanded, the enterprises would have been shut down. For that very reason, the policies needed to implement such a regime were not undertaken, and the underlying structure of the virtual economy remained intact—value producers are still subsidizing value destroyers. Costly restructuring that could make an enterprise more competitive was still inhibited by fear of tax consequences and an end to subsidies. The economy remained stuck in the virtual economy trap.[19]

The power of that trap is clearly huge. A 70 percent real depreciation ought to be a large enough shock to change the expectations of all the players in the virtual economy. Nevertheless, if such a shock is viewed as temporary, and if departing from the behavioral strategies of the virtual economy has long-term consequences, it should not be a surprise that agents are wary. Agents will change their behavior only if they can be persuaded that the policy regime has changed. In Russia after the crisis of August 1998, however, agents never did expect that the policy regime would

19. See Ericson and Ickes (2001) for an analysis of the restructuring trap in the virtual economy.

change, because at precisely that point there was a more important national policy agenda. The period after the 1998 financial crisis has shown— through the accession to power in Russia first of Yevgeniy Primakov and then of Vladimir Putin—that economics, and especially market economics, was not the priority of Russia's top leadership; national security and domestic stability were. Those concerns had in fact formed an important part of the environment that had constrained the economic reform effort from the beginning, but only after the 1998 crisis did their importance become so explicit.

Russia's Impossible Trinity

Previous chapters have emphasized the economic obstacles to Russia's reform. As daunting as they were, they still do not represent the full context in which Russian reformers were operating. The task of creating a market economy was to be undertaken at the same time as Russia democratized and built a new state. Unlike China, for example, Russia was trying to democratize and to create a market economy simultaneously. Even these twin challenges fail to present the full picture. After all, most postsocialist economies faced these same problems.

What distinguishes the Russian situation with regard to these challenges is that of national security—security in a very broad sense, including traditional security vis-à-vis the external environment, as well as social cohesion and territorial integrity. Of course all postsocialist economies experienced dramatic changes in the external environment. In Russia, however, changes in the external environment exacerbated the twin challenges of democratization and creating a market economy. Because Russia was the imperial center of the Soviet Union, the demise of the latter had important nation-building consequences for Russia. In other former Soviet republics, this demise created the challenge of independence—a force that enhanced nation building. Likewise, in other postsocialist economies, changes in the external environment were more favorable, enhancing the ability of those countries to meet these challenges.

At the outset of transition there appeared to be good reason to think that Russia's security burden would decrease. The end of the cold war seemed to offer an end to the arms race and, hence, a reduction in the cost of meeting the needs of national security. At the same time, however, Russia still inherited some daunting security requirements. Indeed, in important respects, the challenges facing Russia increased with the breakup of the

Soviet Union, establishment of new national borders, and the loss of its former alliance structure. Equally important, Russia had a greatly reduced capacity to meet those security needs. Its economy was only about 60 percent of the size of the Soviet Union's. With the breakup of the USSR, some 30 percent of the Soviet defense-industrial base was now located in foreign countries (the other former republics of the USSR). Hardly a single production chain remained intact.[20]

The suddenness of Russia's economic contraction[21] relative to its security needs put it in a unique situation, and it created a much more complex interrelationship between economics, politics, and security than any other country had. For instance, while part of the motivation for undertaking market economic reform was to create a sustainable economic base for the nation, including its ability to defend itself, Russia's abysmally low level of economic performance meant that it would have had to spend more than a democracy can sustain in order to have adequate defense. During the Soviet era, the deteriorating productive capacity of the system meant that the USSR could not meet its defense imperative, even with all the force of a totalitarian regime to extract resources for its priority purposes. A post-Soviet, *democratic* Russia with an economic base barely one-third as large (owing to the combined effect of the geographical breakup and the subsequent output contraction) could not possibly sustain levels of spending commensurate with the defense establishment, and the security needs, it had inherited. Similarly, while some research suggests that greater democracy has been a boon to economic reform in many countries, the objective difficulty of economic reforms in the Russian context meant that democracy was perceived by many as riskier to national cohesion than otherwise might be the case. Economic reform is always a wrenching process, but if reform is too painful, then democracy and freedom become a threat to a radical restructuring, as people can protest.

For Russia, trying to simultaneously fulfill three imperatives—building democracy, establishing a market economy, and ensuring national survival while simultaneously redefining alliance structure and borders—was an unbearable burden. To borrow the phrase coined by Robert Mundell in a very different context, Russia's trinity of imperatives was, *under the specific*

---

20. Post–Soviet Russia's inherited security burden is discussed in detail in Steinbruner (2000, especially pp. 13–14, 47–52, 109–14).

21. By contraction we mean the reduction in size of the economy due to the geographical breakup of the Soviet Union, not to the reduction in GDP, or what is sometimes called the Great Contraction.

circumstances the nation experienced when it entered its transition, an "impossible trinity."[22]

In using this term we do not mean to suggest that the attainment of these three goals of security, democracy, and a market economy is impossible in principle. Modern western nations are a case in point. There it is often taken for granted that the goals go hand in hand. But the apparent self-evidence of their compatibility, and even complementarity, in the western cases made it especially hard to see that it was not going to be possible in the same way for Russia. As we showed above, the economic and political preconditions alone were unique for Russia. However, what made the trinity truly impossible for Russia was the security component.

Initially, the trinity did not appear to be a problem. Both inside and outside Russia there was a broad view that security could be, and even should be, deemphasized. It was believed that the Soviet Union's excessive military burden had stemmed less from legitimate security concerns than from its exaggerated international (even imperial) ambitions. With the demise of communist rule, it was therefore assumed that Russia would naturally scale down its international ambition relative to its economic importance. The logic was that if Russia were to reform its economy and develop democracy, then the nation's security problems would automatically solve themselves, since they would "become like everybody else." These are exactly the ideas to which even Vladimir Putin initially subscribed, as he says in the quote that introduces this chapter: get the economy and democracy development right, and there will be no security problem. However, pretending that the security imperative did not exist did not make it so. As Putin put it, "life and practice" suggested otherwise.

Illusions Dispelled

Objective reality, misperceptions, and policy mistakes all combined to change the consensus that security concerns could be put on the back burner. Two events were critical. One was the first Chechen war, begun in 1994. It highlighted the discrepancy between Russia's security needs and its economic capacity. The second event was NATO enlargement. As much as the West's rhetoric had tried to justify Russia's deemphasis of traditional security, the behavior of western policymakers often flew in the face of what they said. With the eastward expansion of NATO, Russia perceived

22. Mundell used the term to describe a nation's attempt to simultaneously have a fixed exchange rate, an independent monetary policy, and a regime of relatively high capital mobility.

U.S. policy as proof that it still was in an adversarial relationship with the West. This was apparent long before the NATO campaign in Kosovo. It became evident that security no longer could be ignored.

Once the security imperative reemerged into the field of vision of the population and the policymakers, it became clear that they would have to make trade-offs. If security were to be given its full due, the other two main components of the policy agenda—democratization or marketization—would have to be deemphasized. Pressure was particularly strong not to allow strict adherence to market reform to preclude defense spending. Market reform required limits on budgetary spending to control inflation, but national cohesion required greater defense spending, and the required levels of spending were incompatible with democracy, given the low level of economic capacity. The three imperatives were thus in conflict.

The solution that emerged—spontaneously—was that of offsets. The means of coping was to requisition resources through nonmonetary means—the familiar mechanisms of offsets, barter, and the like. It should not be a surprise that the whole system of offsets began in this way, when ministers responded to the inadequacy of budgetary resources by issuing offsets in 1994. Thus the virtual economy allowed for greater defense spending than would otherwise have been politically feasible.[23] Defense industry had suffered greatly in the Russian transition, but things would have been much worse had not the virtual economy protected many defense plants from the full impact of market reform. Enterprises in the military-industrial complex became the paradigmatic Ms. That is, they were value-destroying enterprises whose relational capital allowed them to receive infusions of value from value adders such as Gazprom.[24]

The virtual economy helped slow the deterioration of the security situation, but at the cost of undermining the long-run potential of the economy. The virtual economy not only enhanced nontransparency; it also protects and enhances the value of relational capital. In the virtual economy, survival is the imperative, not restructuring. It therefore ensures stability, but only in tenuous form. The country avoids collapse, but only at the cost of digging itself deeper and deeper in a dead-end system. Throughout the 1990s the degeneration of the virtual economy was causing the sorts of problems described and analyzed in earlier chapters. However, the problems were

23. Gazprom's participation now also involves an element of national purpose. Even if this is not recognized by Gazprom's owners, it explains why the government has an even greater incentive to bribe them (with sanctioned leakage) to participate.

24. For the impact of market reform on the Russian defense industry, see Gaddy (1996, especially chapter 6, "Responding to Market Rules").

largely hidden as organizations (enterprises, households) adapted to solve them on an individual basis.

The bottom-up nature of the virtual economy was inadequate for serious revival of specific sectors.[25] Vital national interests could not be prioritized. The weakness of the public sector—the state—was key. Not only was it underfunded at all levels, but the weakness of the central government was exacerbated by the virtual economy's natural tendency toward more localism. The constituent units of the public sector began acting without control, for reasons of pure survival. The danger in Russia of regional autonomy is not primarily *political* fragmentation of the country. The more immediate threat is the one to national security and national survival as a result of the economic consequences of the virtual economy: value is kept locally. Under such circumstances, it is impossible to have effective policies for a national state, specifically for *national* security.

In Russia, concern for national security in a broad sense centered primarily on the weakness of the state and threats to territorial integrity. Vladimir Putin's analysis illustrates this point. Speaking to the journalists who interviewed him for the book *Ot pervogo litsa* [In the first person], he stated:

> You know, to be honest, everything that's been done in recent years, especially in the sphere of preserving the state, has been. . . . How can I put this in a way that doesn't insult anyone? . . . It's been amateurism. . . . Believe me, already in 1990–91 I knew perfectly well, as arrogant as this may sound, that with the attitude toward the army that prevailed in society, the attitudes toward the secret services, especially after the fall of the USSR, the country would soon be on the verge of collapse. This brings me to the Caucasus. Because, after all, what essentially is the present situation in the Northern Caucasus and in Chechnya? It's the continuation of the collapse of the USSR. And it's clear that at some point it has to be stopped. Yes, originally I had hoped that economic growth and the development of democratic institutions would halt that process. But life and practice showed that this did not happen.[26]

25. There is a particular irony here. The "bottom-up," unorganized nature of the virtual economy is one element that most resembles a true market economy. This led many people to erroneously blame "the market" for undermining the state and its capacity to give adequate attention to security. In fact, it was not the market, but the virtual economy, that most weakened the state. Market reform in Russia was bad *not* because it gave people market incentives that conflicted with state interests. Market reform—as implemented in Russia under its initial conditions and security constraints—had deleterious effects because it created the virtual economy.

26. Gevorkyan, Timakova, and Kolesnikov (2000, p. 133).

The Dilemma

By the end of the 1990s, any Russian leader would have been faced with a dilemma: How is it possible to satisfy the security imperative and maintain democracy when the resulting virtual economy results in erosion of the economic base? Improving long-run economic performance requires rolling back the virtual economy, but how could this be done in the context of policies designed to strengthen the state, enhance national security, and stabilize the social and political situation?

To understand the severity of this dilemma, it is important to realize how strong the forces were that resisted change. The virtual economy is not an optimal state of affairs, but it does represent equilibrium behavior on the part of agents. Given that other agents are behaving in this way, it is not optimal for any individual agent to depart from these strategies. Quite the contrary, the longer the virtual economy goes on, the more committed people are to it. This does not happen because the economy gets better, or even more tolerable. Instead, as the economy deteriorates agents become even more dependent on these behaviors. Therefore, the dilemma was that while Russia could continue as before, it could not dismantle the virtual economy via piecemeal reforms. At the same time, the comprehensive reforms that are needed to make a difference violate the impermissibility constraint. The virtual economy creates a bias against serious economic reform because it furthers survival. This bias is, in fact, familiar from the political economy literature as the status quo bias.[27] In Russia it has its own peculiar features.

The status quo bias in Russia is reinforced by two phenomena that we have discussed in previous chapters. The first is the loot chain, the notion that people's incomes depend on a complex and nontransparent process of redistribution of value in the virtual economy that not even participants themselves comprehend. This enhances the uncertainty that is always associated with reform. Given people's uncertainty over how they would fare in a transparent system, they prefer to stick to the current state. Even if they believe that the aggregate economy will improve as a result of moving to the market, individual-specific uncertainty may cause a person to oppose any change. Furthermore, because the virtual economy guarantees that such uncertainty will be widespread, the status quo bias is quite powerful.

The second cause of the status quo bias is the process of personalization of social safety nets in Russia. As value runs out in the degenerative virtual economy, the active part of the economy shrinks. As the two preceding

27. See Fernandez and Rodrik (1991).

chapters showed, shrinkage has negative effects on the manufacturing sector (especially the waste of human capital), the household sector, and the government (public) sector. As the public sector fails to perform its role as safety net and protector, the population has to rely more and more on its personalized, household safety nets. People have no other buffer. In effect, they self-insure.[28]

The self-insurance generated by personalized safety nets enables households to cope, albeit quite imperfectly, with a shrinking public sector. Personalization exacerbates the bias against reform because any serious effort to dismantle the virtual economy would threaten precisely these informal networks that agents have created to self-insure, thus adding to their uncertainty. Hence, the risks to individuals of policies that would generate a more transparent regime are quite severe.

Consider the bargain that households in Russia would face in choosing to eliminate the virtual economy. The more transparent regime would increase aggregate resources. In principle, then, publicly provided safety nets could replace personalized ones. Because the former are more efficient than the latter, households would be better off if such systems could be established. However, this possibility is not sufficient to induce households to support reform. Households would also have to believe that public systems would actually be created, and would function effectively, to replace the personalized ones. In other words, they would have to expect that the extra resources would not be diverted to other ends. In the context of the Russian transition, such an expectation would be very hard to generate.

The status quo bias is thus reinforced by the cynicism concerning government policies that has developed during the transition, not to mention the Soviet period. This cynicism implies that households will question policies that improve aggregate performance and promise government support for those who lose in the bargain. Personalized safety nets may be highly inefficient, but viewed from the individual standpoint, they have the advantage that the particular individuals are in charge—there is no reliance on Moscow to deliver promised outcomes. The history of Russian governments that have failed to pay pensions and wages on time makes it very difficult for households to believe that they will be adequately insured if they choose to give up their personalized safety nets.

28. One key benefit of personalized safety nets is that—much like relational capital in general—they are well suited to a regime where contract enforcement is weak. In such circumstances, agents must use self-enforcing contracts. Personalized relations satisfy this criterion because they involve transactions between agents who know and trust one another.

The status quo bias suggests that it will be extremely difficult to exit the virtual economy via democratic consensus. Indeed, the desire for stability is so strong in Russia today that it has become a new societal imperative. Putin stated this in his open letter to the Russian people in December 1999, when he wrote that Russians long for "stability, certainty, and the possibility of planning for the future—their own and that of their children—not one month at a time, but for years and decades. They want to work under conditions of peace, security, and a stable legal order." In this document he linked stability explicitly to the absence of radical policy changes. "Russia has reached its limit as far as political and socioeconomic upheavals, cataclysms, and radical transformations are concerned," Putin wrote.[29] Exiting from the virtual economy requires precisely such cataclysmic changes.

If this strong societal mandate for stability rules out such comprehensive reforms, what options are then left for Russia? One is market reform through coercion. Putin appears, at the moment, however, to prefer to maintain some form of democracy. Another approach would be to reject the goals of democracy and a market economy altogether and return to the Soviet system of political repression and economic compulsion. It does not appear that Russians want to choose this path. Moreover, the desire for stability itself would tend to rule out a return to a Soviet-type command economy. An alternative, and more likely, way out of the dilemma is to adjust Russia's current political and economic systems to make them more compatible with the security imperative.

Rather than completely sacrificing the goals of democracy and the market economy, this compromise, or third way, approach would involve *redefining* these imperatives in a way that relieves much of the burden. One can think of this as a new experiment: a different, Russian-style democracy and a Russian-style market. The latter, we believe, would mean a modified virtual economy. This seems in fact to be Putin's preferred solution. He is in effect proposing to replace the impossible trinity, in which democracy and a market economy were defined in western terms, with a new trinity of imperatives: (1) a paramount emphasis on national security; (2) a virtual economy reformed so as to suit the priority of the security imperative; and (3) a political order based on stability, minimal personal liberties, and the "Russian Idea." The new trinity is a true *Russian* trinity. Putin is betting that it will be a *possible* one.

29. Putin (1999).

A Reformed Virtual Economy

Making the virtual economy compatible with the security imperative means addressing the two principal weaknesses of the degenerative virtual economy: excessive looting (or what we call bad leakage) and an anarchic distribution of value. It is straightforward to argue that reducing leakage will leave more resources for preferred uses. The critical point is to reduce only the *bad* leakage: some leakage is needed to induce value producers to contribute. Specifically, this refers to Gazprom, the most important contributor of value to the system and, hence, the greatest beneficiary of good leakage. If a crackdown on leakage hits the wrong type of leakage, it could be counterproductive. An example of the kinds of policies that are already being adopted in Putin's Russia is shown in box 9-2.

A Russian government that acted to reduce the leakage would not only retain more value for priority ends. It would also change the perception of the state in the eyes of society and thereby help reduce the extreme self-protection of households and institutions that has, among other things, made the public sector so fragmented and ineffectual. The virtual economy emerged in part because increasingly throughout the 1990s, institutions, enterprises, regions, and individuals realized they had to protect themselves from predators, not only because the state failed to, but worse: because the state was itself authorizing the predation and sanctioning the looters. Realizing that the biggest threat to their survival was the state and its looting, enterprises and households reacted first of all by not paying taxes. This created a vicious circle, when government institutions and employees had to steal in order to survive. Regional governments used barter and offsets to try to keep some locally generated wealth at home.

The purpose of reducing the bottom-up, spontaneous distribution of value characteristic of the virtual economy is to allow national priorities, rather than a raw struggle on the principle of survival and/or relations, to determine who receives the value. From the national government's point of view, the problem is that relations with regional officials are critical to survival. One could thus interpret a policy of greater centralization of value distribution as a revaluation of relational capital. It would be incumbent to invest more in relations with national officials, and, for example, the relational capital of defense enterprises could rise.

This program for a reformed and more efficient virtual economy would effectively mean a division of the economy into priority and nonpriority sectors. Although this resembles the Soviet system, there are in fact important

BOX 9-2. Reducing Leakage in a Reformed Virtual Economy

"In the Southern Federal District, so-called commissars of the plenipotentiary representative have started being assigned to all of the region's joint-stock enterprises with a state stake of 10 percent or more. A list of the first fifty enterprises is now ready: it includes fifteen river and sea ports, twenty-three electric power stations, and twelve oil and gas complexes.

Plenipotentiary representative Viktor Kazantsev's brigade of commissars will set off for the region's enterprises with a view to defending state interests there by prompting the enterprises to make fuller and more timely payments on all of the due disbursements into the budget, and particularly taxes.

In Rostov Oblast the representatives of the plenipotentiary representative are already dealing with problems connected with the resuscitation of the car plant in Taganrog and the supply of scrap metal for the Taganrog Metallurgical Plant's furnaces. Other enterprises are next in line.

Deputy presidential plenipotentiary representative Viktor Krokhmal specially emphasized that this is a question of specialists' being assigned, rather than officials. "These are managers with a sufficiently high level of skills, who have an excellent grasp of the situation at the joint-stock companies to which they will be delegated. The only quality that should decisively distinguish such a specialist

differences. It would not be a command economy, because it would not be administered from the top down, or from the center out. There would, however, be "coordination." Inside the virtual economy, things would continue in principle as before, albeit with new, more explicit priorities—and undoubtedly also with new mechanisms for value distribution yet to be invented.

At least ideally, this system would also differ from the Soviet system in the degree of compulsion it involved. In the Soviet system, the priority sector exploited the nonpriority sector. Compulsion was necessary. Here there would be, at least initially, less compulsion. The parts of the nonpriority economy outside the virtual economy would not be directly exploited, but rather left to subsist on their own in accordance with the model of shrink-

from his colleagues in the board of directors is his resolve to defend state interests."

Whereas today approximately $3 billion in tax payments comes in from the south's enterprises, soon this sum will have to be doubled. The main burden in carrying out this task will be shouldered by the plenipotentiary representative's envoys.

The law on the management of state property, which the State Duma is preparing to adopt, will help the commissars to defend the state's interests.

According to forecasts, it should be ratified in March-April. The document will stipulate both the rights and duties of the state representatives in the boards of directors on the one hand and their responsibility on the other hand.

One of the architects of this law, Mikhail Yemelyanov, a State Duma deputy who has also been involved in managing state blocks of shares in recent years, cited some appalling examples. In 1998, not one of the 4,000 enterprises that involve state capital transferred any dividends to the state. And yet many of them, such as Transneft, had multimillion profits."

Source: "Russia: Southern District Plans for Defending State Economic Interests Viewed," *Rossiyskaya Gazeta* in Russian, January 20, 2001, p. 3 [Report by Vitaliy Kolbasin: "Kazantsev's Commissars Head for Plants and Factories"] [Foreign Broadcast Information Service (FBIS) translated text].

age presented in chapter 7. They would be for all intents and purposes not only outside of the rest of the economy, engaging in minimal or no exchange, but also outside of the state's responsibility. They would receive nothing from the state, but would also contribute nothing to it. There would therefore be no forced requisitioning or forced labor.

Stability versus Change

Assuming that such a program for a reformed virtual economy could ensure stability—precisely because it preserves the virtual economy—could it also succeed in its goal of making more resources available for security? Everything we know about the virtual economy suggests that ultimately the answer is no. A reformed virtual economy might well appear to improve in the short term, just as the economy did after 1998, but it would still be moving toward a dead end, albeit one that was pushed slightly further away. The long-term problem of the Russian economy remains the legacy of fundamentally value-subtracting enterprises. Even by official Soviet standards, a huge proportion of equipment in Russian industry was physically obsolete when reform began in 1992. The Russian economy needed massive modernization. It has not had it. As a result, a physical plant that was generally old and noncompetitive to begin with is now ten years older and even less competitive. Less drastic, but still important, has been the loss of human capital. People who worked in those noncompetitive industries who felt that they had a chance in the new market economy left and tried their chances there. The people who have remained behind tend to be the least productive and/or the most risk averse.

Another way to think of this is in terms of r-d space. The amount of investment needed to make Russian enterprises competitive—the distance d that enterprises must traverse—increases with time. The initial d with which enterprises began the transition is relative to the world standard. If the world standard is advancing, then an enterprise that simply maintains the current level of efficiency will see its distance *increase*. Hence, the payoff to that enterprise from investing to reduce distance will decline over time.[30] Delayed restructuring increases the margin that must be overcome for an enterprise to become competitive. In effect, there is a rightward drift of the position of all enterprises in r-d space in an economy where modernization lags behind world norms.

In the short run a virtual economy with reduced leakage and more centralized value distribution will achieve growth from *lack of change*, absence of radical transformation. However, this is self-limiting. The inherent contradiction is that part of the growth will be virtual. In other words, it represents more value destruction. Even an increase in the production of low-d goods will not necessarily crowd out value-subtracting activity; it may actually support more of it. To get sustained growth, value destruction must be reduced dramatically. However, that would mean shutting down old enterprises, opening new ones, and moving people massively from their factories, their cities, and their regions. This is hardly the stability and pre-

---

30. The need to restructure grows over time as the enterprise falls further behind the global standard. The net return to investment in restructuring also declines as the gap that must be closed has increased. Relative to investing in relational capital, the return to investing in distance reduction declines with increasing d.

dictability that is the societal imperative in Russia today; it is revolutionary change.

Reconciling strong and sustainable growth with stability is thus a circle that cannot be squared. It is not enough to gear up the old Russian economy. The country must modernize and radically reallocate resources. Then, however, the stability-enhancing mechanisms of the virtual economy themselves become the obstacle. The only way out is radical reform and acceptance of the inevitability of dislocation. The question is how? This question is the subject of the next chapter.

CHAPTER TEN

What Is to Be Done?

In previous chapters we have attempted to analyze how the virtual economy developed and how it works and to explain the negative consequences of its persistence. In this final chapter we consider a program of reform that could eliminate the virtual economy. As we have emphasized, exiting from the virtual economy is the only way that Russia can successfully compete in the global economy.

Our starting point for thinking about a strategy for exiting from the virtual economy is a theme that recurs throughout this book: The virtual economy is a complex system that emerged during transition through adaptation of behavior and institutions. It is not mere stagnation in the course of development to the market, but rather an evolutionary path away from the market. Therefore, the first step is to dispel any illusion that Russia will just grow out of this phase of its development. The second step is to realize that, because of the evolutionary nature of the virtual economy, reform today is a different problem than it was a decade ago. Eliminating the virtual economy today is a much harder task than implementing market reform in the immediate post-Soviet economy. Now more than ever, incrementalism and technical solutions that focus on the symptoms rather than the causes will almost certainly fail to achieve their goals.

The final preliminary step to take before developing the exit strategy is to ask whether there are any lessons to be learned from past reform efforts.

Our intent here is not to join in a complicated and ultimately rather fruitless debate about who or what was to blame for failures in the economic transition. Instead, we want to focus on the most important factors that led to the emergence of the virtual economy. We pose a fundamental question, put most starkly: Was the virtual economy an unavoidable outcome of Russia's attempt to introduce a market economy?

Was It Inevitable?

Any answer to the question of whether the virtual economy was an inevitable development in Russia must confront the issue of what is the appropriate counterfactual. That is, was there a plausible alternative course of development? Some might argue that the economies of central Europe or China provide just such information. These economies also have made a transition from a Soviet-type economy and appear to have done so much more successfully. They did not end up in the virtual economy trap. Their experience should provide clues about how an alternative transition might have proceeded in Russia.

It turns out that while these cases are informative, their value for assessing the inevitability of the virtual economy is rather limited. There is a long and oft-cited list of reasons why Russia differs from both central Europe and China.[1] The list begins with Russia's natural endowment—its inhospitable climate and vast size. Other factors are related to the distinctive nature of Russia's communist system: it had this system longer (and therefore suffered from greater misallocation of resources) than the other economies. It had by far the largest defense sector in the Soviet bloc. Moreover, while the Soviet-type system was imposed on the other economies, it was indigenous to Russia. That is where it developed, and it necessarily developed with certain Russian characteristics inherent in it. Both the central European and Chinese economies enjoyed the important advantage of having another usable past to which they could revert.

Finally, there is the issue of the incentives to break with the old system and replace it completely. The fact that the Soviet-type system was imposed in central Europe meant that a break with the communist past could be treated as liberation rather than as a repudiation of those nations' own history. This was not the case in Russia. The central European economies have

1. There is a great tendency to always want to treat each case as special. All postsocialist countries have their own unique characteristics, but we will argue that Russia does in fact qualify as a special case.

been given a huge positive incentive to succeed in market reform: they are trying to join Europe, and their admission to Europe is contingent on success in market reform. The urgency of not wasting what may well be a one-time opportunity greatly concentrates interest on reform.

The list of Russia's distinct disadvantages in overcoming its old system is long. However, even if these reasons are accepted, they only imply that the likelihood of successful market reform was lower in Russia than in the other economies. This is an important point, but it does not address the more fundamental question; that is, why Russia, but not the other countries, ended up on an *alternative* evolutionary path. Was such a path available to the other economies, but they did not take it? Or was none there?

Our argument is that the *interaction* between market reform policies and some very specific initial conditions led to the virtual economy in Russia. Policies that were effective elsewhere in making the transition to the market had different consequences in the Russian case. In other words, the same policies, undertaken with the same degree of political resolve in other countries, would not necessarily have produced the virtual economy.

We can reduce the critical initial conditions in Russia to three key factors. First, the sheer scope of loss-making enterprises in Russia meant that imposing hard-budget constraints would have doomed a large number of enterprises to closure.[2] Second, the closure of those nonviable enterprises would have had social and political consequences far greater than in other countries. Third, Russia had an asset that was a potential way to avoid this fate, namely, relational capital.

These are all ideas that we have developed and discussed in depth in preceding chapters. The first and third factors above are summarized by the concept of r-d space. If the same scale could be used to plot the distribution of enterprises of various transition economies in the same r-d space, Russia's distribution would be much more concentrated in the eastern and northern parts. That is, the Russian enterprises have higher market distance, d, and higher relational capital, r. The second factor—that is, the social and political consequences of shutting down enterprises on the vast scale that would be dictated by strict market discipline—is summed up by the notion of the impermissibility constraint. Although r-d space does not directly capture the concept of impermissibility, it does so implicitly because of the way in which impermissibility affects relational capital, r.

---

2. "A large number" can be interpreted in two ways: large compared with how the same policies impacted on Central European economies, and large in terms of what is feasible for a society to absorb.

These three factors characterize the initial conditions in which transition took place. However, what was critical for the actual evolution of the virtual economy was the fact that the reformers in Russia failed, to varying degrees, to recognize the existence of these three factors, the interconnections between them, and the reactions they would provoke on the part of agents when the economy was subjected to conventional market reform measures. We examine each of the three factors in turn.

As regards the first—the effects of imposing hard budget constraints—it is not as if the reformers did not know that many enterprises would fail if they were forced to operate according to the rules of a market economy. The problem was in estimating the ratio of those enterprises that could survive to those that could not. This has been referred to as the ratio of "won't adjusters" to "can't adjusters," *walca*.[3]

Russia's reformers, and most observers, worked under the assumption that this ratio was rather high. That is, they saw the main problem as a lack of will, not lack of ability, to restructure.[4] Consequently, the reformers reasoned, what was needed were credible policies to alter the expectations of the won't adjusters—the enterprises that were capable of changing, but just did not want to. With tough policies, the won't adjusters would be forced to change their attitude. This approach makes sense as long as the ratio is high. In that case, the payoff to tough policies is high and the costs are manageable. Most enterprises *can* adjust, and the number of casualties will be low. But if *walca* is low, tough policies have far different consequences. Then the casualties overwhelm the system, and the reforms cannot be continued. After the fact, it is argued that "if only the reform had been credible . . . ." In other words, if only the leaders had been even tougher and more persistent, enterprises would have changed, but this ignores the real problem.

Most observers still fail to recognize the true *walca* ratio in Russia. They still do not fully appreciate the nature of the Soviet system, and in particular the ways in which Soviet pricing distorted the true magnitudes of the economy.[5] This is why so many discussions of Russia's future emphasize the failure of policy rather than the role of structure and why proposals for the future focus on things like tax reform or ending corruption. It is assumed

---

3. This idea was introduced in Ickes and Ryterman (1994).

4. Hence the emphasis on cutting state subsidies to enterprises and on changes in ownership structure as the key to restructuring. See, for instance, Boycko, Shleifer, and Vishny (1995).

5. It was precisely this illusion about the true legacy of the Soviet period that made it possible for our metaphor of the privatization lottery to even partially explain the nature of reform in Russia.

that the policy settings were wrong and must be adjusted to enable Russia to advance. The notion is that reform will take place if only there are proper incentives.

The failure to recognize the true *wa/ca* ratio could be interpreted as a misapplication of the evolution principle. Reformers behaved as if they believed that with new rules Soviet enterprises could evolve into market-like firms.[6] Changes in the environment were supposed to cause changes in enterprise behavior, and enterprises would adapt to the new environment. However, evolution does not work that way, especially in the face of cataclysmic events. Individuals do not evolve, species do. In any population those members that are best suited to the environment will thrive. A change in the environment alters the relative fortune of different members of a population—those with differential advantage survive. When the environmental change is cataclysmic, however, the entire species may become extinct. The dinosaurs did not evolve when the environment was drastically shocked—they died. Other species that were able to survive the cataclysm took over the ecological space freed by the extinction.

Of course, with human institutions, strategies can be changed so the institution can adapt to the new environment. Former Soviet enterprises need not behave in the same manner as before. Indeed, this is just what the reformers counted on. But even if the enterprise can develop new strategies, it cannot change the fundamentals that determine the payoffs from those strategies, in other words, the inherited poor capital stocks.[7] In the case of Russia, opening to the market threatened to make many—too many— enterprises essentially extinct. Unlike the real dinosaurs, however, Russia's industrial dinosaurs possessed an alternative asset—relational capital—that had a positive payoff in their vastly altered environment.

The second part of Russia's Soviet legacy was the enormous social significance of these same nonviable enterprises and, consequently, the dire

6. Peter Murrell was an early critic of the view that enterprises could change their behavior with a change in the ownership regime. See, for example, Murrell (1992).

7. In other words, behavior may be malleable, but if the organism is still unsuited to its new environment, no amount of behavioral change can avert the ecological crisis. In Russia of the 1990s, the idea was to induce changes in enterprise behavior by having consultants and seminar leaders teach modern business strategies. One can imagine analogous seminars that might have been designed in the Late Cretaceous Period to teach the dinosaurs how to survive. Drawing on lessons learned from the success stories of the new environment—small prehuman mammals—the consultants would explain that dinosaurs should "Eat meat, be small, live in tiny crevices." One suspects that the consultants would probably have been paid even if the dinosaurs failed to successfully restructure themselves to become rat-like placental mammals.

consequences of their failure. Their gigantic employment numbers, though certainly important, were not the only problem. What made them even more important was their role as "city-forming enterprises," to use the Soviet terminology. In communities ranging in size from smaller towns to those with populations over a million, virtually all the important municipal services were connected to the enterprise sector. Some of the larger cities were more extreme in this regard than smaller ones. They were all in fact agglomerations of company towns. Up to 60–80 percent of the industrial labor force worked in a handful of giant enterprises, each forming a city of its own.

Reform schemes tended to ignore this problem. Policy dictated that the social assets be divested from the enterprises and handed over to the city governments for management. This strategy assumed that there was somewhere, at the core of the "enterprise-city," an entity that "had" all these social assets. In too many cases, this was not true. The enterprise's production activities and social-service activities had co-evolved. There was no such thing as a company that had taken on too many non-core-related activities. That was the western perception; the Russian reality was that the production entity and the social assets were one. The result was that when formal policies were forced through to separate the social assets from the plant, those assets often collapsed.

The third part of Russia's Soviet legacy—relational capital—was the most critical and least appreciated. Relational capital may have been the most important difference of all between Russia and the central European economies. Relational capital did exist in central European economies, but it was less of an issue there because officials had less value to circulate. Russia, however, had an abundance of energy resources that could be used to contribute value. This energy abundance made it possible for Russia to pursue policies that were too costly in other economies. Energy wealth gave a higher value to relational capital in Russia than elsewhere. Even if the Czech Republic, say, had shared all the problems of Russia, the demise of the Soviet trading bloc, the Council for Mutual Economic Assistance (CMEA), put an end to energy subsidization. The Czechs therefore had no choice but to undertake real reforms. In resource-abundant Russia, officials had plenty of value to disburse. This allowed relational capital to maintain, and even enhance, its critical importance in the transition.

Let us recapitulate the three key factors and their effects. (1) The nonviability of Russia's enterprise sector, reflected in its extremely high *wa/ca* ratio, meant that too many enterprises *would die* if they were subjected to a true hard-budget constraint. (2) The impermissibility constraint meant that the enterprises *could not be allowed to die*. (3) Russia's energy abundance and the value it gave to relational capital meant that the enterprises *did not have to die* because they could circumvent the hard-budget constraint. Nevertheless, all this now prompts the question, What could have been done differently to account for these factors?

Had they fully understood the implications of points (1) and (2), policymakers could have designed a policy package to deal with the inevitable economic and social side effects of reform. Instead of assuming that divestiture of social assets from enterprises would automatically lead to the desired result, policymakers would have developed a concerted policy of building public safety nets from the beginning. This of course would have been a vast undertaking, but it would nevertheless have been necessary, since it would have been the only way to avoid the personalization of safety nets. In the absence of actually functioning public safety nets, enterprises remained at the core of the personalized system. This did not make people more mobile. It did not break the attachment to job and place that would be essential for Russia to reallocate resources.

Dealing with relational capital presented the biggest problem. Awareness of the importance of relational capital could have suggested policies to deal with both the source of the relational capital's value (primarily the energy sector) and the vehicles for its transmission (the directors of the value-destroying enterprises). The key issue is control over the value of the energy sector. But how could policy toward the energy sector actually have been changed? One option might have been to retain full state ownership of Gazprom. However, even in the late days of the Soviet period, resources were already being diverted from Gazprom and other state-owned enterprises. Second, the reformers might have effected greater turnover among officials, both in government agencies and in enterprises. Such a measure would have seriously devalued relational capital because this asset is both individual and enterprise specific. Many central European countries pursued such personnel turnover policies much more resolutely, largely as a by-product of the general purge of communists from all policymaking positions in those countries. Russian reformers may have made a political calculation that too much turnover would jeopardize stability. Or they may have realized that they faced a human capital constraint: there simply was not enough personnel to replace old enterprise management and to staff revamped ministries and government offices—hundreds of thousands of people who would be both able and willing to play by the new rules. More important is the fact that relational capital played a role in the economy. Given the initial ratio of *wa/ca*, it would be hard to operate the economy without relational capital. That is, change of the formal rules alone would not be sufficient. The fundamental mistake was the belief that merely eliminating the old formal system would force the players to play by the new formal rules.[8]

Our arguments above are in part a criticism of shock therapy. Not only did the proponents of shock therapy underestimate the importance of formal safety nets and social concerns in general,[9] they also were guided by blind faith in the automatic nature of radical reform. At the same time, our suggestion to severely reduce the value of relational capital is a way of saying that more of a shock needed to be delivered to the enterprises. However, the critical link is the idea that only with a greater commitment to social safety nets could the greater shock have been implemented. The people needed to be protected and given maximum opportunities to move out of the old world and into the new.[10]

In any event we know that the virtual economy did evolve. Even if different policies had been pursued, we can never know for certain if the Russian economy would have evolved in a different manner. All discussion of counterfactuals boils down to speculation. The real question is what can be done. Here we must reiterate: the problem today is not the same as the one that faced the reformers of the early 1990s. Today, the virtual economy exists.

Restructuring "Russia, Inc."

The virtual economy approach dictates two indispensable features of any program for real reform of the Russian economy: it must be all encompassing and it must recognize the impermissibility constraints. A program has to be comprehensive because the virtual economy is a system and it must be attacked as such. It cannot be treated successfully in piecemeal fashion. The program has to recognize impermissibility constraints because

8. Again, this point was recognized by Murrell (1992) at the time, but the point was generally ignored in the literature.

9. Blame here should not stop with the Russian reformers: precious little support for social safety nets was forthcoming from the West during the heyday of shock therapy.

10. It is precisely when shock therapy is implemented without social safety nets that the enterprise director becomes the savior of the enterprise's workers and other members of the local community. This is an enhancement of his relational capital, and it therefore strengthens his ability to resist market reform.

it must be feasible. It is of course essential to have a technically correct program, that is, one that focuses on the economic fundamentals that underlie the virtual economy. However, a purely technical analysis is insufficient, for it neglects the social and political constraints that limit which policies can actually be implemented. The impermissibility constraint must be considered from the beginning.

To force ourselves to think about the problem of reform in the proper way, we will look at Russia's problem as an exercise in corporate restructuring, albeit one conducted under peculiar conditions. That is, we treat the entire Russian economy as if it were a single bankrupt corporation that has been handed over to external receivers. At the same time, the receivers will still have to take into account constraints of a noneconomic nature, because this bankrupt company has stakeholders whose rights, both formal and informal, must be respected.[11] We then consider how external receivers would analyze this peculiar firm. We develop a restructuring plan based on this analysis, keeping in mind the need to satisfy the impermissibility constraints.

This approach has two advantages. The first is that we avoid the incremental and partial approach from the beginning, since we will be looking at Russian reform from the vantage point of someone who has complete power and authority to deal with the system as a whole. While it might seem that it is a complete fantasy to imagine restructuring the economy as a whole (it is hard enough to implement isolated economic policies in Russia), our purpose is not to make a blueprint. We use this approach because it allows us to consider the problem of the virtual economy comprehensively and because it allows us to see how the assets in Russia could be used more profitably.

A second advantage of our approach is that it allows us to set aside temporarily the question of the political incentives of the leadership. External receivers have the authority to implement a restructuring plan. They can consider the problem without having to consider politics. This lets us analyze what is feasible and would work. Of course this is only a first step. Political realities cannot be ignored.[12] Once a clear idea of what needs to be

11. As in normal bankruptcies, attention is paid to loss of key personnel.

12. The distinction between *politics* and *political realities* is important. We stress that the receivers can ignore politics. That is, because they have full authority, the receivers are not subject to political pressure from interest groups and so on. However, they cannot ignore political realities: they do have to take into account social and political circumstances. They must satisfy the impermissibility constraint.

done emerges, we can return to the issue of political incentives and external preconditions.

We begin by imagining that the Russian economy is a single company, with many divisions. It is of course not uncommon to think of Russia as a multidivisional firm.[13] Usually the idea is that the enterprises are the divisions. Oil, gas, and other resource enterprises might be thought of as profitable divisions and companies like Tutayev, the diesel engine manufacturer featured in chapter 2, as the unprofitable ones. In our exercise, however, the divisions are Russia's *regions*—the various oblasts and other federation subjects. We do this to emphasize the role of regional authorities in preventing restructuring. Thus the governors of regions will be "territorial divisional directors."

In addition to the territorial divisions, we have one functional division, Gazprom. It is the source of the overwhelming volume of the company's cash flow. In our story, the original top management of Russia, Inc., allowed the territorial division directors to collude with the Gazprom division to divert income from the shareholders. This is making the company poorer. Moreover, resources are running out—by 2003 the Gazprom division itself may be in serious difficulty. This clearly critical situation is the setting in which the outside receivers are called in.

As the receivers attempt to get a grasp on this company, they immediately recognize that it has some very peculiar characteristics. They are, for instance, generally aware of the role of Gazprom as a profitable division. They realize quickly that this curious, quasi-autonomous division plays an inordinate role in this company. The relationship between the Gazprom division, the central management, and the directors of the other divisions is extraordinarily complex. As a functional division rather than a territorial division, it is not strange that Gazprom has some of its own operations within all the other divisions, but it appears that it also operates as a parallel central management. It seems like the only thing holding the company together. It is not clear, however, whether Gazprom acts a proxy for central management or is acting on its own.

The external receivers would observe that in Russia, Inc., the majority of divisions live off a few. It would also not take long for the receivers to note that the division directors had seized control of cash flow in the company, and that they had succeeded in this endeavor thanks to their collusion with

13. Analyses that treated the Soviet economy as "USSR, Inc.," were much less far-fetched. That system did resemble a structure with a single owner, namely the Communist Party of the Soviet Union.

Gazprom. This collusion has greatly weakened central authority within the company, which has made it difficult to implement a coherent strategy of reform.

Despite these insights the receivers might still be puzzled as to why the directors of weak divisions would want to stay on board rather than jump ship and look for better positions elsewhere. Further analysis might lead to the conclusion that it is the chance to skim off some of the revenue brought in by Gazprom that is critical. An even more important finding is that the territorial division directors need to keep their divisions operating in order to be able to tap into this reservoir of funds. As long as they can maintain their divisions in operation, they can continue to be claimants for the corporation's funds. The problem, however, is that there are too many claimants for the amount of cash that the Gazprom division can produce.

Under the current configuration of Russia, Inc., it is evident to the receivers that the first problem central management faces is a lack of information. There are problems, questions, and paradoxes everywhere. Despite the pretense of normal accounting and so on, this company is almost completely nontransparent. Division management has clearly been engaging in practices that weaken the company's overall health and viability. Yet no one seems to know for sure what is going on or even how healthy the company is. The divisions use virtual strategies to hide losses, and this increases the noise that clutters information about performance. For instance, various indexes of performance seem good, but that does not jibe with what a minimal amount of due diligence says about the reality of operations. It is common practice to temporarily shift assets (cash) to make a particular index look good.

The receivers need to obtain accurate information about which divisions are loss making and, more important, the extent of their losses. Without accurate information about the structure of loss making in the corporation, management is in a poor position to initiate restructuring. The receivers are interested not only in financial information, but also in the technical potential and human capital resources of the divisions. The external receivers would issue an order for a thorough and comprehensive audit of the various divisions to ascertain their actual contributions to the overall enterprise. This would be the process of accounting for the economic value of transactions, to peer behind the veil created by the virtual accounting.

Having collected this information, the receivers now face the much more difficult stage of recommending proper action. They need to stop subsidization of the loss-making divisions by those that actually generate profits.

Had this been a conventional corporate restructuring, the method of preventing cross-subsidization would be straightforward. The receivers would simply shut down each division's unprofitable lines and allow viable lines of business to remain. However, our receivers would recognize that they are dealing with an unconventional case. First of all, the audit they ordered in the earlier stage showed that the ratio of viable lines to unviable is small in nearly every single division. Second, the extraordinarily complex contractual obligations this company has to its employees constrain the receivers in eliminating the sources of loss.[14] Thus the receivers cannot simply close loss-making divisions immediately. Moreover, ruthless shutdown policies may worsen morale throughout the company. Finally, this is a company where nearly all those involved, whether managers or workers, have adapted their behavior for years, even decades, to the expectation of continued subsidies. This means that even the profitable lines are highly infected by the bad practices. It is therefore not at all obvious that the old activities are reformable.

Therefore, rather than adopting the conventional remedy of excising the loss-making activities from each division, the receivers decide they will have to do just the opposite. They will remove the viable lines of business from the divisions and leave the unviable ones behind. They propose to "migrate" the profitable activities into a limited number of the old divisions that seem to have the best prerequisites for future development.

While the receivers are confident that this migration approach is the correct one under the circumstances, its implementation poses two major challenges. First, the receivers must elaborate some general principles about which divisions will be the target, or destination, divisions. That is, they must determine what kinds of divisions have a future. Note that this is not necessarily the same as determining which divisions currently are profitable and which are not. The idea is to project which divisions would have the greatest potential for future development if they could obtain the best employees and capital from the other divisions.

The second concrete task is to decide how to induce people to leave the loss-making divisions. In this company, employees cannot be ordered to

---

14. These obligations are the corporate analog to political costs of shutting down enterprises in one-company towns, for example. In a corporation, many workers in a loss-making division would have contracts that prevent immediate termination. In a political organization, there are social obligations that are not contractual in a legal sense, but are understood, and whose abrogation may have political consequences.

move.[15] They have the right to stay put. The receivers therefore have to devise a voluntary approach. They must provide positive incentives, while still recognizing the company's financial constraints. The receivers decide on a principle of severance bonuses. That is, they will offer lump-sum payments to workers willing to move to target divisions. Such bonuses will have to be large enough to induce some households to move—perhaps equal to six months' wages. The bonuses will be financed from the savings realized by reducing subsidies to loss-making divisions.

Using severance bonuses to encourage movement of factors has several advantages. One important effect is that compensation reduces the backlash that may be expected to result in the "loser" divisions, the ones left off the list of target divisions. This is not just a matter of buying off resistance. Severance bonuses also promote self-selection by giving an incentive to those who have the best chances to make it elsewhere to leave first. Some factors may be better off in another division but are unable to try because of lack of finance or some similar constraint.[16] A severance bonus would enable such factors to move. Indeed, setting the bonus at the right level can separate the more productive from the less.[17] This has the added benefit that those that do move to another division are the most likely to succeed.

A critical component of the receivers' approach to restructuring is to insulate the growth divisions from the practices of the old ones. It is vital to prevent a resurrection of the deleterious practices of resource diversion. Of course, they will set up new accounting systems that do not allow virtual strategies, but this is feasible only if the prospective growth divisions have no obligations and no relational capital. Therefore, the growth divisions must be shielded. It is also necessary to prevent growth activities from moving into loser divisions, because the virtual economy will leech on to them, with the potential for recreating the problem that the reformers are trying to eliminate.

What about the loser divisions? As the most productive employees accept the offer of severance bonuses to move, these divisions become even less viable than before. Nevertheless, they are still staffed by stakeholders with

15. Under current conditions workers actually face negative incentives to move due to wage arrears. These tie workers to their current enterprises, and regions, to be able to collect the forced loans that they have made to their current employers. See Friebel and Guriev (2000) for an analysis.

16. One is tempted to say workers here, but other factors of production are also tied. Capital is difficult to move because of uncertainty over property rights and obligations to tax authorities in the current region—the analog to contractual obligations.

17. At least one can separate them in an expected value sense, so that agents with higher expected values in a new region move.

contractual obligations that cannot be easily abrogated. If it is too expensive—considering the total costs, including the obligations to employees—to simply shut them down, then the receivers reason that the best solution is to continue to shrink them in size beyond even what results from the migration of employees. They will be allowed to continue operating, but on a lesser scale. By insulating the loss-making divisions, a shrunken rump of the old Russia, Inc., can continue to operate, at a much lower cost to the corporation overall. This too involves self-selection; it utilizes the self-preservation skills of those who choose to stay. It is important to leave these people with the opportunity to move away from these divisions.

The receivers are convinced that this solution is not only financially feasible for the company, but also more equitable than simply shutting down loss-making divisions. After all, the workers in those divisions were not responsible for the errors of the management. Indeed, the managers themselves bear less responsibility, as the enterprises they inherited from the Soviet period were not even intended to be viable in a market economy. Even more important, the program of induced migration combined with planned shrinkage is more voluntary as well. This reduces (though it does not eliminate) the chance of a backlash that would jeopardize the overall restructuring program.

Clearly, this entire plan depends critically on more central control over the company. Central management needs not only to control information, but also to control cash flow. Without control of cash flow, central management cannot cut the deals—making severance payments and other charges needed to induce the loss makers to accept the changes—that would be necessary to begin shrinking and eventually closing down loss-making divisions.[18] Central control will also be needed to insulate the target regions from the pernicious effects of relational capital.

The external receivers' recommendation to centralize control over the company runs counter to advice that is frequently heard. Other companies, it would be argued, seem to be quite successful in going in the opposite direction—giving more autonomy to the divisions. One such example is the notoriously successful USA, Inc. However, the receivers would realize the futility of trying such a strategy in the specific case of Russia, Inc. Such an approach would be intended to alter incentives so that directors of lagging divisions would improve performance, but the receivers would reckon that

18. Central management will not be able to appropriate the whole cash flow, however; it will have to distribute some of the savings to Gazprom to get it to cooperate with the changes. The simplest way to effect this change is to make an offer to Gazprom backed up by a threat to eliminate it as an independent division.

this will not work in this case. The main problem is, again, that so many divisions are nonviable. They were developed for noneconomic reasons. Hence, improvements in the incentives that are faced by division directors would not cope with this fundamental problem.[19] It is not just improvements within divisions that will solve Russia's problems. Hard choices about the fate of various divisions must be made, and this will require more central control.

A second important reason why the receivers back away from the decentralization strategy is fear that they cannot alter incentives enough to devalue relational capital. Hence, they are afraid that autonomous division directors will compete with one another in adopting and emulating bad practices rather than good—that they will act to enhance the value of relational capital rather than reduce it.

To sum up, the receivers' approach to the bankrupt Russia, Inc., consists of seven components that are derived from the key concern—managing and controlling relational capital. First, they remove the pretense about the way the company has been operating up to now. Second, they acquire the necessary information about the state of the company in order to make critical decisions for the future. Third, they elaborate a principle for restructuring that is based on moving assets from a large number of the old loss-making divisions into a number of divisions that are regarded as better situated for growth. Fourth, they draft a policy of awarding severance bonuses in order to encourage self-selection. Fifth, they do not shut down loss-making divisions, but instead encourage them to shrink. Sixth, they insulate the growth divisions from the loss makers. Finally, as a prerequisite for actually implementing all of these, the new management seizes control of cash flow and stops the leakage.

A Real-World Version

How does this allegorical corporate restructuring exercise relate to Russia, the nation? Russia is not a corporation, and its political leaders are not external receivers. We must think of a real-world version of these solutions that translates to the national political structures while still retaining the value of our corporate analogy—namely, that we took a comprehensive approach to the problem.

19. This false allure of the decentralization approach stems from the same erroneous perception of the viability of enterprises that governed the reformers' overall approach to market reform. That is, they overestimate the *wa/ca* ratio. They believed that the main problem was one of incentives and credibility, not of structure.

We begin in the same way as in the exercise. The first principle was, Eliminate the pretense. This is an especially critical step in Russia because of the obstacle of the status quo bias. Pretense reinforces the status quo bias because it makes the current situation appear viable—and almost economically logical. At the same time, a proper accounting that unearths the nature of the transactions in the virtual economy will help make clear to the public the type of changes that are necessary. The goal is not to focus on corrupt practices and unleash scandals; it is to understand the size and direction of the value transfers. We want to know concretely how they occur and how they can be avoided.

Obviously, the critical role of the resource sector—the main value pump of the virtual economy—must be made clear. This will focus mainly on Gazprom—the real Gazprom—but our receivers will also take into account other value-producing parts of the economy. The size of the transfers to the value-destroying part of the economy must also be revealed. With value flows more transparent, the situation shows itself to be precarious and perhaps not self-sustaining. One important benefit of revealing the extent of these transfers will be to make it clear to the public the type of changes that will be needed.[20]

A proper audit will not only show the weakness of the old economy, but will also suggest important principles of a new economy. First, it will become clear that there is a significant geographical element to the nature of transfers in the economy. A large part of the problem is that too much economic activity is located in the wrong places. The vagaries of Russia's climate play a special role. Russia, as it is currently populated, is not only too far to the north; it is also too far to the east.[21] The reason is that in Russia the isotherms—lines of constant temperature—resemble lines of longitude, rather than lines of latitude, as in most parts of the world. This means that regions that are farther to the east are significantly colder than those in the west. Russia's eastern regions thus suffer from a double blow; they are too far from potential markets and in too cold a climate. These observations apply not only to the areas of the Far East and eastern Siberia, but even to

20. Knowledge is a first step, but changing this situation will not be easy, given how large a share (in terms of employment) of the economy may be revealed as value destroying.

21. While Russia and Canada have the same proportion of their territories north of the Arctic Circle, Russia has about one hundred times the share of its population in that region. Of course, Canadian location is determined in large part by the proximity of markets—along the U.S. border—but this also emphasizes that in Russia location is largely independent of market-related forces.

what some might consider the "heartland" of modern Russia, the Urals and western Siberia.

The geographical distribution of Russia's industry was greatly altered by noneconomic decisions. In particular, the decision to move Russian industry to the Urals before and during World War II was made for reasons of security. Millions of workers were moved to not merely inhospitably cold, but inhumanely cold, regions in the gulag. Moreover, industrial location decisions throughout the Soviet period were made without consideration of transportation costs. This means that enterprises in Russia bear an extra burden of climate and transportation costs. These burdens may have been (barely) manageable in the closed Soviet economy, but they place a very heavy toll on producers in a more open market economy. Hence, reform will require that these location burdens be reduced. This is why we have emphasized the importance of self-selection to encourage shifts in industrial location.

These considerations suggest some principles for choosing the critical regions for development. One might speculate that a sustainable Russian economy would require a shift in the distribution of economic activity to the west and south.[22] This would move activity closer to external markets and, most important, to better climates. Another likely development will involve a change in the size distribution of cities in Russia. In most of the world, the size distribution of cities follows Zipf's Law, an exponential distribution.[23] Russia, however, deviates from this "natural" pattern in a rather distinctive way. The most notable abnormality of the size distribution of Russia's cities is that the cities in its second tier (the ten or so cities that rank below Moscow and St. Petersburg) are too small. At the same time, however, in terms of the earlier temperature argument, the cities currently occupying these places ought not to be the ones that grow further because they are too cold. It is quite likely, therefore, that serious reform will involve significant changes in both city location and city size in Russia. Some large cities in the

---

22. Actually, to the southwest. Moving to the south would be of little value in the eastern part of the country given the isotherms in Russia.

23. Zipf's Law as applied to city sizes is the following. Order a country's cities by population (the largest city is number 1, the second largest is number 2, and so on). Then draw a graph in which the logarithm of the rank of each city is plotted on the y-axis and the logarithm of the population of the city is plotted on the x-axis. The result is a straight line with slope of -1. A recent article refers to the Zipf's Law distribution of city sizes as "the most robust regularity in all of economics." See Gabaix (1999). To date, however, the only serious attempt to provide a microeconomic explanation for the phenomenon is Axtell and Florida (2000).

western regions will grow at the expense of large cities in the Urals and western Siberia.[24]

Beyond some general principles of this type, it is hardly advisable to plan in detail what Russia should look like. While this is a process that cannot be planned, it is nevertheless one that has to be planned *for*. The most important point is that policies must facilitate, and certainly should not obstruct or contravene, natural mobility of factors of production inside Russia. The leadership has to be ready to promote change and mobility, *wherever* it might lead. To take one example, if indeed these general principles of movement of activity westward are valid, the idea of "repopulating" the eastern parts of Russia should be abandoned.[25] In addition, the use of severance bonuses to induce migration should be targeted to destinations that have greater economic prospects—those in the western regions.

Not only must people move, but profitable and potentially profitable businesses will need to move as well. This calls for extra comment. One might be tempted to argue that being the only efficient enterprise in a region is an advantage. However, this simply ignores the fact that in a virtual economy environment such an enterprise becomes a value pump for the rest of the region. These businesses need to be moved to more profitable regions. Notice that even within an enterprise in a losing region—an Igor—the possibility exists to move some parts of the business to a new region. Just as there is cross-subsidization *across* enterprises within a region, there is also cross-subsidization across activities *within* an enterprise. Under current conditions, this is necessary for survival. The loss-making activities may enhance relational capital—certainly cutting them would reduce it—but a successful restructuring program would separate them. This is critical to shrink the virtual economy and reduce loss-making activities. Hence, it is necessary to conduct triage on an enterprise level as well as on the regional level.

---

24. We are currently exploring some of these issues in our project "The Cost of Cold." In a typical simulation that we conducted to try to determine optimal city development in Russia, cities in the Urals and western Siberia that today have populations of a million to a million and a half ended up with around 250,000–500,000. These "shrunken" cities include Yekaterinburg, Chelyabinsk, Perm, Ufa, Novosibirsk, Omsk, and Krasnoyarsk.

25. The repopulation idea is current policy in Russia. For instance, in a February 2001 speech President Putin called for programs to reverse the trend of emigration from Siberia and the Far East: "We must substantially raise the attractiveness of in-migration into the regions east of the Urals. This will require serious government decisions in both the political and economic spheres. . . . We must make clear and definite commitments to create the objective conditions for economic revival [of Siberia and the Far East]." Putin (2001a).

The problem with conducting triage on an enterprise level is both lack of information and lack of authority to undertake such a process (after all, there are shareholders). Once again this is where the combined policies of self-selected migration to new regions and subsequent insulation of these regions from practices of the old ones can help. The enterprise can perform its own triage because the profitable activities will be protected from the virtual economy in the new region. Moreover, there may be a positive externality in this practice. Even for those value-adding enterprises that stay in the old region—that refuse to migrate—the potential threat that they *might* migrate will reduce the extent to which officials can extract value. Hence, the option of migration will also reduce the level of virtual economy activity in the old regions. The key point here is that without the possibility to move to a profitable region, the value producer is hostage to the virtual economy in his region. To reduce value diversion, profitable operations must have an outside option.

The proposed reallocation of people and economic activity should not be considered terribly radical in content. These movements are natural developments. They would make Russia closer to Europe, closer to markets, and warmer. In fact, this is precisely the movement that would have happened naturally had not Soviet locational policies worked in the direction opposite of what was happening in the rest of the world. This movement is just a correction of the processes that have increased Russia's market distance, d, by locating its industry and population in economically nonviable regions. Making Russia competitive necessitates accelerating the reversal of these locational mistakes.

While the population movements may be natural in terms of economic fundamentals, they nonetheless involve a massive reallocation of activity and of resources, and the most important of them is people. Such reallocation is a process that will risk stability. It will threaten notions of personal and national security, especially for a Russia that sees a special mission in its continental size. This provides a challenge to reformers. They cannot simply move people involuntarily; indeed, the force of this plan is voluntary movement through severance payments. Given that these intended movements mirror patterns that have happened elsewhere in the world, perhaps they will be easy to generate in Russia as well. These movements ought to be welfare enhancing. However, to garner public support for the program, the Russian government must make sure that this is recognized by the population.

Preconditions

A final step in generating a truly feasible program of economic reform remains. Technical feasibility is insufficient. We must also consider the conditions that are necessary for a successful reform program to be implemented. Russian reform is not being imposed by a foreign power. A successful reform is one that attacks the virtual economy *and* is implementable. Three preconditions appear most important. These are recentralized domestic political authority, an appropriate economic environment, and reassurance for both the leadership and the population that the benefits of reform outweigh the costs, that is, that there is a reason to reform.

Political Centralization

The critical step for implementation of the program devised by the receivers in the corporate restructuring allegory was centralization of authority and of resource flows within the company. This is also the most important prerequisite for the real-world version. To date, Russian reform has been crippled by the ability of regional authorities to pursue policies that promote their regions at the expense of the nation as a whole.[26] Because such policies preserve and increase the value of relational capital, they enable enterprises to postpone serious economic reform. To reverse this situation, the value of relational capital must be reduced dramatically, and this requires a shift of authority from the regions to the center.

Political centralization does not mean weakening democracy or individual rights. Quite the contrary: one main purpose of centralization is to liberate individual citizens to locate themselves and their economic activity to more sensible areas. In order to make resources more mobile, however, physical and human capital cannot be held hostage to relational capital. This means that excessive federalism must be reined in. The responsibilities of the center and the regions must be more clearly defined, especially with regard to taxation.

Some would argue that the opposite approach—empowering the local governors so that they can compete with one another—is the proper reform for Russia to undertake. The argument for devolving more authority to the regions, based typically on comparisons with Chinese reforms, is an impor-

---

26. This includes, for example, barriers to internal trade set up by "red-belt" governors intent on maintaining price controls. See Berkowitz and DeJong (1999).

tant one, so it is worth consideration here.[27] The basic argument for the Chinese approach is straightforward. It assumes that Russia's problems stem from the inadequate incentives that face local officials. Increases in regional incomes are taxed away by the center, which redistributes income across regions on the basis of need more than success.[28] If regional governors saw their power enhanced so that more of the fruits of success stayed within the region—as is purported to be the case in China—they would seek to build larger local tax bases. Giving governors the right to keep more income in their own regions would be an incentive to improve the economic climate and to compete to make their regions more hospitable to new investment.

Although the Chinese approach to federalism is often held to offer important lessons for Russia, it is unlikely that such devolution would have a positive effect in Russia. The reason is that this analysis ignores the role of relational capital.[29] Devolution would strengthen the role of relational capital at the regional level. The fallacy that underlies the suggestion to devolve authority to the regions is similar to that we encountered earlier when discussing enterprises. We described in an earlier chapter how the expectation that market competition would lead to a shakeout of inefficient producers foundered on the rocks of relational capital. The inefficient producers did not simply vanish; instead, they exploited relational capital to survive. Perceptive managers learned from that competitive exercise that they must enhance their relational capital. Regions, too, live in r-d space. If r is valuable, then regions will compete based on their r. Success depends on the environment.[30] If r is still valuable, then decentralizing authority will not

27. See, for example, Roland (2000, chapter 11) and the references therein. See also IMF (2000).

28. See, for example, Narayan (1999).

29. Why does relational capital not doom Chinese decentralization? Resource endowment is a significant factor, but perhaps equally important, in China local officials are still members of the Communist Party. The party contains control mechanisms that limit (but certainly do not eliminate) the value of relational capital. The importance of central control in limiting the discretion of local officials to stifle growth is examined in Blanchard and Shleifer (2000). Moreover, the Chinese party rotates lead cadres across regions. This greatly reduces the incentives facing enterprise directors from investing in relational capital: by the time good relations are established, the official may have moved to another region where he is of little help. The role of rotation in improving the incentives of officials in hierarchies is not new. See Ickes and Samuelson (1987).

30. Douglass North emphasized this point in discussing a bad institutional environment in Africa: "The organizations that develop in this framework will become more efficient—but more efficient at making the society even more unproductive and the basic institutional structure even less conducive to productive activity. Such a path can persist because the transaction costs of the political and economic markets of those economies together with the subjective models of the actors do not lead them to move incrementally toward efficient outcomes." North (1990, p. 9).

improve incentives. Transfers are critical to survival, and they will not be reduced if governors are still powerful.[31]

The Economic Environment

Reform must be not only technically and socially feasible, but also financially feasible. Dismantling the virtual economy is a question of both stimulating the viable parts of the economy to reduce their distance to the market and shrinking the unviable parts. An effective way to assist both processes is to keep the value of the ruble as low as possible. A cheap ruble offers a window of opportunity for serious reform in several important ways. First is the conventional argument that it increases the competitiveness of industry because it helps create a proper environment in which market-oriented enterprises can survive. It reduces d.

Second, a cheap ruble enhances the coffers of the central government. This is an important consideration given the need to pay severance bonuses to encourage movement to new regions. In addition, it will be less costly to support those parts of the virtual economy that cannot be eliminated immediately. Ruble depreciation makes the value-adding part of Russia's economy (which is predominantly cash based) larger in ruble terms relative to the value-subtracting part that lives in the virtual economy. Hence, the nonmonetary transactions that are needed to subsidize production at value-destroying enterprises shrink in ruble terms.

Although the cheap ruble can reduce the size of transfers from outside Russia that would be required to help with reform—indeed, a large enough depreciation would make it possible for western aid to be sufficient to buy off the virtual economy—there are trade-offs. Depreciation on that magnitude would also further impoverish the Russian people, and there is no way to impose such a fall in the standard of living without actually being an occupying power. How ruthless one can be depends on the difference between, on the one hand, restructuring a company within a market economy and, on the other, restructuring the whole country with no external absorptive capacity.[32]

A Reason to Reform

Even if a viable reform plan is developed and the organizational and economic preconditions to fulfill it are met, would-be reformers still face

31. This is the clear implication of Ericson's industrial feudalism model. See Ericson (2001).

32. Obviously it would be very different if Russia were, for instance, the fifty-first state of the United States; East Germany's provinces were in just this way successfully incorporated into West Germany.

one more hurdle: they have to gather the political momentum to implement the plan. In today's Russia, this means convincing both themselves and the broader population that there is a reason to reform. Notice the double-edged nature of the problem. It is not only the public that must be given a reason to undertake reform; the leadership must also be induced to launch reforms that are inherently disruptive and politically threatening.

The failure of previous reform efforts to live up to promises has not only generated great cynicism but has also led to the development of the self-protection schemes (the personalized safety nets) that are so critical to the virtual economy. Cynicism and self-protection have created an inertia that successful reform must overcome. This is no easy task. To overcome the inertia, the public must be assured on at least two fronts. First is the size of the benefits of reform relative to the costs: the public must see a potential reward big enough to warrant undergoing another wave of social upheaval—one greater, in fact, than that they already experienced in the decade of the 1990s. Second is the issue of credibility: the public must believe that the rewards from successful reform will actually accrue to them.

Even assurance on these two fronts is insufficient for reform to be implemented. The leadership must overcome its own inertia as well. This means, at the very minimum, that the implications of the impermissibility constraint must be met. To implement reform the leadership must be confident that the short-term negative effects of reform will not threaten the very survival of the nation.

The experience of eastern Europe gives an idea of the role that reward can play in creating the conditions for viable reforms. A critical element in the success of reform in the so-called Visegrad countries—Hungary, Poland, and the Czech Republic—was the promise of integration into Europe. The prize was membership in the European Union (EU).[33] This prize concentrates attention and creates a setting where costly reforms are undertaken. The question is whether EU accession can be enough of an incentive for Russia. Perhaps not, but the eastern European case suggests something of the size of the prize that would be needed; it is at least a lower bound on the size of the prize. After all, the Visegrad countries undertook their

33. Fischer and Sahay recognize the role of potential EU accession in their discussion of differences in transition performance across countries. "For many countries, the prospect of joining the European Union has been a powerful spur to reform. The absence of that prospect for the OFSU countries (the former Soviet Union minus the Baltics) except perhaps eventually Ukraine must be among the factors retarding reform." Fischer and Sahay (2000, p. 22). Roland (2000, pp. 180–84 and 338–39) analyzes the EU accession effect and its impact on transition success.

reforms under initial conditions less unfavorable than Russia's, and they did so before a virtual economy had crystallized. For Russia to emerge from its current state of development will require at least as great an effort, and it will thus take at least as great a prize to create a movement for such effort.[34]

The size of the prize is not the only issue, however. To alter incentives in Russia enough to make a difference, EU accession must also be a promise that Russians can believe. Given how much it would cost Europe to admit Russia in its current state, accession could happen only if Russia actually made progress on serious reform. This is the conundrum: Russia needs a credible hope of admission in order to launch true reform. At the same time, Europe will never promise accession until it is persuaded that Russia's commitment to serious reform is real.

Is there a way out of the stalemate? Perhaps greater U.S. involvement could assist in the process of Russian accession to the EU. EU accession for Russia makes sense for the United States. Russian integration into the west is clearly in America's own interest. Such an outcome would certainly enhance international security and create a real peace dividend. The dividend might, in fact, be large enough for the United States to compensate the EU sufficiently to make the promise of accession real.

For the United States to become directly involved in the issue of Russian accession to the EU, it would have to be elevated to the status of an American national priority. The United States would have to recognize the stake it has in a real integration of Russia into the west. To realize such an outcome would require development of a triangular arrangement between Europe, the United States, and Russia. To be sure, this would require each of the three parties to make a huge commitment and assume significant risks, since each would be tying its future to that of the others. It would also be costly. Russia, of course, would bear the direct burden of change. Europe would assume much greater problems in achieving its own agenda. The United States, meanwhile, would inevitably have to extend itself to have co-responsibility for a part of the world that many hoped had graduated fifty years after World War II.

The advantage of U.S. involvement on such a scale is that it enhances the reward for the leadership in Russia as well as the public. A tripartite effort to integrate Russia with the west reduces the threats to national survival that

34. It is fairly clear that entry into the World Trade Organization (WTO), although a much more likely prospect for Russia than EU accession, would be an inadequate substitute for it. WTO membership is almost surely an insufficient prize to capture the attention of the Russian public.

real economic reform implies. It signals that economic reform is a policy not to weaken Russia but to strengthen it in the long run. It can thus encourage Russian leaders to undertake a comprehensive reform program, and it may overcome the obstacles that a troubled decade of reforms has created.

We do not present EU accession as a "magic bullet" for Russia. It is neither a necessary nor a sufficient condition for a true reform project. It is not sufficient, because even with such a prize to coordinate beliefs and provide reassurance, real reform will still require leadership to see through disruptive changes in the economy and in society. EU accession is no panacea in this regard. Nor is it a necessary condition for reform, because eliminating the virtual economy is beneficial to Russia on its own terms. After all, it is the virtual economy that prevents Russia from integrating into the global economy and that limits the growth of real incomes. Given the inherent inefficiency of the virtual economy, net benefits can be obtained by its elimination. What EU accession does is enhance the rewards from elimination of the virtual economy, and it concentrates expectations. However, it does not alter the fundamental point—that the virtual economy is an obstacle to Russian prosperity. Without the prospect of EU membership, implementing a true reform project is more difficult. This means that even greater leadership will be needed.

Regardless of the merits of the idea of Russian EU accession, disagreements on that issue or on any of the specific proposals we have offered in this chapter should not detract from the importance of two facts that will apply to any alternative proposal for serious economic reform. First, true reform cannot be purchased on the cheap. The fundamental problems of the Russian economy stem from the interplay of poor initial conditions, the legacy inherited from the Soviet period, and the impediment to serious reform represented by relational capital. These factors have created the environment in which the virtual economy could flourish. Because the virtual economy represents a stable adaptation to this environment, there is no cheap and easy way out. Second, Russia must shoulder the effort to extricate itself from its trap. Given the far-reaching and disruptive nature of the reforms that are required, it is evident that no sovereign country can accept such policies imposed from the outside. To be implemented, true reform— elimination of the virtual economy—must be embraced from within.

An Example
of Barter to
Evade Taxes

This appendix presents two examples of how barter can facilitate the evasion of taxes. The examples use bilateral barter for ease of exposition. Most barter in Russia is multilateral. It would be easy to add enterprises to the barter chain without changing the force of these examples, but the bilateral case makes the source of the tax gains most transparent.

Example A

This example has two enterprises, which use one another's output as input.

Two enterprises: Gazprom, Norilsk Nickel

Two goods: natural gas, metal products

Metal output, y_M, is given by: $y_M = 0.5\, y_G$

Gas output, y_G, is given by: $y_G = 2\, y_M$.

The market price of gas (P_G) and metals (P_M) equals 1 ruble, so the relative price is unity. If Norilsk were shut down, Gazprom could import metals at a price of 1 ruble. Therefore, Gazprom is indeed profitable at initial prices, and Norilsk is not. Under these conditions, metal production is not actually profitable, since it takes two units of gas, with a market value of 2 rubles, to produce one unit of metals, which is worth 1 ruble. Suppose that the tax rate on profits is 100 percent and that there are no labor costs of production.

We consider two cases. The first case is a monetary economy. Suppose for simplicity that there is an artificial trading company. It pays each producer the market price (1 ruble) for its output and sells the output to the other enterprise at the market price. Assume that it does this at zero cost. These transactions are carried out with money. Gazprom's profits are equal to 1 ruble, and taxes paid are 1 ruble. Norilsk loses money and pays no taxes. Gazprom's and Norilsk's accounts can be written as in table A-1.

Now suppose that instead of engaging in monetary exchange, the enterprises barter with one another. In this transaction, the barter price (to Gazprom) of Norilsk output is raised to 2 rubles. The external price of Norilsk output is unchanged, but the price that is recorded in this transaction is doubled. The same physical transaction occurs. Norilsk receives two units of gas from Gazprom (valued at 2 rubles) and ships one unit of metals to Gazprom (now priced at 2 rubles). The new accounts are shown in table A-2.

The effect of the increase in the price of metals is to reduce Gazprom profits and, hence, taxes. This one-unit saving in taxes can be shared between the two enterprises. That is, a side payment from Norilsk to Gazprom that is less than one unit will make both enterprises better off.

Example B

Now we alter the example to include labor and make clear that barter can still reduce tax incidence when there are loss makers. Continue to assume that the price of gas and metal products are both 1 ruble and that each process requires use of the other good as input. Gazprom uses one unit of metal output, and Norilsk uses two units of gas. Each process requires labor, according to

(a) $y_G = \alpha_G L_G$

(b) $y_M = \alpha_M L_M.$

The wage rate is equal to unity, and each enterprise has two units of labor. Let $\alpha_G = 2$ and $\alpha_M = 0.5$, and let the tax rate on value added be 1/3. Gazprom thus produces four units of output, selling two units to Norilsk and another two to the market. Norilsk sells all its output to Gazprom.

Table A-3 shows what happens in a monetary exchange.

TABLE A-1. Monetary Exchange

Category	Gazprom account	Norilsk account
Revenues	2	1
Costs	1	2
Profits	1	-1
Taxes	1	0

TABLE A-2. Barter

Category	Gazprom account	Norilsk account
Revenues	2	2
Costs	2	2
Profits	0	0
Taxes	0	0

TABLE A-3. Monetary Exchange

Category	Gazprom account	Norilsk account
Revenues	4	1
Labor costs	2	2
Materials costs	1	2
Profits	1	-3
Value added	3	-1
Taxes	1	0

TABLE A-4. Barter

Category	Gazprom account	Norilsk account
Revenues	4	2
Labor costs	2	2
Materials costs	2	2
Profits	0	-2
Value added	2	0
Taxes	0.67	0

Now suppose that Gazprom and Norilsk engage in barter and raise the price of metal to 2 rubles. Table A-4 shows the new accounts.

Compare tables A-3 and A-4. Norilsk's tax obligation is unchanged (at zero), since it does not have positive value added in either case. However, Gazprom's taxes have declined by 0.33 rubles. Nevertheless, there has been no change in physical flows. The simple accounting of barter allows the two enterprises to reduce total tax payments by one-third of a unit of output.

Comment

Why does this work? The asymmetry is because Norilsk is a loss maker. Clearly, if Norilsk were not initially losing money, then this change would cause its profits (and, hence, taxes) to increase by the same amount as Gazprom's decline. In both examples the comparison between the monetary and barter transactions has nothing to do with the "real world." Whether in barter or in money, the same physical transaction takes place between enterprises, the same physical transformation takes place in the production process, and the same physical output results.[1]

In the first example (without labor), the two enterprises together have cut tax liability by one unit, which they share (compare table A-1 with table A-2). In both examples, both enterprises are better off from a barter transaction that uses a price that is higher than the market price. Norilsk is producing negative value added whether or not barter takes place, but in the barter transaction this is hidden from view. The federal budget is worse off because of the loss of tax revenues. Notice also that industrial production is higher even though tax revenue decreases (something that should sound familiar in light of the discussion early in chapter 2).

This is not the end of the story. Hiding the reality makes it easier from a policy standpoint to allow Norilsk to continue to destroy value, therefore making the country as a whole worse off. Another way to think about this is that hiding reality through barter makes it harder for reform-minded policymakers to shut down value destroyers.

Essentially, Gazprom is buying tax losses from Norilsk that are valuable to the former but not to the latter. The two enterprises share the benefit. It is interesting to note that if Gazprom produced something that was not an input into domestic production, it could not get this benefit. It would export the good, and value added in Russia would be higher. The survival of the loss makers allows a privately beneficial transaction that is socially inefficient.

---

1. Notice that Norilsk may also benefit from the barter transaction because it could use this inflated price to value the output it uses to pay taxes in kind that are not based on profits.

Selected Data and Findings from the Karpov Commission Report

Troubled especially by the growing rate of nonmonetary payments of taxes, in the spring of 1996 the Russian federal government appointed a special interagency commission to study the problem of nonpayment of cash to the federal and regional budgets. The commission was headed by Petr A. Karpov and came to be known as the Karpov Commission. In the course of its work, the commission conducted an enterprise-by-enterprise examination of the actual books of 210 of Russia's largest companies.

The official name of its report, presented in December 1997, was "On the Causes of the Low Rate of Collection of Taxes (Nonpayment to the Fiscal System), General Causes of the 'Payments Crisis,' and the Possibility of Restoring the Solvency of Russian Enterprises."

This appendix summarizes some of the findings presented in the report. (All of the data cited refer to the period covered by the commission's audits: 1996 and the first half of 1997.)

1. The cash component of Russian large enterprises' earnings is extremely low. The average cash share of earnings for all enterprises studied by the Karpov Commission was 27 percent. In nearly 90 percent of the enterprises, cash constituted less than half of total enterprise earnings. For

TABLE B-1. Cash as a Share of Enterprise Revenues

Percentage

Cash as a percentage of total enterprise revenues	Percentage of enterprises surveyed
> 50	11
40-50	5
30-40	10
20-30	17
10-20	28
<10	30

TABLE B-2. Cash as a Share of Total Enterprise Revenues, by Sector of Industry

Percentage

Sector	Cash as a percentage of total enterprise revenues
Nuclear power	5
Gas	9
Electricity production	13
Chemical	16
Coal	20
Ferrous metallurgy	21
Machine building	23
Oil	31
Auto manufacturing	41
Railways	49
Wine and liquor	63

almost 60 percent of them, cash represented less than 20 percent of their gross revenues (see table B-1).

2. The cash component differs starkly among the various sectors of industry, ranging from less than 15 percent in the gas and electrical power sectors to more than 60 percent in the alcohol industry, as shown in table B-2.

3. Enterprises' cash earnings are inadequate to meet the various claims on that cash. The sum of the current wage bill and current tax bill exceeds the enterprises' cash resources, without taking into account any cash payments due to suppliers or other creditors (see table B-3).

4. Many enterprises do not earn enough cash even to pay wages. For 31 percent of enterprises, the cash component of earnings was so low that it did not even cover the wage bill. Many of those enterprises had to resort

TABLE B-3. Enterprise Cash Revenues and Claims on Them

Categories of revenue and claims	Trillions of rubles	As percentage of cash revenues
Gross revenues of enterprises	319.3	—
Of which, in cash	87.4	100
Current wage bill	38.1	44
Current tax bill (total amount due to all types of budgets and extrabudgetary funds, including the federal pension fund)	69.5	80
Cash actually paid to the federal budget and the federal pension fund	7.0	8

TABLE B-4. Federal Tax Performance of Large Enterprises

Category	Trillions of rubles	As percentage of amount due
Total federal taxes due	29.9	100
Amount paid in cash	2.3	8
Amount paid in noncash form	18.9	63
Amount not paid	8.7	29

to paying wages in kind or had to create money surrogates of their own (scrip).

"Among the enterprises in this category are OAO Dal'vostugol' [coal], OAO Rostsel'mash [the giant agricultural machinery and defense plant in Rostov], OAO Avtodizel', OAO Yuzhuralmash, OAO Sevuralbaksitruda, OAO Korshunovskiy GOK, OAO Yakutenergo, GP Kalinskaya AES [nuclear power], OAO Ryazanskaya GRES [hydroelectric], OAO Altayenergo, GP Kurskaya AES [nuclear power], and others."

5. Because they lack cash, large Russian enterprises pay only about 8 percent of their taxes in cash. More than 60 percent of what they owe is paid in offsets (nonmonetary form). Nearly 30 percent of taxes are not paid at all, as shown in table B-4.

6. The Karpov Commission believes that most enterprises pay such a small share of their taxes in cash because they are unable to: "Our analysis revealed that in practice *over 80 percent of the enterprises are incapable of paying their obligations to the fiscal system in cash* because they simply do not earn a large enough share of their own revenues in cash form" [emphasis in original].

TABLE B-5. Cash Revenues and Cash Tax Payments
Trillions of rubles

Name of enterprise	Cash revenues	Amount paid in federal taxes	Of which, paid in cash
Moscow Railways	9,759	654	0
Gorky Automobile Plant [GAZ]	4,200	774	0
Samaraneftegaz [oil]	2,895	978	0
Sakhalinmorneftegaz [oil]	1,432	319	1.5
Total	18,286	2,735	1.5

However, there are some enterprises that do earn enough cash to pay taxes, but are nevertheless permitted to pay in nonmonetary form. One of the most egregious examples is the Nizhny Novgorod–based automobile manufacturer, GAZ. It earned 4.2 trillion rubles in cash in the first half of 1997, thereby incurring federal tax obligations of 714 billion rubles. During that same period it actually paid the budget 774 billion rubles, but all of that was in the form of offsets. *"It did not pay one single ruble in cash to the budget"* [emphasis added]. Some major cash-earning enterprises that were allowed to pay taxes in noncash form are shown in table B-5.

Further Comments on Value Destruction

Value destruction (or negative value added, NVA) is a much more severe condition than loss making. An enterprise loses money when the revenue (market value) it receives is less than the costs of production. Costs of production, however, include nonpurchased inputs (labor and capital services). In order for the enterprise to be a value destroyer, it is not enough merely to lose money: its losses must exceed the cost of its primary (nonpurchased) inputs. An enterprise can thus be loss making without destroying value. Indeed, this is usually what happens when an enterprise is a loss maker. Another way to put it is that in value destruction the contribution of labor and capital services in the production process is actually negative. The enterprise transforms the purchased inputs in a manner that makes them worth less than what was started with.

In formal terms the condition for negative value added is

$$P_i z_i - P_M M < 0,$$

where z_i is the output of enterprise i, P_i is the price of that output, M is the materials purchased to produce the output, and P_M is the price of the materials.

Loss making implies that profits are negative. The condition for loss making therefore is

251

$$\pi_i = P_i z_i - P_M M - wl - rK < 0,$$

where π_i is profits of enterprise i, and w and r represent the rental costs of the primary inputs labor, l, and capital, K.

In other words,

$$P_i z_i - P_M M < wl + rK.$$

Negative value added and loss making are equivalent if $wl + rK$ is equal to 0. This would be true only if an enterprise paid no capital or labor costs at all.

An NVA enterprise has losses so big that they are greater than the value of the primary (nonpurchased inputs). That means that the application of labor and capital to the purchased inputs results in less value than existed at the beginning of the process.

What happens when an enterprise is able to delay paying for its material inputs? Suppose that in any period, enterprise i pays only the fraction $\gamma < 1$ of its material costs. Then it is possible that the enterprise is financially solvent even if it is actually destroying value. This would be true when

$$\pi_i + wl = P_i z_i - P_M M < 0 < P_i z_i - wl - \gamma P_M M.$$

This is possible when material arrears are larger than wage costs. Notice that in this case some other enterprise is essentially lending, *involuntarily*, to enterprise i. An example would be a manufacturing plant whose material inputs come from Gazprom. This is the canonical case considered in this book. On average, of course, arrears on inputs and on sales will balance one another. However, a truly profitable firm can subsidize the production of a value destroyer. Indeed, this is the essence of the virtual economy.

Because the standard notion of negative value added is so strict, it may be useful to work also with a weaker notion of negative value added. Let us then call the notion considered above, in which we consider only the value of *purchased* inputs (and thus do not include the cost of capital), strong negative value-added (SNVA). We will define weak negative value added (WNVA) as including the costs of replacing capital explicitly. That is, suppose that revenues are sufficient to cover material costs exactly. This enterprise contributes nothing to value added, and it loses revenue at the rate of its capital costs. Because revenues are insufficient to cover the depreciation of capital, the productive capacity of the enterprise is decreasing over time. This is the situation—where net revenues are insufficient to cover depreciation—that we view as WNVA, that is, a situation where value is being destroyed in the weak sense. The capacity to produce national income, in this case, is transient. Over time, national income will fall, because capital must be replaced.

The notion of WNVA is useful because over short periods it is feasible for such an enterprise to operate. Of course there are insufficient revenues to pay wages, but if workers accept arrears the enterprise can continue to produce. An even weaker version of the notion occurs when revenues are sufficient to meet some wage costs. Now the enterprise suffers no cash-flow problem, yet productive capacity is deteriorating as production continues. This represents a slow erosion of an economy's productive capacity. It will be important when we discuss the long-run future of the virtual economy.

We must be careful with this notion. Consider the situation of an enterprise with large sunk costs earning negative profits. Because the assets are sunk, the opportunity cost of using these resources in production is zero (assuming that there are no operating costs of using the capital). As long as revenues exceed the variable costs of production, it is advantageous for the firm to continue production. In such a situation, production adds to national income. However, this is not a case of SNVA, because value added is positive.

An interesting case in the Russian context occurs when the nominal wage rate exceeds the opportunity cost of labor. This is important in cases where workers continue to work at enterprises even when wages are not paid in full. Let $\tilde{w}$ be the true opportunity cost of labor, where $\tilde{w} < w$. Then it is possible that at nominal (virtual) wages the enterprise is a loss maker, but at the actual opportunity cost of labor it may not be:

$$P_i z_i - wl - P_M M < 0 < P_i z_i - \tilde{w}l - P_M M.$$

Because the workers receive less than they are promised, it is sometimes argued that these arrears represent lending by the workers to the enterprise. In fact, however, if the enterprise pays the promised level of wages (where they get the revenue is another story), this is actually a gift to the workers. However, this also means that at such an enterprise it may not always be appropriate to speak about wage arrears when full wages are not paid. Labor only appears to be undercompensated, because nominal wages exceed the true value of labor's contribution. (Note, however, that even at the inflated level of wages the enterprise is producing value added.)

At the same time, however, if we think about the promised excess portion of the wage—the part over and above the true value of labor—as being part of the redistributionist "deal" that the virtual economy represents (see chapter 5), then the situation becomes more complicated. There may be some extra amount beyond the true wage that ought to be regarded as "equitable." Arrears are tolerated to a certain level, but not beyond. This is analogous to the deal with Gazprom: how much of its export earnings it is allowed to keep, how much it subsidizes the rest of the economy, and so on.

When we speak of negative value added in a closed economy, we are typically referring to an enterprise rather than an industry. In a closed economy it is almost always the case that a sector contributes value added, because as production levels decrease, market prices have to rise. This is an obvious contrast to the case in an open economy, where external prices provide a ceiling on how high the price of output can rise. Even if a sector is contributing value added, however, enterprises within that sector can destroy value if they are particularly inefficient. In a market economy such firms are weeded out. If inefficient enterprises continue to produce due to an absence of exit in a planned economy, such enterprises can routinely use more valuable inputs than the output they produce.

A discussion of value destruction should consider some notion of steady-state prices. In a recession, prices may decline due to lack of demand, but this may be temporary. Of course, even in recessions prices rarely fall so far as to make the value of output less than that of purchased inputs. Moreover, during recessions firms in market economies typically reduce output and maintain prices, rather than the other way around. The obvious reason is that continuing to produce the same volumes as before would result in greater losses. Only when subsidies of some type are expected may a producer choose to maintain production in the absence of demand.

It is also important to note that the response to value destruction must depend on how transient the phenomenon is. When prices are liberalized it may be that value added is negative at some enterprises because production must adjust to the new world prices. What is critical to note about Russia, however, is that negative value added in 2002 can no longer be ascribed to transient lack of adjustment. Industrial production has, according to official statistics, shrunk by 30 percent since 1991. Some of this decline in production must be the abandonment of production that was destroying value. By 2002, however, the continued existence of any value destroyers cannot be due to slow adjustment to the market, but, rather, to the active adaptation of enterprises to the virtual economy.

Russian enterprises in 1992 suffered two types of shocks that affected the calculation of value added. There was both (1) internal liberalization—freedom for agents to choose what to produce and consume independent of central planners, thus to set domestic prices freely—and (2) external liberalization—introduction of world market prices. Because these changes occurred at the same time, we do not really know what "Russian" (free market) domestic prices were/are. Hence, we also do not know which enterprises might have been value adding at these never-existing domestic prices. It could thus be argued that by combining the internal and external liberalizations, reform created too great a shock to enterprises. It may have made the distance needed to catch up to the world market too large for most enterprises. Realizing that, enterprises may have given up on adjustment and retreated inward, eventually ending up in what we now call the virtual economy.

Suppose, instead, that there had been only internal liberalization, while fairly heavy protection against the world economy was maintained. Under such circumstances, it is likely that more enterprises would have attempted a first stage of adjustment, thus at least giving us a better sense for deciding which would be viable in a second phase of adjustment, with or without protection.

The Director's Decision Problem

In this appendix we consider the enterprise director's decision problem. We begin with the static optimization problem that concerns the allocation of effort, and hence production, at a point in time. We then consider the dynamic optimization problem to solve the investment problem.

Static Problem

The static problem for the director is to allocate his own effort between time spent on production of hard goods and that spent on production of soft goods.[1] In other words the total amount of effort, $\bar{e}$, must be divided between time spent producing hard and soft goods: $\bar{e} = e_h + e_s$ (where e_h is the effort devoted to producing hard goods and e_s that required to produce soft goods). We suppose that effort is the only variable input that the director chooses.

1. Of course it is not just the production itself to which the director devotes his time. He must also see to it that the goods are sold. For hard goods, the director must devote effort to production and marketing. Less effort is needed for production of soft goods, since the same old goods are being produced. Instead, effort must be expended on maintaining good relations. To continue to sell soft goods, the enterprise must have relational capital.

Production is given by

$$y_h = f(e_h, d, r) \qquad \text{(D-1)}$$

for hard goods, and by

$$y_s = g(e_s, r) \qquad \text{(D-2)}$$

for soft goods. We assume that $f_{e_h}, g_{e_s} > 0$; that is, greater effort devoted to hard (soft) goods production increases the output of hard (soft) goods, and that $f_d < 0$; that is, greater distance reduces the output obtainable from a given level of effort.

Notice the asymmetry in these two production functions. The production of hard goods depends on relational capital, but the production of soft goods does not depend on distance. The former follows because greater relational capital makes it easier to procure inputs, and that helps any type of production, including that of hard goods (hence, $f_r > 0$). However, the production of soft goods does not depend on how competitive the product is in the marketplace.

We assume that the prices of hard and soft goods differ. If p is the market price of the hard good and we let τ be the tax rate on hard goods, then $p(1 - \tau)$ is the after-tax price of hard goods. Let $\hat{p}(r_{it})$ be the price of soft-goods production. Notice that this depends on the enterprise's level of relational capital. This suggests that the price of soft goods is enterprise specific. The relative price of hard goods in terms of soft goods can thus be written as

$$\rho \equiv \frac{p(1-\tau)}{\hat{p}(r_{it})}.$$

The existence of the tax wedge means that the output produced by a Russian enterprise will have two prices: one is a market price (when the resources are used to produce hard goods) and the other an informal shadow price (when the resources are used to produce soft goods).[2] This "tax" wedge offsets the standard advantage of monetary transactions over nonmonetary: transactions costs are much lower for the former if both

2. These taxes create a wedge between the prices of hard and soft goods. This wedge is a key determinant of the composition of the enterprise's output. When taxes are increased on hard goods, there will be a relative shift to production of more soft goods. The converse is also true, but the adjustment occurs with a lag, because agents must be sure that the change is not transitory. To move production from soft to hard goods opens the enterprise to more scrutiny. If there is uncertainty about the duration of the price change, the supply response may be less than expected. This probably accounts for the rather slow response to the devaluation of August 1998. Relative prices for hard goods rose dramatically, but the response of suppliers was rather desultory at first.

types of receipts are taxed similarly. However, nonmonetary transactions involve greater possibilities for evasion, and hence, the after-tax return to such transactions may be greater.[3] The problem for the enterprise manager is thus to allocate effort to equate the marginal returns between soft and hard goods production.

Since effort is the only variable input, profits are equal to net revenues, which in turn depend on net output and price. Hence the profit functions for hard and soft goods are

$$\pi_h = p(1 - \tau)f(e_h, d, r) \tag{D-3}$$

and

$$\pi_s = \hat{p}(r)g(e_s, r), \tag{D-4}$$

where $p(1 - \tau)$ is the price of hard goods net of taxes, and $\hat{p}(r)$ is the price of soft goods, which is an increasing function of the enterprise's stock of relational capital.

Effort choice also depends on the relative price of hard and soft goods, ρ. To see how, we need to examine the director's static optimization problem—that is, to maximize total profits, given by

$$\Pi \equiv \pi_h + \pi_s = p(1 - \tau)f(e_h, d, r) + \hat{p}(r)g(e_s, r), \tag{D-5}$$

subject to a constraint on total effort,

$$e_h + e_s = \bar{e}, \tag{D-6}$$

and to the enterprise's cash constraint,

$$p(1 - \tau)f(e_h, d, r) \geq m_t, \tag{D-7}$$

where m_t is the amount of inputs that must be purchased in cash during period t.

The first-order conditions from this problem yield[4]

$$\frac{p(1 - \tau)}{\hat{p}(r)} = \frac{g_{e_s}}{f_{e_h}}. \tag{D-8}$$

---

3. As we will see, however, the enterprise may also face a cash constraint: a minimum amount of cash needed to operate. This creates a minimum level of monetary sales below which the enterprise cannot fall.

4. Assuming that the cash constraint is not binding and concavity of the production choices, we obtain an interior solution for effort levels. We will consider the case where (D-7) is binding below.

Notice that diminishing returns to effort mean that the marginal product of effort decreases with increased effort. Hence, (D-8) implies that a higher price of hard goods or a lower tax rate leads to greater production of hard goods relative to soft goods. A higher level of r, however, lowers the relative price and hence implies less production of hard goods.

We can also use (D-8) to infer the effect of increased d on the production of hard goods. Increased d causes f_{e_h} to decrease because it is now harder to produce hard goods with any level of effort (that is, $f_{e_h d} < 0$). This means that the left-hand side of (D-8) increases. Since the relative price of hard and soft goods is unchanged, profit maximization requires that more effort be supplied to production of soft goods and less to hard goods to restore the equality in (D-8).

How does the cash constraint alter our analysis of the director's decision problem? When the cash constraint binds, production at the enterprise is limited by the need to pay for certain inputs in cash. At the margin, cash sales are now more valuable than they would otherwise be. To see this, note that the cash constraint is now

$$p(1-\tau)f(e_h,d,r) = m_t, \tag{D-7$'$}$$

and the enterprise is forced to produce more hard goods than it would otherwise choose. Hence (D-8) becomes

$$\frac{p(1-\tau)}{p(r)} < \frac{g_{e_s}}{f_{e_h}}. \tag{D-8$'$}$$

As long as the enterprise has not yet earned the minimum amount of cash it needs in order to pay absolutely essential costs, the shadow price for assets used to generate cash sales will be high. This means that the enterprise will produce a greater amount of cash goods than it would—given relative prices and its level of d—if it were not so constrained. If the cash constraint is relaxed—say by an increase in the price of cash goods or by a fall in the tax rate—the enterprise will be able to satisfy (D-7) at a lower level of cash goods production, and hence its production bundle will shift toward soft goods. This situation is seen in figure 4-1 in the text (p. 80).

Dynamics

The dynamic decision problem for an enterprise director is to determine how much to invest in reducing distance, i_d, and how much to invest in relational capital, i_r. The objective of the director is to choose these investment levels to maximize the value of the enterprise or the expected discounted value of future profits. The director has limited resources for investment; he can deploy these to invest in distance reduction, to enhance relational capital, or both. These investments will then determine the enterprise's distance and relational capital next period. Thus

$$d_{t+1} = d_t + \phi(i_{d,t}, d_t)$$
$$r_{t+1} = r_t + \gamma(i_{r,t}, r_t) \tag{D-9}$$

where $\phi(\cdot)$ and $\gamma(\cdot)$ are concave functions of investment in distance reduction and relational capital, respectively.[5] Notice that $\phi_1 < 0$: greater investment in distance reduction reduces distance. Similarly, greater investment in relational capital increases the level of relational capital ($\gamma_1 > 0$).[6]

It is important to note that the effectiveness of such investments depends on the current state: a higher value of d_t reduces the return to investing in distance—that is, $\partial^2\phi/\partial i_d \partial d_t \equiv \phi_{12} < 0$. If an enterprise is very far from the market, investing in reducing distance may have very little effect. In other words, if the enterprise produces the wrong thing in the wrong way, incremental investment has no effect; the market still does not want its product. Only a large investment, one sufficient to change the whole scheme of production, can reduce distance for this enterprise. This is less likely to be the case with relational capital: it probably is sensible to assume that $\gamma_{12} = 0$; that is, the level of relational capital does not affect the impact of investment on the stock, so that γ_1 is a constant in the relevant range.

Expression (D-9) presumes that the impact of investment on the state variables is deterministic. It may be more realistic to consider this to be stochastic. For example, distance could rise unexpectedly because of improvements elsewhere in the world economy, or relational capital may fall next period due to a crackdown on tax offsets. Hence, we probably should write (D-9) as

$$d_{t+1} = d_t + \phi(i_{d,t}, d_t) + \varepsilon_t$$
$$r_{t+1} = r_t + \gamma(i_{r,t}, r_t) + \eta_t \tag{D-9'}$$

5. The fact that $\phi(\cdot)$ and $\gamma(\cdot)$ are concave means that there are diminishing returns to investment in any period.

6. We have argued that an enterprise that sits still finds d increasing over time. Hence we really should augment (D-9) with a term that represents the growth of distance over time due to global economic development. Similarly, one could argue that relational capital depreciates over time, so that the enterprise that fails to invest would see its stock diminish. For simplicity we ignore these factors in the model.

where ε and η are mean-zero disturbances. Note that the variances of these disturbances will likely vary by industry, as both technological progress and the possibilities for enhancing relations depend on the type of activity undertaken.

To simplify the analysis it is convenient to assume that the director knows the impact of these investments on future productivity—that is, that the functions $\phi(\cdot)$ and $\gamma(\cdot)$ are known. This confines uncertainty to the future values of the relative price of hard goods and soft goods and to the shocks, ε and η. Investment in either direction thus depends on what the director expects relative prices—in the broad sense that includes taxation—to be in the future. This follows because ε and η are mean-zero disturbances, so that $E_t \varepsilon_{t+1} = E_t \eta_{t+1} = 0$. Hence, for simplicity, we assume in the remainder that directors have perfect foresight.

The director's objective is to choose i_d and i_r to maximize the value of the enterprise, which is the present value of the cash flow. We can write the latter as

$$\pi_t = p_t(1-\tau)f(e_{h,t}, d_t, r_t) + \hat{p}_t(r_t)\gamma(e_{s,t}, r_t) - i_{d,t} - i_{r,t}, \qquad \text{(D-10)}$$

where we are treating $p_t(1-\tau)f(\cdot)$ and $\hat{p}_t(r_t)\gamma(\cdot)$ as net revenue functions for simplicity; all costs of production are subsumed in these functions. Notice that r affects the cost of production for both types of goods, but distance is relevant only for hard goods.

The objective of the director is thus to choose investment paths $\{i_{d,t}, i_{r,t}\}_{t=0}^{\infty}$ to maximize the present value of the enterprise[7]

$$V = \sum_t \beta^t \pi_t, \qquad \text{(D-11)}$$

subject to the evolution equations for r and d, (D-9).

Notice that the impact of a unit investment in i_d or i_r is the product of two forces: (1) the impact of investment on the state variables (r_{t+1}, d_{t+1}); and (2) the effect of the change in the state variable on production. We refer to the former as the *effectiveness* of investment. Thus, for example, the expected impact on total profits in $t+1$ from a unit of investment in distance reduction in t, is given by

$$\frac{\partial \pi_{t+1}^e}{\partial i_{d,t}} = p_{t+1}^e(1-\tau)\frac{\partial f_{t+1}}{\partial d_{t+1}}\phi_1(d_t). \qquad \text{(D-12)}$$

---

7. We assume that effort choices are always made optimally and abstract from them here.

Profits increase with investment in distance reduction—expression (D12) is positive—given that $\phi_1 < 0$ and $\partial f/\partial d < 0$.

The change in profits is the product of three variables: the after-tax expected price of hard goods in period $t + 1$, $((1 - \tau)p^e_{t+1})$, which we assume is independent of such investment; the marginal product of a decrease in distance; and the effect on distance of a unit of i_d. The price term is clearly positive, and the other two variables are negative: reducing distance increases productivity, and investing in distance reduction reduces distance. Clearly the latter two variables are subject to diminishing returns.

The relationship between i_r and future profitability is more complex. The reason is that investing in r affects both soft and hard goods production, the latter through its impact on the cost of production:

$$\frac{\partial \pi^e_{t+1}}{\partial i_{r,t}} = \gamma_1(r_t)\left[\hat{p}^e_{t+1}\frac{\partial g_{t+1}}{\partial r_{t+1}} + \frac{\partial \hat{p}^e_{t+1}}{\partial r_{t+1}}g(e_{s,t+1},r_{t+1}) + p^e_{t+1}(1-\tau)\frac{\partial f_{t+1}}{\partial r_{t+1}}\right]. \quad \text{(D-13)}$$

Notice that the impact of investment in relational capital on profitability is nonnegative. It can be decomposed into three terms, each multiplied by $\gamma_1(r_t)$, the change in relational capital that results from a unit of investment. The first term inside the brackets on the right-hand side of (D-13) is the value of the marginal product of relational capital, which we have assumed to be strictly positive. The second term is the change in profits due to the higher expected (soft-goods) price induced by greater relational capital, which is nonnegative.[8] The last term is the value of the marginal product of relational capital on hard goods production. This last term is also nonnegative, but it is likely to be close to zero for enterprises with very little relational capital; hence, the value of this term is likely to be smaller than that for investment in distance reduction. The reason is that greater relational capital affects the profitability of hard goods only through the effect on costs, while greater distance reduction improves the productivity of hard goods production (either directly or by improving the quality of the good and thus fetching a higher price).

The relevant comparison for the director is the expected net present value of the profit streams generated by i_d and i_r.[9] Using (D-12) and (D-13),

8. This term is a bit unusual. In standard models greater investment does not affect the price of output. However, relational capital is clearly different.

9. Of course, the director must also decide whether to invest at all. Thus the return to investment must exceed the discount rate. We have ignored any opportunity cost of funds. However, there may be investment opportunities available to the director. Clearly GKOs were a superior alternative to investment at many enterprises before August 1998. Yet the ability to invest *externally* may require cash, which implies that the opportunity cost of investing in distance reduction may differ from that of relational capital.

and assuming that investment has only one-period effects,[10] we find that

$$\frac{\partial \pi^e_{t+1}}{\partial i_{d,t}} \overset{>}{<} \frac{\partial \pi^e_{t+1}}{\partial i_{r,t}} \Leftrightarrow$$

$$p^e_{t+1}(1-\tau)\frac{\partial f_{t+1}}{\partial d_{t+1}}\phi_1(d_t) \overset{>}{<} \gamma_1(r_t) \begin{bmatrix} \hat{p}^e_{t+1}\dfrac{\partial g_{t+1}}{\partial r_{t+1}} + \dfrac{\partial \hat{p}^e_{t+1}}{\partial r_{t+1}}g(e_{s,t+1},r_{t+1}) \\[2ex] +p^e_{t+1}(1-\tau)\dfrac{\partial f_{t+1}}{\partial r_{t+1}} \end{bmatrix}. \tag{D-14}$$

Given that $\phi_{12} < 0$, (D-14) implies that as d_t increases, the enterprise is less likely to invest in distance reduction. The optimal investment decision for the director is to choose investments so that (D-14) holds with equality.

How does investment choice vary with r? This is more complex. Greater r will have impacts on both sides of (D-14). Greater r lowers input costs, so we assume that $\phi_{13} > 0$; this would mean that the left-hand side of (D-14) increases. What about the right-hand side? We can assume that the impact of investment on the stock of r is independent of the level ($\gamma_{12} = 0$), so the impact will depend on the terms in the brackets.

The force of our arguments suggests that the sum of terms in the brackets will increase with r, at least for a large range of plausible values. When r_t is very low, an enterprise will benefit little from investment in relations. An enterprise with low relational capital will be unable to appropriate the benefits of informal activity. The low-relations enterprise will not be able to find purchasers of soft goods, nor will it be able to obtain inputs through informal means. This is a hurdle that must be overcome before the enterprise can appropriate the benefits. Once r achieves this critical level, the returns to investing in relational capital will increase.

This suggests that at very low levels of r, investing in reducing d may dominate. As the stock of relational capital increases, the returns to invest-

10. This is equivalent to assuming a two-period model. In a more general formulation we would compare the discounted sums of the change in profits. For example, the change in value from an investment in distance reduction would be

$$\frac{\partial V_t}{\partial i_{d,t}} = -i_{d,t} + \sum_{k=0}^{\infty}\beta^t\left[p^e_{t+k}(1-\tau)\frac{\partial f_{t+k}}{\partial d_{t+1}}\phi_1\right].$$

Notice that we would expect that

$$\frac{\partial f_{t+k}}{\partial d_{t+1}} \to 0$$

as $k \to \infty$. We would have a similar expression for r.

ing in relational capital will increase. We can further understand the dynamics by returning to the r-d space diagram. Our concern is to understand the trajectory an enterprise will follow given some initial conditions for r and d. In figure 4-2 in the text we consider three possibilities that differ only in the value of r_t (points A, B, and C). To see how the decisions of these three enterprises differ, it is convenient to use a simplified version of (D-9), where we assume that $\phi_1 = -1$ and that $\gamma_1 = 1$.[11] Then we could write (D-9) as

$$d_{t+1} = d_t - i_{d,t}$$
$$r_{t+1} = r_t + i_{r,t}$$
(D-9″)

In figure 4-2 our concern is with the direction of motion; thus it is useful to look at the changes in distance and relational capital:

$$\Delta d \equiv d_{t+1} - d_t = -i_{d,t}$$
$$\Delta r \equiv r_{t+1} - r_t = i_{r,t}$$
(D-15)

Now consider a point like C in figure 4-2. Relational capital is very low. From expression (D-14) we know that the return to investing in relational capital is likely dominated by distance reduction at such a point. Hence, to equate the marginal returns from investment in both directions, the enterprise will invest more in distance reduction, driving down the marginal return so that equality in (D-14) can be restored. This means that $-\Delta d > \Delta r$ for such an enterprise. The enterprise faces a greater attraction to the west than to the north.

Now consider the enterprise at point A. Relational capital is very high. Hence the return to investing in relational capital is higher than at point C. If r is sufficiently high, then, to equate the marginal returns, the enterprise will have to invest more in r than in distance reduction. Hence, for an enterprise like A, we would have $-\Delta d < \Delta r$; the enterprise is pulled more to the north than to the west. Continuity suggests that some intermediate enterprise, like point B, exists where the optimal investment decision pulls in both directions equally. Hence, at point B we have $-\Delta d = \Delta r$.

To complete the analysis we now ask how the critical level of relational capital, $\hat{r}$ (the level of r such that $-\Delta d = \Delta r$), varies as the level of d changes. We know that lower d raises the return to investing in distance reduction for any level of r, but it leaves the return to investing in r unchanged. Consider some enterprise, B′, where $r_{B'} = r_B$, but $d_{B'} < d_B$ by some small

11. This assumption is only made for convenience of exposition. Given that γ is a non-decreasing function of r and that ϕ is a nonincreasing function of d, this assumption does not change the result in the text.

increment, δ. The marginal returns to investment cannot then be equal at B′ if the enterprise invests equally in each direction (as at point B). Hence at B′ we must have $-\Delta d > \Delta r$. This means that the critical value, $\hat{r}$, that causes $-\Delta d = \Delta r$ must increase with lower d. If we then let d vary, we obtain the restructuring boundary, labeled RB in figure 4-3 in the text.

The restructuring boundary divides r-d space into regions where the forces of attraction are stronger to the north and those where it is stronger to the south. Hence, in the region labeled I in figure 4-3 in the text, enterprises face a stronger attraction to reducing distance. In region II, in contrast, the pull is greater to further investments in relational capital. The arrows in the diagram suggest the trajectories that enterprises will follow based on their levels of r and d.[12]

12. Notice that enterprises below the VC line are, by definition, not viable. Thus they loot rather than survive, and the direction of motion is to the southeast.

An
Evolutionary
Model

The virtual economy represents an adaptation. It is not the Soviet system renamed, but rather an adaptation of enterprises to the changes in the economic environment caused by reform and transition. We have suggested thinking of it as a mutation. Incomplete shock therapy failed to wipe out loss-making enterprises. Instead, they mutated into something new. The new strain of enterprises made it harder for market-oriented enterprises to compete. The greater the number of mutant enterprises, the greater the relative disadvantage for market-type enterprises. The reason is that mutant enterprises operate under different rules.

One way to see the effects of incomplete shock therapy is to analyze the evolutionary process of enterprise behavior. Suppose that enterprises can choose to follow one of three different strategies: they can behave like a market-like enterprise, like a Soviet enterprise, or like what we will call a "virtual" enterprise.[1] The relative payoff for each of these strategies will depend on both the enterprise's own strategy and the choices of other enter-

---

1. This terminology is not ideal. The virtual economy refers to an economic system, not a particular type of enterprise. The virtual economy contains both inefficient manufacturing companies and net value-suppliers such as Gazprom. In this appendix we refer to enterprises that use barter and offsets as virtual enterprises, as a second-best type of shorthand.

prises. The former we have already characterized in terms of d and r. Presumably, the greater is the market distance for a given enterprise, the lower is the payoff to choosing the market strategy. Similarly, the payoff for choosing the virtual strategy would be less if an enterprise had a lower level of r. However, relative payoffs will also depend on how other enterprises behave, and that is the focus of this appendix.

Why would the payoff to a strategy depend on the choices of other enterprises? Consider, for example, barter. The cost to a given enterprise of eschewing cash will depend on the difficulty of finding other partners willing to use nonmonetary exchange.[2] This suggests that there is a thick-market externality in choosing the virtual strategy. It may be that the market system is more efficient if all enterprises are market-like enterprises; indeed, we make just this assumption in this section. That, however, is not the critical question for transition. Rather, we want to know if there is a path from the command system to the market economy. While it may be that the market is more efficient if all enterprises are market-like, it still may be impossible for the market system to invade and overtake an economy that is populated primarily by Soviet-type enterprises.

A crucial question for transition is whether the market system can be approached gradually. A simple way to study this question is to see how the choices of strategies evolve based on the populations of the three types of enterprises. Let us denote the market, Soviet, and virtual strategies as M, S, and V strategies, respectively. The payoff that an enterprise receives depends on the strategies that other enterprises are playing. Let $\pi(i, j)$ be the payoff to an enterprise choosing strategy i when all other enterprises choose strategy j ($i, j = S, M, V$). We assume that the payoff to being a market enterprise is greatest when other enterprises choose the market strategy, and it is lowest when all other enterprises follow the Soviet strategy.[3] Hence the payoff to the market strategy is:

$$\pi(M, M) > \pi(M, V) > \pi(M, S).$$

Similarly, the relative payoffs for the virtual and Soviet strategies are:

2. For some empirical evidence on the presence of economies of scale in using barter in Russia, see Guriev and Ickes (2000).

3. This is somewhat counter to the analysis of partial reform presented by Murphy, Shleifer, and Vishny (1992). In their analysis, market-like invaders can prosper in an environment of state-owned enterprises by purchasing inputs from state-owned enterprises at below market prices. The case is not directly related, however, because there is no discussion of how the surplus (bribes) is distributed, and we therefore cannot really discuss relative fitness.

$$\pi(V, V) > \pi(V, S) > \pi(V, M);$$

$$\pi(S, S) > \pi(S, V) > \pi(S, M).$$

Notice also that the market economy is assumed to be socially most efficient, and a fully Soviet economy is least efficient. Thus, $\pi(M, M) > \pi(V, V) > \pi(S, S)$. It is important to recognize, however, that these payoffs refer to outcomes in the transition environment. This means that when all enterprises choose the Soviet strategy, they are playing in an environment without Soviet institutions. It is an economy where all enterprises play Soviet-type strategies (that is, they play by the formal and informal Soviet rules), but where Soviet institutions such as Gosplan no longer exist.

A payoff matrix that illustrates these assumed payoffs is given by:

	Market	Soviet	Virtual
Market	5	0	3
Soviet	0	3	1
Virtual	2	3	4

(E-1)

where the numbers are payoffs to a row strategy against a population of column strategies. Hence, $\pi(M, M) = 5$, $\pi(M, S) = 0$, $\pi(M, V) = 3$ and so on. Notice that the payoff matrix given above has the following features:

—The Soviet enterprise is (weakly) dominated by the virtual enterprise: that is, no matter what the environment, the virtual enterprise always does as well as the Soviet enterprise and sometimes better.

—Against a population of Soviet enterprises the virtual enterprise does as well as the Soviet enterprise.

Most of the payoffs in (E-1) are straightforward. The fact that $\pi(M, V) < \pi(V, V)$ is worth comment. A market enterprise that operates in an economy with many virtual enterprises is under threat precisely because of the fiscal pressure from the government. With many virtual enterprises, enterprises that operate in the monetary economy are prey to the tax authorities. The relative situation of a market-like firm is decreasing in the number of virtual enterprises because the latter are able to barter and use tax offsets to reduce the real value of liabilities. One might also question the assumption that $\pi(M, V) > \pi(M, S)$. If the economy is dominated by Soviet enterprises, the market enterprise would find it very difficult to procure inputs—much harder than with virtual enterprises. This is the logic behind the assumption. One might argue, however, that in the virtual economy the market-type enterprise will, again, be the prey of the tax authorities. This may suggest that it is plausible also to investigate the implications of assuming that $\pi(M,V) < \pi(M,S)$.[4]

Three pure strategy equilibria exist in this game. One consists of all market enterprises; this is the most efficient. A second equilibrium consists of all virtual enterprises. The last one consists of all Soviet enterprises, but this is, of course, weakly dominated. In addition, there is also a mixed equilibrium, q, with ¼ market enterprises, no Soviet enterprises, and ¾ virtual enterprises.

Notice that if there were no Soviet-type enterprises, we would not expect to see any virtual enterprises. The reason is that the "all market" equilibrium dominates the "all virtual" equilibrium. By assumption we have chosen the all-market equilibrium to be the most efficient, and in an environment where the only two types of enterprises are M and V, the system will end up in the "all market" equilibrium. However, when Soviet-type enterprises exist, it is possible that the economy will end up in the "all virtual" equilibrium. The presence of Soviet-type enterprises affects where we end up, even though this strategy is dominated by the others.

To see this, we assume that the population of each type of enterprise depends on its relative performance compared with the other types. Thus, let $p_i(t)$ be the proportion of enterprises that choose type $i = S$, M, or V at time t. We can formulate the change in the population by:

$$\dot{p}_i = p_i \left[e_i A p - p^T A p \right], \qquad (E\text{-}2)$$

where p is the vector of population shares (p_M, p_S, p_V), A is the 3 x 3 matrix of payoffs from (E-1) and e_i is the vector of payoffs for an enterprise choosing strategy i (for example, $e_S = (5, 0, 3)$). The term in the brackets is the difference between the payoff from a particular strategy and the average for

4. Notice that we can do this without altering the pure-strategy equilibria. For example, we can use the alternative payoff matrix:

	Market	Soviet	Virtual
Market	5	2	0
Soviet	0	3	1
Virtual	2	3	4

We have investigated the evolutionary dynamics with this payoff matrix using replicator dynamics, as in the example studied in the text. The qualitative behavior remains similar—there are still two basins of attraction—but the likelihood of getting stuck in the virtual economy is smaller than with the original payoff matrix in the sense that we need a larger initial mutation of virtual enterprises, $p_V(0)$, and the critical value to reach the market economy is lower.

FIGURE E-1. Some Evolutionary Dynamics

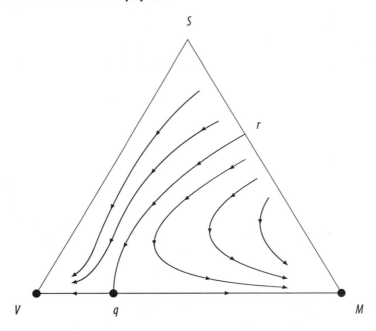

all the enterprises given the current population shares. Thus the growth in the population of any type of enterprise depends on its *relative* performance compared with the average of all enterprises. For initial populations of the three types of enterprises we can see how strategies evolve. In particular, we can study how the basins of attraction are altered by the initial population shares.[5]

The results can be understood with the aid of figure E-1. Suppose initially that all enterprises are Soviet-type. We are at the top of the simplex. Now assume that in period 0 a shock occurs that converts some proportion of these enterprises to market strategies. Further suppose that there is a mutation that creates a virtual enterprise. We can let the initial population of these enterprises be arbitrarily small. For instance, let $p_V(0) = .001$. The resulting dynamics depend on how large is the market shock. The critical value is $p_S(0) = r_S = .625$.[6] If the shock does not bring the share of enterprises

5. The dynamics specified in equation (E-2) are known as the "replicator dynamics" in evolutionary game theory. See, for instance, Weibull (1995) for a further discussion and interpretation.

6. The specific shares are of course dependent on the chosen payoffs in payoff matrix (E-1).

choosing the Soviet strategy below this critical value, the dynamics take the economy to the "all virtual" equilibrium. When the shock is greater than this, however, the economy makes a successful transition to the market. The critical boundary is labeled in figure E-1 as the curve qr.

Another way to think about these dynamics is to consider the basins of attraction. There are two basins of attraction. One is the market economy. The other is the virtual economy. The choices of enterprises eventually take us to one of these basins. In our example, the basins of attraction are given by the regions Vq and Mq along the base of the simplex. As figure E-1 shows, the basin of attraction of the market economy is larger than that of the virtual economy. What would happen, however, if there was a constraint that the proportion of Soviet enterprises could not shrink to zero? That is, suppose that a political constraint requires the continued presence of state-owned enterprises. In a sense this was precisely the case in early transition, primarily with respect to defense enterprises. The effect of such a constraint is to increase the relative size of the virtual economy's basin of attraction. Such a constraint implies that the economy no longer ends up at the base of the simplex—where the share of Soviet enterprises is zero—but at some higher level. Essentially, the base of the simplex shifts up, with the boundary qr unchanged. Given the slope of qr, it is apparent that the probability increases that a virtual mutation will take us to the virtual basin of attraction.

The market economy is evolutionarily stable. The system is immune to *small* mutations. The virtual economy is also evolutionarily stable. The problem is large mutations. When there are both Soviet and market enterprises, the system is vulnerable to the virtual virus.

A key assumption is that when most enterprises are market enterprises, being a market enterprise dominates being a virtual one. However, when the mass of nonmarket enterprises is sufficient, it pays to be virtual. The reason is that when most enterprises are operating with tax offsets and barter, it is very costly to operate only with cash.

This is related to the rotation of the restructuring boundary (RB) curve in r-d space. The RB curve separates the regions where enterprises choose to invest in relations from the regions where enterprises choose to reduce distance. If the boundary rotates counterclockwise, this increases the domain of attraction of the basin in the northeast. The key to pushing market reform is to rotate it clockwise.

Because the virtual economy is a basin of attraction, it may be stable to small perturbations. Thus reforms that might seem effective in market thinking may backfire. Tightening the cash constraint is an example.

Regions in
r-d Space

The discussion of enterprise behavior in chapter 4 treated the government's behavior as exogenous. We assumed that when enterprises choose between producing hard goods or soft goods and between investment in distance reduction or relationship enhancement, they take the government's behavior as given. Even under these assumptions, the problem for the enterprises is complicated enough. It is interesting, especially in the context of the discussion of chapter 8, to consider government policy as an endogenous variable, at least with regard to the willingness to engage in tax offsets in lieu of cash payments. This choice will depend on the characteristics and initial conditions that policymakers face. This is especially true of regional governments.

Just as enterprises differ in their endowments of distance and relational capital, so too do regions. Some regions are endowed with natural resources that can be easily exported, such as Tyumen oblast, with its natural gas. Other regions are dominated by industrial dinosaurs that are characterized by high *d*. This suggests that we classify regions by average distance. We define the average distance of a region as a weighted index of the distances of the enterprises located in the region:

$$\Delta_j = \sum_{i \in I} \delta_{ij} d_i, \tag{F-1}$$

where I is the set of enterprises in a region,[1] and δ_{ij} is the share of enterprise i's output (measured at market prices) in region j.[2] A region endowed with many loss-making enterprises (for instance, Ivanovo) would have a high Δ_j. The key difference between regions with high and low Δ is the marketability of output. A region with low Δ will thus have more cash in circulation, while regions with high Δ will feel the burden of the cash constraint to be much tighter.

Relational capital also varies by region, and it also depends on the relational capital of the constituent enterprises in the region. Hence, by analogy we can write:

$$\Theta_j = \sum_{i \in I} \delta_{ij} r_i. \tag{F-2}$$

Notice that this measure of relational capital at the region level characterizes the enterprises in the region. It measures how dependent they are on relational capital.

A related concept of interest is the relational capital of the local executive, essentially the governor.[3] The relational capital of a regional governor is the result of personal history and investments in maintaining relationships. It will be a function of the characteristics of the enterprises in the region, but it is not equivalent to this. Letting κ_j be the relational capital of the governor of region j, we could write $\kappa_j = f(\Theta_j, \Delta_j)$, noting that κ_j is an increasing function of its first argument. This capital is valuable for dealing with the central government and with governors and enterprises in other regions. For example, higher κ_j can get region j a better deal on offsets with Moscow.

We might assume that the selection process for local officials is such that governors are chosen with characteristics appropriate to their region. For example, a high-Δ region would be more reliant on relational capital, so it might choose governors with higher κ_j.

Governor's Decision Problem

We assume that the governor has two policies to choose from: promarket (M) and antimarket (AM). The former involves transparency and satisfying budget constraints, the latter involves nontransparency and evading budget

1. Obviously the size of this set varies across regions.
2. Alternatively, one could use employment shares as the weighting scheme.
3. Though one might argue that the role of the region in the national economy is also important. This is certainly the case in terms of conflict with the central government.

constraints. The promarket policies push the loss-making enterprises out of business; the antimarket policies are designed to keep them operating. One can think of the former as pushing enterprises to reduce d and the latter as pushing them to increase r.

Notice that this choice by the governor will affect the investment choices of the individual enterprise director. If the governor chooses promarket policies, the enterprise director will expect that investing in relational capital will have a lower payoff than if the governor invests in his own relational capital.

We assume that the governor maximizes the present discounted value of welfare in the region,[4] the instantaneous level of which is measured by U_t^G. Let the initial level of regional welfare be given by U_0^G. To analyze the choice of policies, we examine the trajectory of regional welfare under the two reform scenarios.

Promarket Policies. Under this regime the effect of the initial impact is a decline in welfare to U_1^G. The fact that the effect of promarket policies can be negative may seem surprising, given that loss-making enterprises are put under pressure and must adjust or shrink. Restructuring is almost always costly in the short run. Moreover, regions are not autarkic; relational capital in one region can be used to obtain value produced in other regions. Hence policies that limit its use may cause a deterioration of performance even if they only attack inefficient structures.

The magnitude of the initial decline with promarket policies is determined by the initial state of $(\Theta_{jt}, \Delta_{jt})$. Suppose that these values are high. High Δ_{jt} means that enterprises, on average, suffer with promarket policies. If the enterprises have high relational capital (if the region has high Θ_{jt}), then they suffer from a reduction of their relational capital as a result of promarket policies. Hence the drop in welfare, $U_0^G - U_1^G$, will be larger.[5]

If regional distance were smaller, then the negative effect might be smaller. Indeed, if distance is small enough then the impact could be positive. In either case, it is clear that over time, promarket policy improves welfare to $\hat{U}^G$, which is greater than U_0^G.[6] Nevertheless, for a considerable

---

4. For simplicity we have ignored uncertainty and assume that the governors have perfect foresight.

5. This is easiest to see if regional welfare depends on regional output. Promarket policies devalue relational capital, and this reduces production of soft goods. The greater average distance is, the greater this decrease in production will be. If the immediate effect of promarket policies on hard output is limited, then regional output decreases, as does welfare.

6. It has to be welfare enhancing in the long run because value destruction is eliminated. However, this takes time, and it depends on the assumption that in the long run all subsidies are eliminated.

FIGURE F-1. Promarket Policy

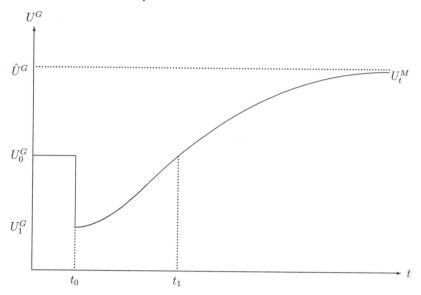

period of time welfare remains below the initial level. The duration depends on the initial level of Δ_{jt} and on the trajectory of U^M_t over time (see figure F-1).

Of course, the trajectory of U^M_t depends on the investment decisions of the enterprise. Our argument is that more promarket policies induce enterprises to choose distance reduction rather than investment in relational capital. One could perhaps argue that when policies are more credible, the beneficial impact of promarket policies will happen more quickly. If policies are unclear, enterprises hedge their bets and devote less to distance reduction, which is the only effective policy in the long run.

It is useful to consider the amount of time it takes for welfare to return to its original level. In figure F-1 this happens at time t_1. Let $\tau_M \equiv t_1 - t_0$ be the duration of the period before the promarket policy raises welfare back to its initial level. It is easy to see that τ_M will be larger the higher initial Δ_{jt} is.

Antimarket Policies. What about antimarket policies? The governor could invest in protectionist type policies that depend on regional Q_{jt} and encourage investment in relational capital. In that case initial welfare actually rises if there are enough enterprises that have both high d and high r.

FIGURE F-2. Antimarket Policy

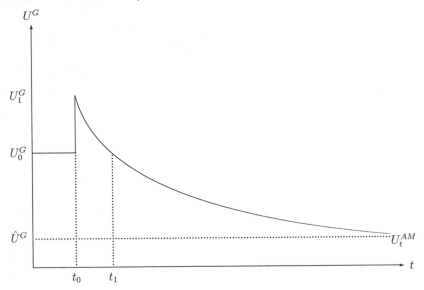

These enterprises need such policies, and the governor is rewarded for supporting them. Let the initial impact of such policies move welfare to U_1^G in figure F-2.[7]

In the long run, however, antimarket policies are self-defeating, so welfare is reduced, eventually to a point below the initial level of welfare. Let t_1 be the time at which welfare drops below the initial level with antimarket policies. Then the length of this period, $\tau_{AM} \equiv t_1 - t_0$, along with the governor's personal rate of time preference, is a crucial determinant of his decisions. The greater τ_{AM} is, the more likely the governor will be to choose the antimarket policy.

What does τ_{AM} depend on? As with the case of promarket policies, the initial state of the region is a crucial determinant. If Δ_{jt} is high, the initial benefit of the antimarket policies is higher, as it is in the case when Θ_{jt} is higher. A larger effect ought to make the duration larger as well, though this is not completely certain. Higher Δ_{jt} means that enterprises are very unsuited to the market. As time passes, antimarket policies may lose their effectiveness, and enterprises that concentrated on relational capital may collapse suddenly.[8] It will also depend on the ability of the governor to translate his

7. If, however, most enterprises were low d, that is, if Δ_{jt} were low, then the welfare impact could be negative.

8. Thus the trajectory in this case may not be the smooth path depicted in figure F-2, but rather a sudden collapse at some future date.

relational capital into resources. This depends, partly, on the attitudes of the center.

Notice how the governor's choice of antimarket policies affects the investment decisions of enterprises. Enterprise directors will invest more in relational capital rather than in distance reduction. This will make adjustment more difficult in the long run, as the region becomes more addicted to such nonmarket policies.

Impermissibility

The framework we have developed is useful for analyzing impermissibility. As we have discussed in the text, impermissibility is a constraint on policies that prevents unacceptable outcomes from being implemented. We can think of this as some lower bound to acceptable welfare levels. Let this lower bound on welfare be given by $\underline{U}^G$. This implies that if the negative shock of promarket policy in a region is large enough, promarket policy violates the impermissibility constraint.[9] In this case promarket policies cannot be implemented intact. Adaptations and adjustments to the policies will ensure that welfare does not cross this lower bound.

Decisionmaking

To choose between promarket and antimarket policies, the governor must compare the value of the two. Let U_t^M be the level of welfare under the promarket policy at time t, and similarly let U_t^{AM} be the level of welfare under the antimarket policy. The governor calculates the discounted value of the difference in welfare under the two trajectories:

$$\Gamma \equiv \int_{t_0}^{T} \left(U_t^M - U_t^{AM} \right) e^{-\rho t} dt, \qquad (\text{F-3})$$

where T is the terminal period of the governor's planning period and ρ is his rate of time preference. If $\Gamma > 0$, promarket policies lead to higher welfare over the planning horizon. Notice that as T gets large, the integral in (F-3) will certainly become positive. This follows because promarket policy produces higher steady-state welfare. Nevertheless, in finite horizons this need not be the case, because the term in the parentheses is negative in the first few periods of reform. More important, however, even if $\Gamma > 0$, governors may still choose antimarket policies. The governor may be more concerned about the immediate future than about the consequences down the road.

9. Obviously, this happens when $U_1^G < \underline{U}^G$ in figure F-1.

FIGURE F-3. Promarket Policy in a Low-Δ Region

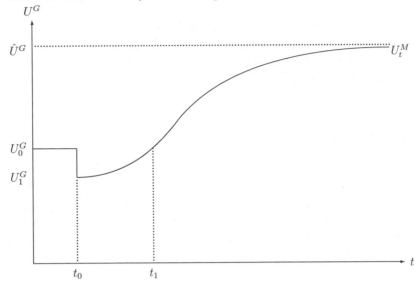

The more impatient the governor is, the less likely he will be to choose pro-market policies. This is clear from (F-3): the higher the rate of time preference, the less likely that $\Gamma > 0$ for finite T.

It would be interesting to add to this some uncertainty. A governor may not last out his term. One could analyze this problem in a manner that is similar to time preference. Indeed, uncertain duration of office acts in a way similar to impatience. Indeed, one can think of ρ in (F-3) as the sum of real time preference and the instantaneous probability of being thrown out of office.

Low-Δ Regions

The analysis so far has considered what may be called typical regions. What if a region has enterprises with very low d—that is, what if it is a low-Δ region? In such a region the initial shock of promarket policy is smaller, and the ultimate net gain is larger. The path of welfare looks more like figure F-3.

The welfare path of antimarket policies is also different in the low-Δ region. In this case the cost of imposing the antimarket policies is larger because the low-d enterprises in the region suffer significantly. Hence in this case we have a path that looks like figure F-4.

FIGURE F-4. Antimarket Policy in a Low-Δ Region

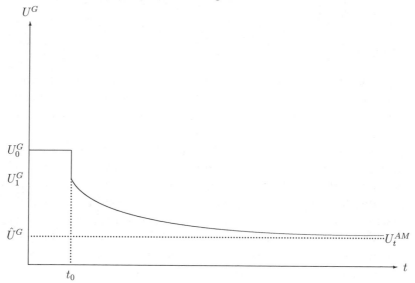

In figure F-4 the initial shock of antimarket policy is negative, and performance deteriorates further over time. Antimarket policies hurt most enterprises in the low-Δ region (especially if they are also low-r as well).

Clearly, in a low-Δ, low-Θ region the governor is going to choose the promarket path, since even in the short run the impacts will be positive.

Bifurcation

If regions differ with regard to initial levels of (Θ_{jt}, Δ_{jt}), then we should expect a bifurcation in regional outcomes. Low-Δ regions will tend to choose promarket policies. High-Δ regions will choose antimarket policies. This will influence the investment decisions of enterprises, thus reinforcing the region's (governor's) decisions. Hence the paths that regions follow will diverge. Notice that this divergence does not require enterprises to move between regions. The decisions of governors will influence investment decisions in such a way that the divergence occurs.

These diverging paths result in the regions' ending up with starkly different policy environments. The promarket regions will tend to rely much less on virtual economy strategies, while in the other regions reliance on these strategies will become even more intense. These different policy environments are likely to be quite stable, making it very difficult for a future governor to alter them.

Addiction

In the equilibrium we observe that in some regions reliance on tax offsets and other virtual strategies grows over time. Officials in such regions become addicted to these sources. This is the consequence of policies that dissuade enterprises from investing in distance reduction.

As the enterprise invests in relational capital, the recipient of this investment becomes dependent on it. Enterprises and officials become mutually dependent on offsets and bribes. It is not too farfetched to compare this with the relationship between a pusher and his junkie. The more the junkie uses drugs, the more addicted he becomes; the pusher in turn has an incentive to get the junkie addicted.[10] The same phenomenon is at work in the virtual economy. The more an enterprise adopts such strategies, the more dependent it becomes on them. Producing goods that cannot be sold for cash but can be used to obtain tax offsets makes it harder to exit this trap in the future. Just as using drugs saps the health and vitality of the drug addict, the enterprise that produces for tax offsets rather than for the monetary economy concedes the battle to remain competitive.

It is important to emphasize why this addiction weakens the enterprise over time. The enterprise that does not invest in reducing d finds its competitive conditions worsening over time. This is a condition of operating in a globally competitive environment. Stagnation does not mean that d remains constant. Instead, it increases as other enterprises enhance their productivity. Hence, just as with the drug addict, the enterprises become more addicted to the behavioral strategies adopted to ensure survival. They may be myopically rational, but they worsen the enterprise's opportunities over time.

Thus the addiction to the behavioral strategies associated with the virtual economy increases the difficulty that an enterprise or region will face if it tries to escape this equilibrium. The enterprise that chooses to invest in r rather than in reducing d becomes more dependent on the region's continuing to accept offsets and barter. The region that encourages tax offsets encourages enterprises to invest in r rather than reducing d. These enterprises are thus more dependent on future tax offsets. Just as with drug addiction, the virtual economy is a condition that is painful to overcome.

10. As Tom Lehrer noted, "He gives the kids free samples, Because he knows full well, That today's young innocent faces, Will be tomorrow's clientele. . . "

References

Abel, Andrew. 1990. "Consumption and Investment." In *Handbook of Monetary Economics,* edited by Benjamin M. Friedman and Frank H. Hahn. North Holland.

Akoryan, A. 1992. *Industrial Potential of Russia: Analytical Study Based on Fixed Assets Statistics to 1992.* Commack, N.Y.: Nova Science Publishers. Cited in Gertrude Schroeder, "Dimensions of Russia's Industrial Transformation, 1992 to 1998: An Overview," *Post-Soviet Geography and Economics* 39 (5): 243–70.

Aoki, Masahiko. 2001. *Toward a Comparative Institutional Analysis.* MIT Press.

Arsent'yeva, N. M. 1997. "Skrytyye ten'yu: sotsiologicheskoye issledovaniye tenevoy ekonomiki" [Hidden by the shadow: a sociological study of the shadow economy]. *EKO* 1997 (10): 143–51.

Aslund, Anders. 1999. "Why Has Russia's Economic Transformation Been So Arduous?" Paper presented at the World Bank's Annual Bank Conference on Development Economics, Washington, D.C., April 28–30.

Axtell, Robert L., and Richard Florida. 2000. "Emergent Cities: A Microeconomic Explanation of Zipf's Law." Mimeo. Brookings.

Berglof, Erik, and Gerard Roland. 1998. "Soft Budget Constraints and Banking in Transition Economies." *Journal of Comparative Economics* 26 (1) March: 18–19.

Berkowitz, Daniel, and David N. DeJong. 1999. "Russia's Internal Border." *Regional Science and Urban Economics* 29 (5): 633–49.

Black, Bernard S., Reinier Kraakman, and Anna Tarassova. 2000. "Russian Privatization and Corporate Governance: What Went Wrong?" *Stanford Law Review* 52: 1731–1808.

Blanchard, Olivier, and Andrei Shleifer. 2000. "Federalism with and without Political Centralization: China versus Russia." Working Paper 7616. National Bureau of Economic Research (March).

Blasi, Joseph R., Maya Kroumova, and Douglas Kruse. 1997. *Kremlin Capitalism: Privatizing the Russian Economy.* Cornell University Press.

Boycko, Maxim, Andrei Shleifer, and Robert Vishny. 1995. *Privatizing Russia.* MIT Press.

Boyd, R. Forthcoming. "Population Structure, Equilibrium Selection and the Evolution of Norms." Proceedings volume for Conference on Economics and Evolution held at the International School for Economic Research, University of Siena, June 1997, edited by Ugo Pagamo. Cambridge University Press.

Breach, Al. 1999. "Russia: Now a Competitive Exchange Rate—The Revival of the Real Economy." Global Economics Paper 22. Goldman Sachs (July 23).

Cohn, Stanley H. 1979. "Soviet Replacement Investment: A Rising Policy Imperative." In *Soviet Economy in a Time of Change.* Joint Economic Committee of the Congress of the United States. vol. 1: 230–45.

Coleman, James S. 1988. "Social Capital in the Creation of Human Capital." *American Journal of Sociology* 94: S95–S120.

Commander, Simon, and Christian Mumssen. 1998. "Understanding Barter in Russia." Working Paper 37. European Bank for Reconstruction and Development (EBRD) (December).

Cox, Donald, Zekeriya Eser, and Emmanuel Jimenez. 1997. "Family Safety Nets during Economic Transition: A Study of Inter-Household Transfers in Russia." In *Poverty in Russia: Public Policy and Private Responses*, edited by Jeni Klugman. Washington: World Bank.

Dewatripont, M., and E. Maskin. 1995. "Credit and Efficiency in Centralized and Decentralized Economies." *Review of Economic Studies* 62: 541–55.

Dixit, Avinash, and Robert Pindyck. 1994. *Investment under Uncertainty.* Princeton University Press.

Ericson, Richard E. 1988. "Priority, Duality, and Penetration in the Soviet Command Economy." RAND Note N-2643-NA. The RAND Corporation (December).

————. 1999. "The Structural Barrier to Transition Hidden in Input-Output Tables of Centrally Planned Economies." *Economic Systems* 23 (3): 199–244.

————. 2001. "The Post-Soviet Russian Economic System: An Industrial Feudalism?" In *Russian Crisis and Its Effects*, edited by Tuomas Komulainen and Iikka Korhonen, 133–59. Helsinki: Kikimora Publications.

Ericson, Richard E., and Barry W. Ickes. 2001. "A Model of Russia's Virtual Economy." *Review of Economic Design* 6 (2).

Fernandez, Raquel, and Dani Rodrik. 1991. "Resistance to Reform: Status Quo Bias in the Presence of Individual-Specific Uncertainty." *American Economic Review* 81 (5): 1146–55.

Fischer, Stanley. 2001. "Exchange Rate Regimes: Is the Bipolar View Correct?" *Journal of Economic Perspectives* 15 (2): 3–24.

Fischer, Stanley, and Ratna Sahay. 2000. "The Transition Economies after Ten Years." Working Paper WP/00/30. International Monetary Fund (February).

Fitzpatrick, Sheila. 1999. *Everyday Stalinism: Ordinary Life in Extraordinary Times: Soviet Russia in the 1930s.* Oxford University Press.

Fox, Merritt B., and Michael A. Heller. 1999. "Lessons from Fiascos in Russian Corporate Governance." *New York University Law Review* (October).

Friebel, Guido, and Sergei Guriev. 2000. "Should I Stay or Can I Go? Worker Attachment in Russia." Working paper, New Economic School (NES), Moscow (November).

Fukuyama, Francis. 1995. *Trust: The Social Virtues and the Creation of Prosperity.* The Free Press.

————. 2000. "Social Capital and Civil Society." Working Paper WP/00/74. International Monetary Fund (April).

Gabaix, Xavier. 1999. "Zipf's Law for Cities: An Explanation." *Quarterly Journal of Economics* 114 (3): 739–67.

Gaddy, Clifford G. 1996. *The Price of the Past: Russia's Struggle with the Legacy of a Militarized Economy.* Brookings.

Gaddy, Clifford G., and Barry W. Ickes. 1998. "To Restructure or Not to Restructure? Informal Activities and Enterprise Behavior in Transition." William Davidson Institute Working Paper 134. University of Michigan.

————.1999. "An Accounting Model of the Virtual Economy in Russia." *Post-Soviet Geography and Economics* 40 (2): 79–97.

————. 2001a. "The Cost of the Cold." Unpublished Pennsylvania State University working paper (May).

———. 2001b. "How to Think about the Post-Soviet Output Fall." Mimeo (March) (econ.la.psu.edu/~bickes/ickres.htm).

———. 2001c. "Stability and Disorder: An Evolutionary Analysis of Russia's Virtual Economy." In *Russia in the New Century: Stability or Disorder?*, edited by Victoria E. Bonnell and George W. Breslauer. Boulder, Colo.: Westview Press.

Gevorkyan, Nataliya, Natal'ya Timakova, and Andrey Kolesnikov. 2000. *Ot pervogo litsa. Razgovory s Vladimirom Putinym* [In the first person. Conversations with Vladimir Putin]. Moscow: Vagrius.

Götz, Roland. 1999. "How Virtual Is the Post-Soviet Barter Economy?" Mimeo. Bundesinstitut für ostwissenschaftliche und internationale Studien, Cologne, Germany (October).

Graham, Carol, and Stefano Pettinato. 2002. *Happiness and Hardship: Opportunity and Insecurity in New Market Economies*. Brookings.

Grossman, Gregory. 1963. "Notes for a Theory of the Command Economy." *Soviet Studies* 15 (2).

———. 1977. "The 'Second Economy' of the USSR." *Problems of Communism* 26 (September-October): 25–40.

Guiso, Luigi, Paola Sapienza, and Luigi Zingales. 2000. "The Role of Social Capital in Financial Development." Working Paper 7563. National Bureau of Economic Research (February).

Guriev, Sergei, and Barry W. Ickes. 1999. "Barter in Russian Enterprises: Myths vs. Empirical Evidence." *Russian Economic Trends*, no. 2 (1999), pp. 6–13.

———. 2000. "Barter in Russia." In Seabright (2000).

Guriev, Sergei, and Dmitry Kvasov. 1999. "Barter in Russia: The Role of Market Power." Mimeo, New Economic School, Moscow.

Hendley, Kathryn, and others. 1997. "Observations on the Use of Law by Russian Enterprises." *Post-Soviet Affairs* 13(1): 19–41.

Hendley, Kathryn, Barry W. Ickes, and Randi Ryterman. 1998. "Remonetizing the Russian Economy." In *Russian Enterprise Reform: Policies to Further the Transition*, edited by Harry G. Broadman, 101–20. Washington: World Bank.

Hewett, Ed A. 1988. *Reforming the Soviet Economy: Equality versus Efficiency*. Brookings.

Ickes, Barry W., Peter Murrell, and Randi Ryterman. 1997. "End of the Tunnel? The Effects of Financial Stabilization in Russia." *Post-Soviet Affairs* 13 (2): 105–33.

Ickes, Barry W., and Randi Ryterman. 1993. "Roadblock to Economic

Reform: Inter-Enterprise Debt and the Transition to Markets." *Post-Soviet Affairs* 9 (3): 231–52.

———. 1994. "From Enterprise to Firm: Notes for a Theory of the Enterprise in Transition." In *The Postcommunist Economic Transformation*, edited by Robert Campbell. Westview Press.

———. 1997. "Entry without Exit: Economic Selection under Socialism." Mimeo, Pennsylvania State University.

Ickes, Barry W., and Larry Samuelson. 1987. "Job Transfers and Incentives in Complex Organizations: Thwarting the Ratchet Effect." *Rand Journal of Economics* 18 (2): 275–86.

IET (Institute for the Economy in Transition). 1999. "Rossiyskiye predpriyatiya v 1996–1997 gg" [Russian enterprises in 1996–1997] (www.online.ru/sp/iet/prom96.rhtml), March 2.

IMF (International Monetary Fund). 2000. *World Economic Outlook* (May).

IMF (International Monetary Fund). 2001. *International Financial Statistics*.

IMF and others. 1991. *A Study of the Soviet Economy: Joint Study of the IMF, World Bank, OECD, and EBRD.*

Interfax. Various issues. Interfax Weekly Statistical Report. Moscow.

Johnson, Simon, Daniel Kaufmann, and Andrei Shleifer. 1997. "The Unofficial Economy in Transition." *Brookings Papers on Economic Activity* 1997 (2): 159–221.

JP Morgan. 1999. "How Much Debt Relief Does Russia Need?" October 15, 1999.

Karpov Commission Report. 1997. "O prichinakh nizkoy sobirayemosti nalogov (neplatezhey fiskal'noy sisteme), obshchikh prichinakh 'krizisa platezhey' i vozmozhnosti vosstanovleniya platezhesposobnosti rossiyskikh predpriyatiy" [On the causes of the low rate of tax collection (nonpayments in the fiscal system), general causes of the "payments crisis," and the possibility of restoring the solvency of Russian enterprises]. Report of the Inter-Agency Balance Commission chaired by P. A. Karpov. Moscow (December).

Khalin, Dmitriy. 1999. "Investitsionnoy sfere neobkhodim kapital'nyy remont" [The investment sphere needs major repair]. *Ekonomika i zhizn'*, no. 12 (March).

Kiss, Yudit. 1999. *The Transformation of the Defense Industry in Hungary.* Bonn International Center for Conversion. Brief 14 (July).

Kontorovich, Vladimir. 1988. "Lessons of the 1965 Soviet Economic Reform." *Soviet Studies* 40 (2): 308–16.

Kornai, Janos. 1992. *The Socialist System: The Political Economy of Communism*. Oxford.

Kukharenko, V. 1998. "Sovershenstvovaniye bazy sel'skogo stroitel'stva" [Improving the base of agricultural construction]. *Ekonomist*, no. 11: 87–91.

Latynina, Yuliya. 1999. *Okhota na izyubrya* [Deer hunt]. Moscow: Olma Press.

Ledeneva, Alena V. 1998. *Russia's Economy of Favours*. Cambridge University Press.

Leitzel, Jim. 1995. *Russian Economic Reform*. Routledge.

Malov, A., and Ye. Mayn. 1997. "Ekonomicheskoye polozheniye predpriyatiya" [The economic situation of the enterprise]. *Ekonomist*, no. 8: 30–41.

McKinnon, Ronald. 1993. *The Order of Economic Liberalization: Financial Control in the Transition to a Market Economy*. Johns Hopkins University Press.

Morozov, Alexander, Brian Pinto, and Vladimir Drebentsov. 2000. "Dismantling Russia's Nonpayments System: Creating Conditions for Growth." Technical Paper 471. World Bank (June).

Murphy, Kevin, Andrei Shleifer, and Robert Vishny. 1992. "The Transition to a Market Economy: Pitfalls of Partial Reform." *Quarterly Journal of Economics* 107 (3): 889–906.

Murrell, Peter. 1991. "Can Neoclassical Economics Underpin the Reform of Centrally Planned Economies?" *Journal of Economic Perspectives* 5 (4): 59–76.

———. 1992. "Evolution in Economics and in the Economic Reform of the Centrally Planned Economies." In *Emergence of Market Economies in Eastern Europe*, edited by Christopher K. Clague and Gordon C. Raussen. Blackwell.

Narayan, R. Badri. 1999. "An Examination of Intergovernmental Transfers in the Russian Federation." Ph.D. dissertation. Pennsylvania State University.

Nash, Roland, and Yaroslav Lissovolik. 2000. "Reforming Russia: A Reality Check from the Regions." Renaissance Capital Research Report. Moscow (September).

North, Douglass C. 1990. *Institutions, Institutional Change, and Economic Performance*. Cambridge University Press.

OECD (Organisation for Economic Co-operation and Development). 1995. *OECD Economic Surveys: The Russian Federation 1995*. Paris.

———. 1997. *OECD Economic Surveys: The Russian Federation 1997.* Paris.

———. 2000. *OECD Economic Surveys: The Russian Federation 2000.* Paris.

Ovcharova, Lilia, Evgeny Turuntsev, and Irina Korchagina. 1997. Unpublished report submitted to the Economics Education and Research Consortium (EERC), Moscow.

Pickering, Thomas. 1996. "Farewell Address to the American Business Community." Renaissance Hotel, Moscow, October 21, 1996.

Promyshlennost' Rossii [Industry of Russia]. 1996. Moscow: Goskomstat Rossii.

Putin, Vladimir V. 1999. "Rossiya na rubezhe tysyacheletiy" [Russia on the threshold of a new millennium] (www.government.ru:8080/government/minister/article-vvp1.html).

———. 2001a. "Vystupleniye na soveshchanii po voprosam tarifnoy politiki v Sibiri i na Dal'nem Vostoke" [Speech to the meeting on questions of utility rates policy in Siberia and the Far East] (February 16) (www.president.kremlin.ru/events/161.html).

———. 2001b. "Vystupleniye Prezidenta Rossiyskoy Federatsii V. V. Putina na Delovom sammite ATES" [Speech of the President of the Russian Federation V. V. Putin at the APEC Business Summit], Shanghai, October 19 (www.president.kremlin.ru/events/341.html).

Putnam, Robert. 1993. *Making Democracy Work: Civic Traditions in Modern Italy.* Princeton University Press.

Roland, Gerard. 2000. *Transition and Economics.* MIT Press.

Rose, Richard. 1998. "Getting Things Done with Social Capital: New Russian Barometer VII." Studies in Public Policy 303. University of Strathclyde, Scotland.

Rossiyskiy statisticheskiy yezhgodnik [Russian statistical yearbook]. Various years. Moscow: Goskomstat Rossii.

Russian Economic Barometer. Various issues.

Russian Economic Trends. Monthly update. Various issues. Russian-European Centre for Economic Policy (RECEP). Moscow. (www.recep.org)

Seabright, Paul, ed. 2000. *The Vanishing Rouble: Barter Networks and Non-Monetary Transactions in Post-Soviet Societies.* Cambridge University Press.

Shcherbakova, L. A. 1998. "Tara kak zerkalo rossiyskikh reform. Promyshlennyy kompleks: perekhod v novoye kachestvo ili v nebytiye?"

[Tara as a mirror of Russian reforms. The industrial complex: transition to a new quality or to non-existence?]. *EKO* no. 8: 59–70.

Shleifer, Andrei, and Daniel Treisman. 2000. *Without a Map: Political Tactics and Economic Reform in Russia*. MIT Press.

Solzhenitsyn, A. 1998. *Rossiya v obvale* [Russia in collapse]. Moscow: Russkiy put'.

Statistical Abstract of the United States. 1990. U.S. Department of Labor.

Steinbruner, John D. 2000. *Principles of International Security*. Brookings.

Stiglitz, Joseph E. 1999. "Whither Reform: Ten Years of the Transition." Annual World Bank Conference on Development Economics 1999. Washington: World Bank.

Tompson, William. 1998. "The Price of Everything and the Value of Nothing? Unravelling the Workings of Russia's 'Virtual Economy.'" University of London (September).

USIA (United States Information Agency). 1998. "Who Protests in Russia." Opinion Analysis M-186-98. Office of Research and Media Reaction (December 8).

Volgin, Andrei. 1998. "The End of the Virtual Economy." Unpublished paper.

Weibull, Jurgen W. 1995. *Evolutionary Game Theory*. MIT Press.

Westhead, Keith, and Derek Weaving. 1999. "Gazprom: Show Me the Money." Deutsche Bank, Russia Oil & Gas Sector Report (September 29).

Woodruff, David. 1999. *Money Unmade: Barter and the Fate of Russian Capitalism*. Cornell University Press.

World Bank. 1996. *World Development Report*.

Yakovlev, Andrei. 1999. "Black Cash Tax Evasion in Russia: Its Forms, Incentives and Consequences at the Firm Level." Mimeo, 1999.

———. 2000. "Barter in the Russian Economy: Classification and Implications Evidence from Case Study Analyses)." *Post-Communist Economies* 12 (3): 279–91.

Yeltsin, Boris N. 1998. [State of the Union speech].

———. 1999. [State of the Union speech].

Young, Peyton. 1998. *Individual Strategy and Social Structure: An Evolutionary Theory of Institutions*. Princeton University Press.

Zhuravskaya, Ekaterina V. 2000. "Incentives to Provide Local Public Goods: Fiscal Federalism, Russian Style." *Journal of Public Economics* 76 (3): 337–68.

Index of
Authors Cited

Index

Adaptation: behavioral, 2–3, 6, 110–11; to hostile environment, 9–10
Addiction: to virtual strategies, 280
Agriculture: paradigm of shrinkage, 162–67; wages in, 166. *See also* Bobino farm story; Krasnodar food production story; Rural Russia
ALROSA: performance in *1999*, 198–99; case study, 200–01
Altayenergo, 249
Arkhangel'sk (oblast): personalization of social safety nets, 169–70
Arrears, wage. *See* Wage arrears
Asia-Pacific Economic Cooperation forum (APEC): Putin on virtual economy, 4n
Auto manufacturing industry: cash payments, 248. *See also* GAZ
Avtodizel', 249

B (government sector). *See* Four-sector accounting exercise; Government; Public sector

Bankruptcy: rarity, 22; redefinition in virtual economy, 126; shrinkage as alternative to, 156
Barter: computing cash value, 39; defined, 25; explanations for, 27–29; hides loss-making enterprises, 246; Igor's Rules and, 65–67; Karpov Commission findings, 247–50; misleading statistics, 97; multilateral chains, 32–33; not synonymous with virtual economy, 4–5, 198; phony investment boom and, 33; price discrimination and, 70n, 96n24, 96n25; reduction after *1998*, 195–96; reduction explained by accounting exercise, 196–98; regional differences, 26–27; surveys on growth, 25–26; tax evasion and, 29–32, 243–46; tight money policy and, 113; transactions costs, 33; Ukraine, 198–99n. *See also* Natural economy; Tax offsets

292